# TRADITIONAL CONSTRUCTION PATTERNS

08FEB26

# TRADITIONAL CONSTRUCTION PATTERNS

STEPHEN A. MOUZON

with SUSAN M. HENDERSON

FOREWORD BY ANDRÉS M. DUANY

A NEW URBAN GUILD PUBLICATION

## McGraw-Hill

NEW YORK   CHICAGO   SAN FRANCISCO   LISBON   LONDON
MADRID   MEXICO CITY   MILAN   NEW DELHI   SAN JUAN
SEOUL   SINGAPORE   SYDNEY   TORONTO

**The McGraw·Hill Companies**

LIBRARY OF CONGRESS CATALOGING-IN-PUBLICATION DATA

Mouzon, Stephen A.
    Traditional construction patterns / Stephen A. Mouzon
    p. cm.
    Includes index.
    ISBN 0-07-141632-3
    1. Building. 2. Architecture. 3. Building-Details-Drawings. I. Title.
    TH155.M68 2004
    721-dc22

2003070171

567890 CUS/CUS 0109876

ISBN 0-07-141632-3

Printed and bound by Von Hoffman.

## DESIGN

Stephen A. Mouzon

## ACKNOWLEDGEMENTS

This book would not have been possible without the love, faith, and patience of Wanda Mouzon.

The numerous contributions of Andrés Duany, Elizabeth Plater-Zyberk and other members of Duany Plater-Zyberk & Company are greatly appreciated and beyond the scope of the brief description afforded by this space.

This book is enormously better due to the depth of knowledge, breadth of vision and hard work of Nancy Bruning and Calder Loth, who worked many frantic hours on the final edits. The book would have been an embarrassment without them.

This book is a publication of the New Urban Guild, which currently includes the following members (in alphabetical order): Erica Albright, William J. Allison, Julia M. Covington, Keith D. Covington, Christopher S. Engel, Frank G. Greene, Milton Wilfred Grenfell, Susan M. Henderson, Gary William Justiss, Matthew J. Lister, Richard E. McCoy III, R. Eric Moser, the author, Louis Nequette, Nathan R. Norris, Van G. Pond, Jr., and Ken Pursley.

McGraw-Hill books are available at special quantity discounts to use as premiums and sales promotions, or for use in corporate training programs. For more information, please write to the Director of Special Sales, Professional Publishing, McGraw-Hill, Two Penn Plaza, New York, NY 10121-2298. Or contact your local bookstore.

# CONTENTS

## FOREWORD

## INTRODUCTION

### CHAPTER 1
~
## THE STORY OF THE LANGUAGES OF ARCHITECTURE

### CHAPTER 2
~
## THREE GREAT THEMES OF TRADITIONAL ARCHITECTURE

### CHAPTER 3
~
## LEXICON

### CHAPTER 4
~
## THE CLASSICAL ORDERS

### CHAPTER 5
~
## BASIC PRINCIPLES

# CHAPTER 6
## ~
# DETAILS

# CHAPTER 7
## ~
# WALLS

# CHAPTER 8
## ~
# DOORS AND WINDOWS

CHAPTER 9
~
# PORCHES AND BALCONIES

CHAPTER 10
~
# EAVES

CHAPTER 11
~
# ROOFS

# FOREWORD

Nothing seems stranger to the layman than the contempt with which certain architects hold other architects.

It is ever thus with tribal warfare.

How would it otherwise be possible that an architect could dislike another having never met, but simply on the basis of a building seen? How is it possible that a style of architecture should be considered to be the only appropriate one "for our time"? How is this possible in an era when we are meant to be categorically open to diversity?

It seems that architecture and its sects constitute the last of the respectable wars. In the profession's modernist schools, suppression of ideas is overtly practiced. At gatherings of the tribal divines and at the oracles, otherwise known as lectures and symposia, there is an irrational blood lust against traditional architecture.

How can such prejudice be sustained? Is it not obvious that we can look with interest upon all styles of buildings, enter them, use them, not be fundamentally harmed and even sometimes be inspired by them? Is it not everywhere observable that both traditional and modernist buildings may perform well or badly, and that this depends on the quality of their design and construction— not their style?

How amazing that this intolerance can be maintained in the teeth of the most sacrosanct of American scorecards: the marketplace. After all, traditional buildings are preferred by the people by crushing margins. In a society that measures success in numbers (the most votes, the most sold, the richest, the fastest, the tallest) traditional architecture wins by a landslide. It is the way (let us conservatively estimate) that 95% of the million new housing units are built in the U.S. every year. In the presence of this physical fact, how can the modernists' dismissal that traditional architecture is "not of our time" be maintained?

Of course, there is the requisite "critical" discourse, by which success in the market is ipso facto degraded for being complicit in capitalism— a quaint conceit. But why should anyone be concerned about such opinions? After all, these editors, teachers, and critics are on the margin, visible only to themselves. Traditionalist architects, with their million annual buildings, with their success, could easily ignore them.

But they should not.

This book responds with the reason why. Yes, traditional architecture appeals. But the fact is, most of the vast production of traditional building is dismal, ranging from the merely inept to the simply hideous. It is now apparent that many architects, even the well intentioned, lack knowledge of the principles of their tradition. This is a fundamental problem, because traditional architecture is intrinsically a body of knowledge. It is not like the modernist styles where architects define the rules of their own game— a self-determined contest in which each is therefore the indisputable champion: No one beats Eisenman at Eisenman's game; and when anyone else enters the field, he changes the rules. It is quite a different story with traditional architects. There are rules. A person who designs a traditional building is entering a field populated by true world champions including Palladio, Schinkel, Lutyens, and Goodhue. It takes extraordinary courage and temerity to do so— or ignorance. And that is, I'm afraid, the general situation: an innocent ignorance that leads inevitably, in the case of traditional architecture, to mediocrity.

These poor results are what sustain the otherwise untenable modernist critique. Modernist critics never attack a good traditional building. It is not the work of Krier or Porphyrios or Merrill that is held up for ridicule; it is always the buildings that deserve it.

And so, it turns out, that the true enemy of traditional architecture is not modernist architecture. The vulnerability of today's architecture is its own poor quality— and that's why this book is important.

The author, Steve Mouzon, is a practicing architect. For over twenty years, he has dedicated himself to the study and design of traditional buildings and places. In search of deeper knowledge and authenticity, his travels have allowed him to accumulate an unparalleled understanding of what can go wrong. Through his experience as a New Urbanist Town Architect, he has seen what almost always does go wrong. And now, with discernment and wit, he has thoroughly catalogued the ideal and the shortcoming. He has produced a manual that is clear, easy to use, and targeted to the most common errors (yes, in the use of traditional language, there are ERRORS). There is no further excuse. Traditional architects can now sweep their own house clean.


Andrés Duany
July 6, 2004

# INTRODUCTION

## THE MOST-LOVED PLACES

T HE best measure of the greatness of architecture is the extent to which it touches the hearts, minds, and spirits of the people who use it. Good work in architecture can move people, just as good work in music, art, writing, or drama does.

How is it possible to recognize architecture that touches and moves people? Generally, the places that move people most deeply are the places they love the most. The most-loved places are the ones they go furthest to see, or the places they go most often, or the ones they pay the most to buy if given the opportunity. The most-loved places are the ones that sit most indelibly in some corner of the mind like an old friend. As one old man put it when describing a long-loved town of his youth: "That's the one place I absolutely must go back to before I die."

Study of the most-loved places over the past two decades has revealed that certain characteristics of the buildings and public spaces occur so often that they establish common patterns. Some patterns emerge around the world and point toward deep and abiding needs common to all of humanity. Other patterns occur nationwide, and are as much a part of a nation's culture as its spoken language. Still others occur region-wide, like a regional dialect of the national language. Patterns occasionally develop on a smaller local level within the region in response to compelling natural features such as the edge of a mountaintop or the seashore. The great beloved places contain patterns on all these levels, making them both a part of the great timeless continuum of the places of mankind and also a potent expression of the aspirations and ideals of a particular people in a particular place.

Some question whether we can still build places such as these that are profound expressions of who we are, and that can sit so indelibly in our memories. They say that humanity isn't capable of building places of such great beauty anymore. But we are, in fact, a richer, smarter, stronger society than ever before. Average people take for granted comforts and conveniences that once were not available even to kings. Our tools are bigger, faster, and easier to use than anything ever seen before. The collected wisdom of the ages is just a mouse click away. The majority of all the scientists who have ever lived are alive today and, by virtue of our technology, are building a knowledge base the likes of which could not have been imagined just a century ago. It would be absolutely tragic if a society so big and smart and strong and rich were to settle for architecture that is inferior to most of what has come before. Yet, that is exactly what has happened for nearly a century. It doesn't have to be that way.

Some people also question the wisdom of building places that resonate with towns such as Charleston or Savannah because they feel that architecture should be "an expression of our age." Why should we be forced to live in an historical museum? Don't most of the architectural academies condemn traditionally planned communities as being nothing but built nostalgia? Those arguments might seem compelling at first glance, until you look at the places they produce.

What aspects of "our age" are buildings meant to express? Today, buildings that are strictly an "expression of our age" often express and reinforce the most negative aspect of modern society, such as disjointedness, separation, confusion, and despair. Architecture has slid so far down this treacherous slope that a legion of newly minted architects aspire to nothing greater than to produce buildings that look as if they had been damaged in a windstorm.

It turns out that the "expression of our age" mantra has actually been a code phrase for the expression of our machines to a century of architects. Architecture that pays deference to the tools rather than to the people that use them is wrong-headed at best, and usually is very destructive to the most-loved places. The preservation movement was founded as a result of this dilemma. Today, the most passionate response evoked by most architecture is found during public efforts to stop projects. As a result, the most civil effect that can be expected of architecture based on machines is to be less offensive.

## Why This Book?

This book is based on the conviction that we can aspire to build great human-based places again that not only avoid offending the citizens that use them, but actually delight them instead. Many of today's technologies make construction of great places easier than it has ever been before in human history, if only we have the knowledge of how to use them. That knowledge, however, has largely been lost over the past 80 years. This loss was partially the result of the combination of the Great Depression and World War II, a fifteen-year period when relatively few and relatively humble buildings were built. But it is just as much a result of the ideas of Modernist architects who had no further use for the old skills and the old knowledge.

The greatest damage done by Modernism, however, was not done by the great Modernist buildings which now probably number over 300 worldwide. Those buildings are the product of genius and should be applauded as such. The harm resulted instead from putting the ideas of Modernism into the hands of average architects. These ideas can be incredibly powerful in the hands of a master architect at the top of his or her game, but almost always produce terrible results when used by anyone else. The fact that these ideas have been in use for nearly a century and have only produced 300 great buildings while serving up countless bad ones is ample testimony to this fact.

There is an even darker side to the act of putting Modernist ideas into the hands of the average practitioner. Because most less-than-famous architects often struggle to pay the bills, they are susceptible to the demands of their clients. Study after study and poll after poll have shown that the public prefers traditional architecture by overwhelming margins. So when faced with the dilemma of paying the rent or staying true to Modernist principles they learned in school, most architects opt to pay the rent. They add just enough of the trappings of traditional architecture to appease the client, but assemble the building with the Modernist tools that only the heroic geniuses should use. The resulting Frankenstein monster is not Modernist by any stretch of the imagination, but neither is it true traditional architecture, either. It is instead a collection of misshapen pieces of traditional architecture stitched together with no clear vision of what the resulting creature should be. Most of us probably can't explain exactly what is wrong with this sort of building because there are just enough traditional pieces thrown in to make it look vaguely traditional at first glance, just as the fictional Frankenstein monster looked vaguely human at first glance, with a head, arms, legs, and body. But in both cases, we immediately know that something isn't right.

The intent of this book is to finally explain in layman's terms the vague sense of unease we've all had with traditional architecture done wrong for the past half-century, and to give people the tools for getting it right again. The first tool is a fully illustrated Lexicon of nearly 240 terms we should all know, but probably don't. It's hard to ask for something if you don't know what to call it. It's also hard to say it if you don't know how to pronounce it, so the Lexicon provides pronunciation on all of the words that are not obvious.

The primary tool, however, is a collection of 108 patterns illustrated as Do's and Don'ts with diagrams and photographs. These patterns represent the most common errors of traditional construction, and are the things we really need to start getting right if we hope to build more of the most-loved places again. Only 3 of the 108 patterns show any Modernist work at all, and it is everyday Modernism, not great Modernism. But this book does repeatedly hold Modernist theories accountable for the damage they have done when applied to traditional architecture.

Although the book discusses theory at times, it is not written in "Architect-Speak." It is written for the mainstream audience, and especially for builders, homeowners, and their architects or designers. While it is not exclusively about residential construction, those who are involved in building or planning to build a home are likely the largest group that will find this book useful. It gives everyone the tools to build substantially better, often at little or no additional cost. Some patterns are more expensive, to be sure, but many of the correct details shown actually save money by being simpler and lasting longer. Other patterns simply re-arrange the things being built without adding materials.

This book owes a significant debt to two earlier publications. The structure of the 108 patterns that constitute the majority of the book (pages 60 - 293) is based on that of Christopher Alexander's *A Pattern Language*, as is the idea that architecture can be expressed as a coherent language of patterns. The content of the patterns found on those pages is an expansion on the architectural codes of Duany Plater-Zyberk & Company. The historical facts upon which this book are based are commonly available in many sources, but were verified in the publications listed in the Bibliography on page 294. Because this information is available in several places, no specific references were footnoted.

# CHAPTER I
~
# THE STORY OF THE LANGUAGES OF ARCHITECTURE

PATTERNS in architecture are much like words in a spoken language. Entire vocabularies of patterns, when combined with rules of usage, create styles, or pattern languages. Some forms of expression, such as a smile or a laugh, transcend words and are considered to be universal. This is the first realm of architecture: the universal patterns. Because these patterns are universal, they are found in architectural languages worldwide. The second realm of architecture includes the patterns common to an entire nation, much as a spoken language is common to an entire nation. These patterns are not often specific to any particular style, but usually are incorporated into many of the nation's styles. The third realm includes the patterns common to a region, similar to the dialect of a specific region. The third realm is inhabited primarily by the environmental patterns. The fourth realm includes the patterns found only in a particular locale within a region. Every building can and should speak in a commonly understood language of these patterns to tell the story of its purpose and its place in the culture it serves. The patterns included in this book are almost all patterns of the first and second realms. Second-realm patterns focus primarily on the architectural traditions of North America and Europe since they are the primary forces that created the places inhabited by the intended audience of this book.

## THE FIRST REALM: THE UNIVERSAL

SOME universal patterns in architecture have occurred throughout time and around the globe to such a degree that they obviously address deep and abiding needs in the human heart and mind. The collection of the universal patterns of architecture often fall into one of the following general categories: those which reflect the vertical or the horizontal arrangement of the human body, those which provide physical comforts, and those which put us in harmony with our world as follows:

Studies have shown that from the earliest days of life, babies prefer patterns that resemble the human face and body to patterns of random shapes. Not surprisingly, built form can reflect the human form in many ways. Most traditional architecture reflects the base-shaft-cap (feet-body-head) arrangement of the human body. This base/shaft/cap assembly can be found throughout a building from its overall shape to the design of columns, door casings, and windows; and even to the smallest details, such as the design of a baseboard.

[4]

Most traditional buildings also reflect the symmetry of the human form, at least to some degree. Although the human body can strike many different poses, from the very formal act of a soldier standing at attention to the very informal and relaxed pose of a teenager sprawled at impossible angles over a couch, the human face is essentially symmetrical at all times. This same sort of symmetry is found pervasively at the face (or entry) of traditional buildings around the world. For an example, just go to an old part of any town, stand in any place you choose except the middle of a park and look in any direction; you're sure to see several. Most entries don't look exactly like human faces, of course, but they do possess the basic symmetry of the human face.

Humans also have some basic physical comforts and delights that are truly universal. For example, we are all naturally drawn to light, and we all enjoy a comfortable place to sit. Window seats, therefore, have fulfilled these needs for centuries. Yet, many architects of the past century have overlooked this basic fact. Other small physical comforts have been overlooked as well, such as the pleasing play of filtered, natural light versus harsh, glaring, artificial light. There are legions of methods for accomplishing filtered, natural light, including window muntins, splayed shuttered openings, or a grape vine trained up over an arbor surrounding the window. Most recent architectural styles reject these options as being historical, and therefore, unacceptable, employing large sheets of glass set in hard-edged frames instead.

Architectural harmony is also part of the first realm, and has been explored and studied since antiquity in the work of the ancient Pythagoreans, their Platonic contemporaries, then Vitruvius, and later his Renaissance followers in Europe and by others on other continents. They observed that nearly all harmonies, whether in music, art, and even nature itself, are determined by very simple proportions. For example, the wavelengths of an octave in music have a 2:1 proportion, whereas a melodic perfect fourth interval, which is formed by playing two notes that are five steps apart, has a 3:2 wavelength proportion. The measure of a human is a 1:1 proportion, meaning that a person's height is equal to the distance between the fingertips of their outstretched arms. This is best illustrated by Leonardo da Vinci's famous drawing of a man inscribed in a circle and a square that became the most recognizable icon of the Renaissance. Other simple but irrational proportions such as the square root of 2 and the Golden Mean (0.618...) have similar effects. These theorists and architects held that architecture crafted around these proportions would resonate with humans and with the universe. Considering these universal patterns, beauty in architecture is not an individualized concept changing with every viewer, but is based on certain timeless, universal principles.

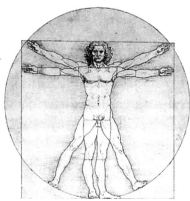

*Leonardo da Vinci,* VITRUVIAN MAN, *pen and ink, 13½ x 9¾ in. Venice, Galleria dell' Accademia, inv. 228.*

# THE SECOND REALM: THE NATIONAL LANGUAGE

JUST as a nation has its own distinct spoken language, it also has a distinct architectural language. Drive from one nation to another in Europe or any other continent, and notice how quickly the character of the buildings changes once you cross the border. Most nations have built up very detailed languages of architectural patterns over the centuries.

[5]

These architectural patterns play the same part in an architectural pattern language as words do in a spoken language. They have been handed down from generation to generation, constituting the collected architectural wisdom of the culture to which they belonged. Patterns, for example, determine how you create a front door, or a porch, or a sunny garden spot.

Why is a common language so important? A pattern language that everyone understands does several critically important things. It tells the story of the nation, its culture, and its place within the larger framework of human history. The pattern language also helps people determine what the building is and how to use it.

A common pattern language tells the story of a culture in several ways. A good building often reads like a family tree, telling us about both our ancient cultural ancestors and our more recent predecessors. For example, the Empire style of the French is composed heavily of classical elements with roots in classical antiquity, but it also incorporates more recent patterns such as roof configurations that are undeniably of French origin.

Spoken language does almost the same thing. English, French, Spanish, Italian, and other western European languages all bear the marks of the ancient Latin from which they're descended. So, too, does the architecture of each of these cultures reflect the heritage of Greek and Roman predecessors, while also telling about the somewhat different course each culture has taken since then. For example, the French Colonial architecture of the United States responded to local issues such as flooding and need for ventilation by building the main level raised several feet above grade, while expressing construction techniques learned from France's Roman colonization by using timber construction with bousillage infill.

Certain patterns are specific to certain building types. A fire station ought to look like a fire station; a post office ought to look like a post office; a city hall ought to look like a city hall; and a school ought to look like a school. Why? Because you should not have to read a sign to know what happens inside a building— you should be able to "read" the building instead. A common pattern language creates communities where the structure, hierarchy, and functions of a town can be understood at a glance, as opposed to the confusing places that modern U.S. cities have become.

A common pattern language also tells how to use a building. One of the first things a building should "tell" its users is how to find the front door. How many times have you wandered around some glass-curtained structure, trying to figure out which glass panel to push to enter the building? Traditional cultures all addressed this issue very clearly: the highest roof often included a front-facing gable, often covering a porch, into which a door was placed with more elaborate trimwork than its counterpart at the loading dock. A visitor could see at first glance where to enter the building.

Many architects are offended by the notion that there ought to be a common pattern language, because they believe it limits their ability to reflect the advances in our changing world. Nothing, however, could be further from the truth. The change is simply evolutionary, not revolutionary. The spoken language is again a wonderful example of how this works. Try to read anything written in fifteenth-century English, and you'll discover just how much English has changed through the ages. Some words fall out of favor and into disuse, while others are invented to address changes that the previous generation couldn't have imagined. But at no time in history has a culture ever decided to discard the entire language and to create something totally new, and especially not just to celebrate some new invention. The English language has evolved to effectively address the needs of the modern world, and architecture can do the same.

## THE THIRD REALM: THE REGIONAL DIALECT

ARCHITECTURAL dialects develop in response to regional climates and available building materials. American colonial structures in the New England states were often built out of plentiful hardwood, whereas brick became the material of choice farther south. They were both Georgian at heart, but the character of each was strikingly different.

For example, the northern most colonies dealt with the problem of harsh winters by pulling all the fireplaces into one great brick chimney in the center of the home. Houses in the South that were too small to include separate kitchen structures usually had chimneys that were pulled out as far as possible, often disengaging from the wall just above the firebox.

New England houses typically were compact with relatively low ceilings, to hold as much heat as possible. Houses from Virginia southward, however, often were spread into long, thin wings. The wings allowed better cross-ventilation. Ceilings were extremely high by today's standards, to allow hot air to rise. The wings often wrapped around outdoor courtyards which could be used as living spaces for much of the year. The walled gardens of Charleston, South Carolina, and the courtyards of the French Quarter in New Orleans, Louisiana, are legendary examples.

Porches tell a similar story. Most northern homes included very little porch space because they could be used only a few months out of the year. Virginia is the northernmost state in which large significant porches are often found. By the time you get to Louisiana, however, they wrap around the entire house, to provide as much shade as possible from the sweltering bayou summer. Southerners' reputation for friendliness and hospitality may well be a direct result of the community-building act of sitting on one's front porch and visiting with neighbors.

The importance of the regional dialects cannot be overstated, since most of the conditions that created them still exist today. Southern houses still can be more comfortable if they are long and thin. Tall ceilings still allow heat to rise. Courtyards are still wonderful places to sit on a summer evening, provided they're oriented to catch the prevailing breezes. Unfortunately, we've become so attuned to the comfort brought by the humming compressor of air conditioners and the false sense of community created by our televisions and computers that we've forgotten how beautiful the regional patterns can be when they are put to work to fulfill our needs. Building materials can now be shipped inexpensively from anywhere, so we don't need to build only with regional materials. Architecture, in other words, has become so easy and cheap that it can be created with very little effort compared to previous centuries. But without effort and commitment, it ceases to be great.

## THE FOURTH REALM: THE LOCAL PARTICULARS

WITHIN a region, localized styles develop that come to have great meaning for that particular place. Sometimes, local styles develop as a result of geography. The sea breezes, the salty dampness, and the views in small seaside communities of a century ago were all strong forces that would render inland architectural patterns ineffectual.

Other times, local styles developed as a result of culture. Many eighteenth-century industrial giants sought out country retreats such as Asheville, North Carolina, and Cumberland Island, Georgia. The prevailing style when most of these places were built was the Shingle Style. The Shingle Style is ubiquitous from Long Island northward, so it carries no special meaning there. To a southerner, however, Shingle Style buildings connote a gracious country retreat.

Today, unfortunately, local patterns rarely exist. Part of this is a result of the pervasiveness of factory-built components that may be shipped anywhere, but the philosophical beginnings of the reason are found in the International Style of the early Modernists, who promoted a style meant to be used anywhere with no regard for local traditions. This attitude has permeated much of Modernism ever since, creating a disregard for local patterns that is all too common amongst mainstream architects.

# HOW THE LANGUAGES WERE LOST

THE heart of Modernism's love affair with the machine has, almost from the beginning, centered on the automobile. Go back and read the writings of the founders of the Modern movement— they're riddled with accounts of exploits such as piling into an early automobile and driving late into the night through the streets of Paris at 100 miles per hour. They exulted over these near-religious experiences and how their eyes were opened to the idea that the new age should be entirely different from everything that came before. Then, they went back to their offices and drew their vision.

Their late-night escapades through Paris heralded what the Modernists hoped would be the death of the entire old monarchy of traditional pattern languages. We were entering a new age of bracing realities and emerging truths, and the age demanded a rethinking of everything. We would live differently, we would work differently, we would eat differently, and we would even sleep differently. The Modernists believed that none of the architectural languages of the old world could even be considered to meet the challenges of the new world. This rejection of all things traditional grew to religious proportions, culminating in Adolf Loos' proclamation that "ornament is sin."

There was, however, a problem Modernists didn't anticipate. Most of the early ones assumed that once they created their mass-produced utopian ideal, the working-class masses would see the brilliance of the Modernist genius and flock to these places. The Modernists didn't realize that you couldn't sell something if you can't communicate with the purchaser, and they had just created an architectural language that was entirely foreign to most people. As a matter of fact, the movement quickly splintered into an entire array of secret languages, since the end result of the movement's insistence on originality was a condition where every great architect was expected to create his or her own language.

Most people rejected "Modernist" architecture in its infancy, and they reject it still today. Modernist architecture may be forced upon people in large doses by the government or by employers. But when people buy their own house to live in, they're going to buy the one with the black cast iron eagle in the gable over the door. The average person has no more appreciation for the machine languages of Modernist architecture than for the squawking machine language of modem noise when she or he signs onto the Internet. By rejecting the architectural pattern languages understood by most people, the architects themselves were also rejected.

The architecture schools soon followed, resulting in several generations of architects stripped of the tools necessary to communicate unless they chose to educate themselves. Today, the best that many architects can achieve are buildings that are sad and hollow cartoons of great buildings of the past. Architecture once communicated a culture's highest aspirations. Architecture that fails to communicate, however, stands mute when it needs to speak. We can do better than that. Indeed, we must do better than that.

## HOW CAN WE REVIVE THE LANGUAGES?

THE greatest changes throughout history have been neither easy nor instantaneous. The struggle to revive the human languages of architecture is a world-changing event, and it will take time.

It appears that we are about halfway into a half-century of renewal of common pattern languages. North America leads most of the developed world, and the southeastern United States is one of the most progressive areas of the country. Traditionally planned towns and neighborhoods are at the vanguard of this movement.

The traditional architecture and traditional town planning movement began as the vision of just a few pioneers. Most were architects. Seaside, Florida (near Panama City in the panhandle), was the first such town. Progress was slow at first, until visitors could see a built picture of the vision. From that point forward, the success has been nothing short of legendary. The public at large voted where it counts: with its pocketbook. *Time* magazine's adulation of Seaside as the "Town of the Century" might even be an understatement.

Huge, popular successes such as Seaside go unnoticed professionally for only so long. Public officials began to see an idea of town planning that made more sense than anything they'd had seen in a century. Most forward-looking civic officials, city planners, and landscape architects around the United States have signed on to the notion of traditional town planning. Only the architects seem unable to face the enormous evidence of the failure of Modernist planning and architectural theories.

Architects might more readily accept traditional town planning ideas if they could separate them from the traditional architecture. But the fact that the general public appears to love the traditional architecture every bit as much as the traditional town planning, seems to be hard for them to swallow. Both traditional town planning and architecture are part of the pattern language, and the average person senses that fact. The early Modernists surmised that average people would see the genius of Modernism's ideas and rush to embrace them for saving the world. Their successors clearly are put off by the fact that the citizenry has finally rushed to embrace a set of architectural ideas, but the ideas they embraced were those of traditional town planners and architects as opposed to their own.

So the majority of the architects are generally coming around very slowly. It may take three or four decades from the beginning of the renaissance for most architects to relearn the languages to a respectable level of fluency. They will then be able to create places just as delightful as their ancestors did. What then? Is the future to be nothing more than a museum of architectural history? No— far from it.

Once society as a whole has relearned the common languages of architecture, the languages can begin to evolve again, just as they have always done since the dawn of time. New construction innovations will emerge, and they will be folded into the industry's bag of tricks. New social realities will arise, to which the common languages will respond. New patterns will arise, and old, irrelevant ones will fall away as architecture learns again to reflect humanity in all its complexity and history rather than just the tools of humans at a single moment in time.

# Chapter 2
~
# Three Great Themes of Traditional Architecture

THE tremendous breadth and variety of styles of traditional architecture are obvious and well documented. Nonetheless, certain themes recur so often in American and European architecture (and arguably that of other cultures also) that they can be considered common themes that transcend any particular style. These themes are not to be confused with universal patterns. Instead, they incorporate many patterns, both from the universal realm and from other realms, and have been recognized for millennia. Nearly two thousand years ago, the Roman architect Vitruvius described them as Commodity, Firmness, and Delight. The Buildings for People theme reflects the core purpose of buildings, which is to serve humanity. This is Commodity. The Apparent Structure theme reflects the core task of buildings, which is to create structures that will not only stand up, but also assure their users by their appearance, sound, and feel that they will continue to do so. This is Firmness. The Celebration of the Act of Building theme reflects the core opportunity of buildings, which is to express the necessities of architecture (light, heat, cooling, water, etc.) in a fashion that brings pleasure and satisfaction to the occupants of the building. This is Delight.

## Buildings for People

TRADITIONAL architecture mirrors humans in a great number of ways. Some reflections are very basic, such as symmetrical entrance facades to mirror the symmetry of the human face, or the composition of base, shaft, and cap, found in everything from columns to entire buildings, which reflected the vertical organization of the human body. Innumerable other reflections of the history, culture, traditions, and even the environment of humans were built into traditional architecture as it developed.

Traditional architecture informs people. Buildings that "speak" in traditional architectural pattern languages communicate many things about themselves to the people who use them. Some of the stories these buildings tell are quite detailed, such as the tale of the layers of architectural history of a particular civilization. Other stories are quite simple, such as how to find the front door.

Traditional architecture does many things for people. Some functions are very utilitarian, such as providing a warm spot of shelter by the fireplace on a long, snowy evening. But the very image created by the words in the last sentence does more than simply describe an act of basic shelter. It hints at pure sensual delights, in the flickering of the firelight and the warmth radiating from the firebricks long after the flames have faded to embers. In any case, the goal of traditional architecture has always been the service of humanity.

Modernist architecture, on the other hand, was focused almost entirely on the machine. Much of the idealism of Modernist architecture was based on the notion that mass-produced buildings would save the world's working classes from their perceived miserable existence at the time by providing cheap, quickly produced housing. The actual buildings were based more on the aesthetic of mass production, however, which is a crucial difference. The only manifestation of true mass-produced buildings is the ubiquitous mobile home, which might therefore be considered the highest form of Modernist architecture.

## APPARENT STRUCTURE

TRADITIONAL buildings are built in such a way that all of the structural elements appear as if they are well capable of standing solid over time. When the structure of a building is apparent, users feel the building is firmer and more secure. This has been achieved using a legion of methods, depending on the time and place in which the building was built.

The biggest influences were the construction materials themselves. In stone construction, massive architectural patterns were created based on the weight of the material. Stone is extremely strong when compressed but less strong when bent, so stone beams could not span very far unless they were very thick since a beam holds up a load by being difficult to bend. Thus, stone columns, such as those found in the temples of antiquity, were usually spaced fairly closely together. The ponderous structural members helped to create the grandest and noblest of all pattern languages. The classical orders of architecture are all based on stone construction.

Brick masonry construction was just as heavy as stone, but the pieces were much smaller, so the architectural patterns were notably different. Brick spans across openings through the act of centering. Centering, at its essence, can be described as a series of wedges laid out so that all the joints between the wedges point to a single center point. Small openings can be spanned with flat brick lintels known as jack arches. Larger openings must be spanned with circular or elliptical arches. Individual bricks are quite small compared to stone structural members, but because many bricks can work together to span an opening, brick vocabularies could become lighter and more open than those of stone. The relative lightness resulted in pattern languages that were somewhat less majestic than those of stone.

The lightest vocabularies of all developed using wood. Wood can span the greatest distances with the least effort. Wood was probably originally used at the dawn of time as individual sticks laid against a log, which hung between the forks of two trees, to create a simple lean-to shelter. People quickly learned that wood was easier to work with when it was dressed down into rectangular pieces. Entirely different systems of connection developed. Stone was heavy enough to simply stack and it would stay put. Brick had mortar to hold it together. Wood pieces had to be pegged, mortised, or nailed together. Lightweight wood structures often required braces to keep them from leaning. An old barn on the verge of collapse illustrates what happens to a wood structure when the bracing is taken away.

Hybrid vocabularies soon developed. A common hybrid system included the strength and grandeur of stone columns, the solidity of brick bearing walls, and the spanning capabilities of wood floor and roof structures. Many traditional architectural patterns have employed this combination. But in any case, traditional structural systems were created according to conservative rules of thumb, with the result that buildings clearly looked as if they could stand up.

Many Modernist styles of architecture, on the other hand, take great delight in appearing to be structurally impossible. Modernist structures are engineered to the least amount of material possible, supposedly to save money, but in reality simply to look impossibly thin.

Unfortunately, many of the prejudices toward thin and insubstantial members have permeated the construction industry. This is largely an issue of cost. There is an assumption that a smaller member is a cheaper member. This is often true, but that fact doesn't always affect the total cost. Reduction in the size of a lintel, for example, doesn't result in an empty spot in the wall; the reduction gets filled in with extra wall material, altering or in some cases eliminating the assumed cost savings.

After a century of exposure, the public has become somewhat desensitized to apparent structural impossibility. Nonetheless, buildings that appear to be structurally sound continue to be perceived as more substantial, better, and therefore more valuable than those that do not.

Many passages within this book refer to the necessity of a building appearing to be structurally sound. It should be exceptionally obvious that simply appearing to be structurally sound is not sufficient. A building should be designed to be structurally sound first. If the resulting structure looks too thin, then the finished surface of the structure should be increased further so that it also appears to be firm and sound as per criteria listed elsewhere in this book.

## CELEBRATION OF THE ACT OF BUILDING

TRADITIONAL architecture celebrated the act of building in an abundance of ways. This tapestry of celebration most often concerned the simplest things, such as gravity and sunlight. Celebration of the act of spanning an opening in a wall resulted in a plethora of different lintels, arches, and headers. Celebration of the connection between column and beam resulted in everything from the cornucopia of bracket forms to the column capitals of the classical orders. Columns themselves celebrated their load-carrying duty in a number of ways, from the slight taper of classical entasis to the way that most column bases spread slightly at the bottom, signifying to the observer the weight that they carry.

Time passed, and building programs and construction technology became increasingly complex. The element that told the story became less likely to be the element that was doing the job. Steel columns began to hold up the weight of the building while classical terra-cotta column casings told the story of holding up the weight, for example. Details such as these were derided by nineteenth-century predecessors of Modernist architects as fake and dishonest, even though the job was still getting done and the story was still being told.

Half a century later, Modernist architecture had its own problems to deal with. One of the foundations of nearly all Modernist styles was the refusal to "tell the story" at all, at least in the traditional sense. Modernists were so focused on with the attempt to "express the new age" that they forgot to let their schools look like schools or to let their fire stations look like fire stations. Modernists were even averse to letting their columns look like columns, preferring instead to have them look like drinking straws. Good sense gave way to the aesthetic of super strong materials and oversimplified assemblies.

These refusals of anything appealing to common sense piled one on top of the other until they created the strangest irony of all. The movement that had begun with the battle cry "Honesty and truth!"

had become the movement in which common techniques and everyday acts of construction were entirely hidden behind a facade of slick stylization.

The pitched roof— that most ancient of techniques of keeping water out of the building— was the first to go. All roofs were to be flat. Structure was the next to be affected. Pipe columns, thanks to the strength of the welded joint, could slam into a beam with no hint of a capital. The steel structure was strong enough to support horizontal ribbons of stone cladding, rendering the otherwise noble stone as little more than fancy (and expensive) wallpaper.

Light fixtures retreated to the cocoon of a tin can. Exterior stairs, which should be the most solid part of a building because they convey people from terra firma to the principal floor of the building, instead became thin ribbons of white, suspended above the ground and then above each other by a nearly invisible steel structure.

Even the technology of joining one piece of material to another became subjugated to the desire for slickness. Moldings, which had been developed over centuries as a method of covering inevitable cracks between materials or planes, were no longer used. Modernists believed workmanship could now be perfect, because machines were going to do everything. The worst problems arose in the joints surrounding the roof, because it is virtually impossible to get one plane to slam perfectly into another in a waterproof manner. Centuries of wisdom were built into that joining of wall and roof at the cornice. And Modernist architecture had purposefully forgotten it all.

The Modernist ideal of honesty, then, became a huge hypocrisy. It is clearly more important for a building to be consistent in the message it communicates than for architects to try to force some fiction of honesty upon the building.

# CHAPTER 3
~
# LEXICON

## WHY DO WE NEED A LEXICON?

THIS chapter sets out a Lexicon of the names of various building parts that are used throughout the rest of this book. Many names have been corrupted in recent times, while others have been entirely replaced with incorrect terms. Few trim carpenters in many parts of the U. S. know either the correct spelling or pronunciation of the word "cornice." A variation of the non-word "Carnish" is most often used, and it is often capitalized, as is its non-mythical cousin, the Cornish hen. Similarly, dormers are as likely as not to be referred to as "doghouses." The quality of construction, incidentally, is often similar to that of the true doghouses. If architecture is to communicate with its users, then its designers and builders should first be able to communicate with one another.

*Italicized terms* used anywhere in this book are defined in the Lexicon. Terms have been included in this Lexicon with which the majority of building owners and/or contractors are unfamiliar. Terms have also been included that are used by contractors but which are unfamiliar to most building owners. Terms in common use everywhere, however, have been excluded. There was no clear need, for example, to define a brick, a door, or a window. Elements of the classical orders of architecture are defined here but assembled in the next chapter.

Terms that describe the same or very similar items have been listed in a single entry with the most common term first such as Porch or Portico. Lexicon items in the list that follows are grouped according to their category in order to be able to compare and grasp the full scope of the family of items. For example, Abacus is listed under Column in the Lexicon so that all of the column parts may be shown together instead of being scattered through the Lexicon according to their alphabetical order.

| TERM | CATEGORY | | | | |
|------|----------|---|---|---|---|
| 5V Metal | Roofing | Architrave | Entablature | Bay | Window |
| Abacus | Column | Astragal | Column | Bead | Molding |
| Abutment | Arch | Astragal | Molding | Beaded Panel | Panel |
| Acanthus | Ornament | Attic | Column Base | Beak | Molding |
| Acroterion | Ornament | Backband | Molding | Bed | Molding |
| Annulet | Molding | Band | Molding | Bed Moldings | Entablature |
| Apophyge | Column | Base | Column | Bevel | Siding |
| Apron | Molding | Base | Molding | Beveled and Rabbeted | Siding |
| | | Base Cap | Molding | Biscuit | Wood Joint |

| Term | Category |
|---|---|
| Board and Batten | Siding |
| Bolection | Molding |
| Bottom Rail | Door |
| Bottom Rail | Window |
| Bow | Window |
| Bowspring | Arch |
| Bracket | Entablature |
| Brick | Molding |
| Broken | Pediment |
| Butt | Wood Joint |
| Campanae | Entablature |
| Campanula | Entablature |
| Capital | Column |
| Cartouche | Ornament |
| Casing | Molding |
| Cavetto | Molding |
| Chair Rail | Molding |
| Cincture | Column |
| Clay Tile | Roofing |
| Clerestory | Window |
| Column | Order |
| Concave | Brick Joint |
| Coped | Wood Joint |
| Corbel | Entablature |
| Cornice | Entablature |
| Cornucopia | Ornament |
| Corona | Entablature |
| Corrugated Metal | Roofing |
| Cove | Molding |
| Crown | Molding |
| Cyma Recta | Molding |
| Cyma Reversa | Molding |
| Cymatium | Entablature |
| Dentil | Entablature |
| Dovetail | Wood Joint |
| Drip Cap | Molding |
| Drop | Siding |
| Dutch Gable | Roof |
| Echinus | Column |
| Egg And Dart | Molding |
| Elliptical | Arch |
| Entablature | Order |
| Entasis | Column |
| Epistylum | Entablature |
| Fanlight | Window |
| Fascia | Entablature |
| Fillet | Molding |
| Finger | Wood Joint |
| Finial | Ornament |
| Flat | Arch |
| Flat | Panel |
| Flush | Brick Joint |
| Flute | Column |
| Foliated | Ornament |
| Frieze | Entablature |
| Gable | Roof |
| Gambrel | Roof |
| Garland | Ornament |
| Gorge | Molding |
| Gothic | Arch |
| Grapevine | Brick Joint |
| Guttae | Entablature |
| Half Hip | Roof |
| Half Round | Molding |
| Head | Opening |
| Header | Brick Course |
| Hinge Stile | Door |
| Hip | Roof |
| Hollow Conge | Molding |
| Impost | Arch |
| Intermediate Rail | Door |
| Jamb | Opening |
| Keystone | Arch |
| Lap | Wood Joint |
| Lock Rail | Door |
| Lock Stile | Door |
| Mansard | Roof |
| Medallion | Ornament |
| Meeting Rail | Window |
| Metal Tile | Roofing |
| Metope | Entablature |
| Miter | Wood Joint |
| Modillion | Entablature |
| Module | Order |
| Mortise and Tenon | Wood Joint |
| Muntin | Door |
| Muntin | Window |
| Mutule | Entablature |
| Necking | Column |
| Ogee | Molding |
| Ovolo | Molding |
| Paneled | Door |
| Paterae | Ornament |
| Pedestal | Order |
| Pegged | Wood Joint |
| Picture Rail | Molding |
| Plank | Siding |
| Plate Rail | Molding |
| Plinth | Column |
| Plinth Block | Molding |
| Pointed | Arch |
| Pulvinated Frieze | Entablature |
| Quarter Round | Molding |
| Quirk | Molding |
| Quirk Ogee | Molding |
| Raised | Panel |
| Raked | Brick Joint |
| Reverse Board and Batten | Siding |
| Reverse Ogee | Molding |
| Roman | Arch |
| Rosette | Ornament |
| Round | Pediment |
| Roundel | Ornament |
| Rowlock | Brick Course |
| Sash | Window |
| Scarf | Wood Joint |
| Scotia | Molding |
| Scroll | Ornament |
| Shaft | Column |
| Shed | Roof |
| Shingle | Siding |
| Shiplap | Siding |
| Shoe | Molding |
| Sidelight | Window |
| Sill | Opening |
| Sill | Window |
| Slate Shingle | Roofing |
| Soffit | Entablature |
| Soldier | Brick Course |
| Springline | Arch |
| Squashed | Brick Joint |
| Standing Seam Metal | Roofing |
| Stile | Window |
| Stool | Window |
| Stop | Molding |
| Stretcher | Brick Course |
| Struck | Brick Joint |
| Swag | Ornament |
| Swelling Conge | Molding |
| Taenia | Entablature |
| Tenia | Entablature |
| Tongue and Groove | Wood Joint |
| Tongue and Groove Beaded Board | Siding |
| Tongue and Groove Flat | Siding |
| Tongue and Groove V-Groove | Siding |
| Top Rail | Door |
| Top Rail | Window |
| Torus | Molding |
| Transom | Window |
| Triglyph | Entablature |
| Tuscan | Column Base |
| Weathered | Brick Joint |
| Wood Shingle | Roofing |
| Wreath | Ornament |

### AEDICULE

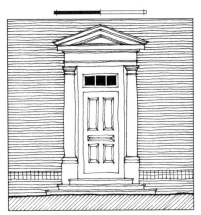

The aedicule (ed-uh-KYOOL) is a door or window opening framed with *columns*, an *entablature*, and usually a *pediment*. It can be viewed either as an extremely enriched *casing* or as a miniature reflection of the *order* of the entire building. A single aedicule is often used for the front door of a building.

### ARCADE

An arcade is a row of arches, just as a *colonnade* is a row of *columns*. An *entablature* and a ceiling may sit above the arches, but the term specifically refers to just the arches and their supporting *piers* and/or *columns*.

### (ARCH) ABUTMENT

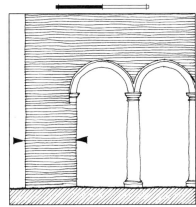

An arch abutment is the solid mass of wall adjacent to or abutting the arch. The abutment is often required in true masonry buildings to resist the horizontal thrust of the arch.

### (ARCH) BOWSPRING

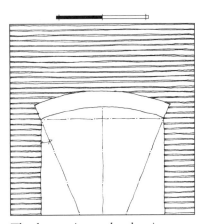

The bowspring arch takes its name from the hunting bow. This type of arch is laid out from a single radius point located well below the *springline* of the arch. In most cases, the sweep of the arch is between 45° and 60°.

### (ARCH) ELLIPTICAL

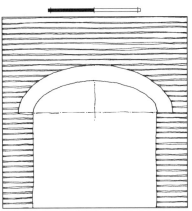

The elliptical arch is exactly one-half of an ellipse. It is usually not a true half-ellipse, but is ordinarily laid out as a series of two shorter radii arcs at the ends and a longer radius arch in the center.

### (ARCH) FLAT, OR JACK

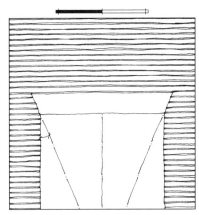

A flat arch, or jack arch, is a *lintel* made up of several wedge-shaped pieces that act structurally as an arch. It can be built of brick or stone. Flat arches can span only relatively small openings.

## (ARCH) IMPOST

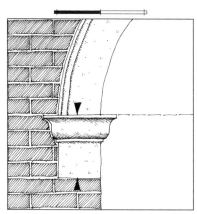

The impost is a block of stone or other masonry material upon which the arch rests. It is usually shaped or enriched, and it occurs immediately below the *springline* of the arch.

## (ARCH) KEYSTONE

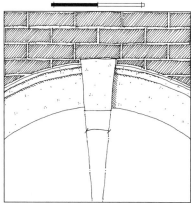

The keystone is the stone at the center of the arch. It is the key to the arch because the arch becomes structurally stable only when it is installed. Keystones are usually larger than the other arch stones and are often adorned with inscribed or applied ornament of many kinds. Keystones occur in *Roman, elliptical,* and *bowspring* arches.

## (ARCH) POINTED, OR GOTHIC

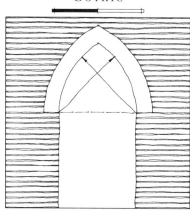

The pointed, or Gothic, arch is constructed of two circular arcs, which are slid toward each other so that they intersect in a point at the top of the arch. This arch type was most commonly used during the Gothic era and during revivals of the style during recent centuries.

## (ARCH) ROMAN

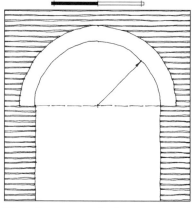

The Roman arch is constructed of a single circular arc that sweeps exactly 180°. The Romans first commonly used it, as its name obviously implies. It has become a part of the vocabulary of many styles since that time.

## (ARCH) SPRINGLINE

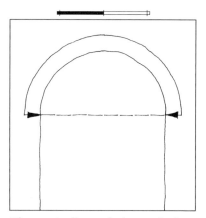

The springline of the arch is a horizontal line that connects the bottoms of the curves of the arch. The radius points of the *Roman* and *Gothic* arches occur on the springline; the radius point of the *bowspring* arch occurs below the springline.

## AXIS

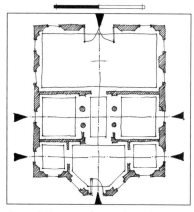

An axis is a regulating line that runs through a building. A series of doors or windows are often aligned along an axis, and building elements are often mirrored on both sides of an axis.

[17]

## BALUSTER

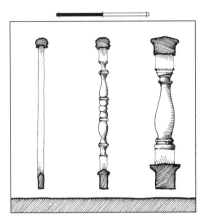

A baluster (BAL-us-tur) is a short post, a series of which are used to support a railing. Simple balusters may be square, whereas more elaborate ones are often turned from thick blocks. Some are shaped to look like miniature columns.

## BALUSTRADE

A balustrade (BAL-us-trade) is a series of *balusters* with their supported railing and with newel posts at each end.

## BARGEBOARD, GABLEBOARD, OR VERGEGBOARD

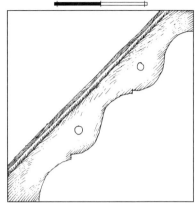

"Bargeboard," "gableboard," and "vergeboard" all refer to the outermost board of the *raking cornice* of a gable. These terms are usually used with Carpenter Gothic or similar styles where this board is cut into sometimes elaborate decorative patterns. The top of the bargeboard occurs flush with the roof deck.

## (BRICK COURSE) HEADER

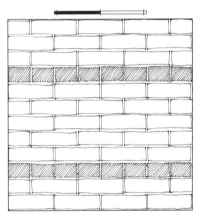

The exposed surface of a header brick is nominally $2^1/_4$" tall and 4" wide. Header courses were once commonly used to tie two *wythes* of brick together. Because they are the same height as a *stretcher* brick, headers can be alternated with *stretchers* to create a number of decorative bond patterns.

## (BRICK COURSE) ROWLOCK

The exposed surface of a rowlock brick is nominally 4" tall and $2^1/_4$" wide. Rowlock courses were also used to tie two *wythes* of brick together; but because they do not match the height of a *stretcher* course, they must be used alone in a course. Rowlock courses are now most commonly used to create brick sills under windows.

## (BRICK COURSE) SOLDIER

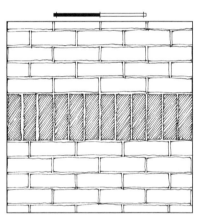

The exposed surface of a soldier brick is nominally $2^1/_4$" wide and 8" tall. Soldier courses were used historically for a number of functions, including belt courses. They are now also used to finish out the top of a *brick veneer* wall, as this is the easiest way to get the top course of brick inserted behind the *frieze* board.

### (BRICK COURSE) STRETCHER

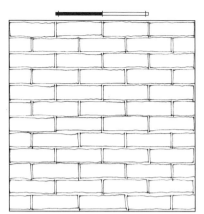

Stretchers are the most common of all courses, making up the vast majority of all brickwork. The exposed surface of a stretcher brick is nominally 8" wide and $2\frac{1}{4}$" tall.

### (BRICK JOINT) CONCAVE

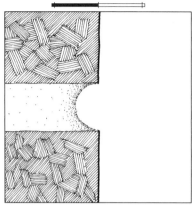

The simple concave tooled brick joint is both the simplest and the most weatherproof joint available. It is created by compressing the mortar with a rounded tool which creates a harder surface that curves out to shed water. It is the joint most commonly found on masonry buildings built before 1925.

### (BRICK JOINT) FLUSH OR RIBBON

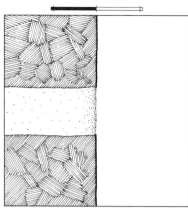

The flush brick joint is achieved by cutting the mortar off at the surface of the brick with a trowel. It is not particularly waterproof because the mortar is not compressed. Ribbon joints also have a flush surface but were carefully tooled to compact the mortar. Ribbon joints are the standard joints for fine-quality Federal-period buildings.

### (BRICK JOINT) GRAPEVINE

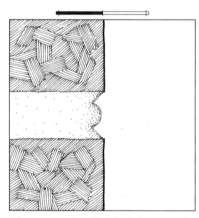

The grapevine brick joint can be any number of slightly different shapes. They are tooled similarly to the *concave* joint, but with a tool that leaves a bead of mortar of various shapes at the center of the joint. It is quite waterproof and was never common due to its more detailed nature, but was found most often prior to 1925.

### (BRICK JOINT) RAKED

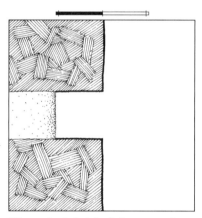

The raked brick joint may have been the most popular joint among architects in the past half-century, but it is notoriously nonresistant to the elements. It also has a fairly harsh appearance because the mortar is in shadow most of the day. This effect makes the brick seem discontinuous from the wall, masking its structural properties.

### (BRICK JOINT) SQUASHED

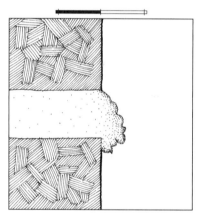

The squashed brick joint is the least weatherproof joint ever to be commonly used. It is also the least orderly. To create this joint, the mason simply squashes mortar out of the joint as he or she places the brick and then leaves it there. Some architects claim that it is rustic, but traditional rustic masons would probably have been ashamed of it.

## (BRICK JOINT) STRUCK, WEATHERED

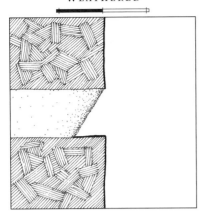

The struck joint (illustrated) is formed by striking downward from the bottom edge of the brick, cutting the mortar off at an angle. It is an unnatural joint type that is doubly susceptible to the weather because it provides a horizontal ledge for water accumulation and a non-compressed mortar surface for the water to soak into. Weathered joints are reverse.

## BRICK VENEER

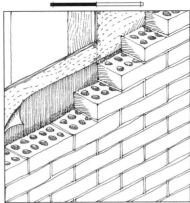

Brick veneer construction consists of a single *wythe* of brick over some other backup wall material such as concrete block or (more commonly) wood or lightgauge metal frame construction. This method has been in common use for most of a century and has been almost the only way of building a brick-finished wall for 50 years.

## BRICK WYTHE

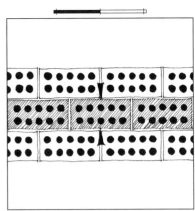

One wythe of brick is a single layer, or wall, of brick. *Brick veneer* construction, by definition, is a single wythe of brick. True masonry walls are built of multiple wythes of brick, concrete block, or other masonry units.

## CHAMFER

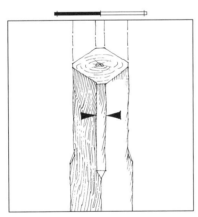

The chamfer is generally the beveling of an edge or corner to produce an oblique plane, often at 45° to the original planes. Small chamfers often occur at corners of walls, *posts* or *pilasters* to lessen the likelihood of damage to the corner.

## COFFER

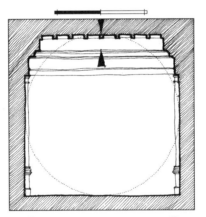

Coffers are recesses into a ceiling, arch, or dome. They are understood today as being a single recess into a ceiling. While this is technically correct, there were traditionally several small coffers in a large ceiling. Coffers are typically square except in the case of coffered domes, where they are wedge-shaped.

## COLONNADE

A colonnade is a row of *columns*, just as an *arcade* is a row of arches. They may be surmounted by an *entablature* and a ceiling, but the term specifically refers to just the *columns*.

### (COLUMN) ABACUS

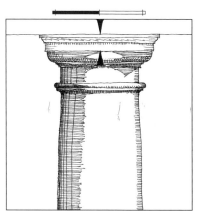

The abacus is the uppermost element of the column *capital*. It is a simple square slab in the simpler *orders*, but gets somewhat more enriched with the more elaborate *orders*.

### (COLUMN) APOPHYGE

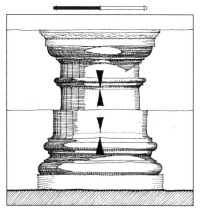

The apophyge (uh-POF-uh-jee) is a *cavetto* that occurs at the top and/or bottom of the *column shaft*, creating a joint with the *capital* and/or *base*. The surface of the apophyge flows smoothly into the surface of the *column shaft*.

### (COLUMN) ASTRAGAL

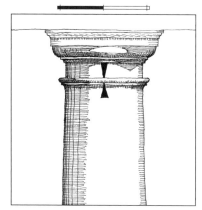

The column astragal (ASS-truh-gul) occurs beneath the *necking* on Tuscan and Roman Doric columns. It typically consists of a small *half-round* molding and occurs above the *cincture* of the *apophyge*.

### (COLUMN) BASE

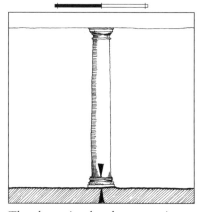

The base is the lowest primary division of the *column*. Some column base types such as the *Attic bases* have been used almost interchangeably across several *orders*. The Greek Doric order typically had no column base whatsoever.

### (COLUMN) CAPITAL

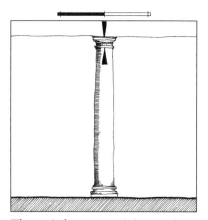

The capital, or cap, as it is sometimes called, is the top primary division of the *column*. Capitals are usually the most distinctive portions of an entire *order*, typically serving to identify the entire *order* much as the human face typically serves to identify the person.

### (COLUMN) CINCTURE

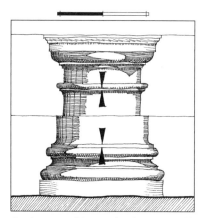

A cincture (SINK-chur) is a small, flat mold that separates the *base* or *capital* from the *apophyge* of the *shaft* (if there is an *apophyge*.) A cincture is a specialized type of *fillet* or *band*.

### (COLUMN) ECHINUS

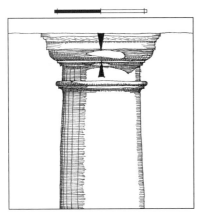

The echinus (uh-KEEN-us) is the uppermost turned element of the *capital*, and it occurs just below the *abacus*. It is usually an elliptical *ovolo* in the Greek orders but is a radial *quarter round* in the Tuscan and Roman *orders*. The echinus often rests upon a *cavetto* or *fillet*.

### (COLUMN) ENTASIS OR DIMINUTION

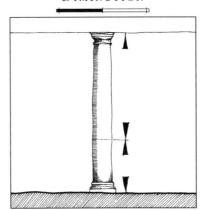

"Entasis" (EN-tuh-sis) is a term that originally described the elaborate optical correction employed by the Greeks on their most treasured buildings. Unfortunately, no one has built to that degree of sophistication for millennia, so the term is now used to describe only one aspect of entasis: the elegant taper or diminution of the classical *column*.

### (COLUMN) FLUTE

Flutes are vertical grooves cut into the surface of *column shafts*. Greek Doric flutes touched each other, coming to a point and running from the *capital* to the bottom of the *column*. Flutes of other *orders* do not touch, leaving a narrow ridge of *column* face between each flute and terminating just below the *capital* and above the *base*.

### (COLUMN) NECKING

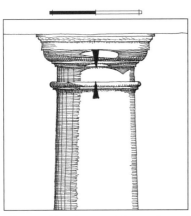

The necking is a straight section of column *shaft* that occurs below the *echinus* and above the *astragal* in the Tuscan and Roman Doric *order*.

### (COLUMN) PLINTH

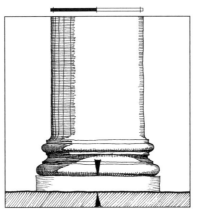

The plinth is the lowest part of the *column base*, and it is usually composed of a simple square-edged block. It carries the greatest weight of any column part, so its plain, stocky appearance is appropriate to its function.

### (COLUMN) SHAFT

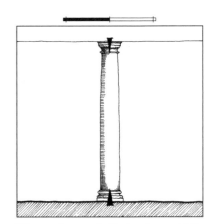

The column shaft is the middle primary division of the *column* and includes everything between the *base* and the *capital*. Every classical *column* has some sort of taper, resulting in the top of the *shaft* being thinner than the bottom of the *shaft*. See *(Column) Entasis*.

### COLUMN BASE - ATTIC

Some variation of the Attic column base is often used in the Roman Doric, Ionic, Corinthian, and Composite *orders*. The simplest version of the Attic base is a round *cavetto* over a round *torus* over a round *scotia* over a round *torus* over a square *plinth block*.

### COLUMN BASE - TUSCAN

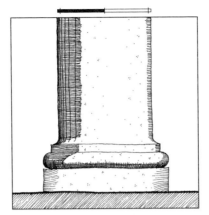

The Tuscan column base consists of a round *cavetto* over a round *torus* over a square *plinth block*. It was typically used only in the Tuscan *order*.

### CORBEL

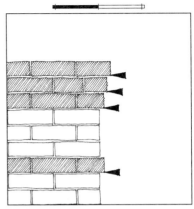

A corbel (COR-bul) is typically a small projection in a wall. It occurs most often in brick walls and is achieved by stepping the brick out $1/2$" to $1 1/2$". The amount of corbel is limited if the brick is cored. Cores are holes in the brick used to reduce shipping weight. Corbel can also mean a small supporting *bracket* or *modillion*.

### CORNER BLOCKS - CASING

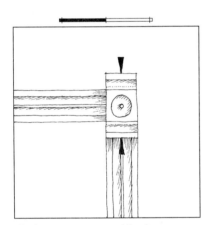

*Casing* corner blocks were enormously popular during the nineteenth-century romantic era. They formed the joint between *head casing* and *jamb casings* and were often elaborately carved, usually with some sort of bull's-eye pattern. They were the same width as the *jamb casings*, but were usually thicker.

### CORNER BLOCKS - TRIM

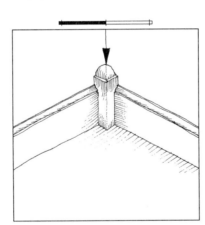

Trim corner blocks most often occur at inside corner joints of trim boards. They were first widely used in the romantic styles of the nineteenth century, and their ends were sometimes elaborately carved. Today's corner blocks are usually very simple, and they are often used to avoid making a proper *coped joint*.

### (DOOR) BOTTOM RAIL

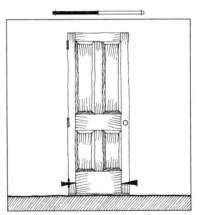

The bottom rail of a door is the horizontal framing member that runs from *hinge stile* to *lock stile* at the bottom of the door. Bottom rails are sometimes fairly tall, to reinforce the bottom of the door, since this area takes a great deal of abuse. Metal kick plates are mounted across the bottom rail to provide greater protection.

### (DOOR) HINGE STILE

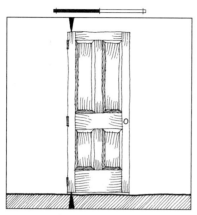

Door stiles are the outermost framing members of a door, running vertically from top to bottom of the door at each outside edge. The hinge stile is the one to which the hinges attach and by which the door is hung.

### (DOOR) INTERMEDIATE RAIL

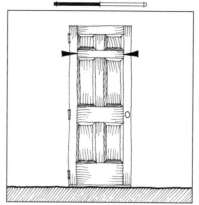

An intermediate rail of a door is any horizontal framing member that runs from *hinge stile* to *lock stile* except the *top*, *bottom*, or *lock rails*. Intermediate rails are sometimes required for strength on very tall doors when the *panels* would otherwise be too tall, but intermediate rails are usually used for aesthetic reasons to achieve a particular design.

### (DOOR) LOCK RAIL

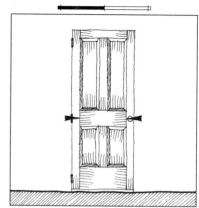

The lock rail of a door is the horizontal framing member that runs from *hinge stile* to *lock stile* at the height of the latch. Lock rails are necessary because the lock area endures the greatest degree of structural stress in a door. Some door designs use a double lock rail with a horizontal *panel* between the two rails.

### (DOOR) LOCK STILE

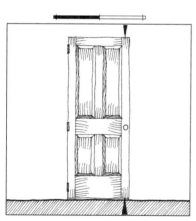

Door stiles are the outermost framing members of a door, running vertically from top to bottom of door at each outside edge. The lock stile is the one into which the lock is set.

### (DOOR) MUNTIN

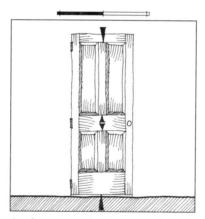

A door muntin is any framing member that does not extend entirely from top to bottom of the door or from *stile* to *stile*. Muntins are most commonly used to divide vertical *panels*.

### (DOOR) PANELS

For centuries paneled doors were both the most common and the most refined types of doors built. Paneled doors are generally constructed of *stiles* (vertical members), *rails* (horizontal members), *muntins*, and panels. All members were usually built of wood until the middle of the twentieth century. See *Panel (Flat)* and *Panel (Raised)*.

### (DOOR) TOP RAIL

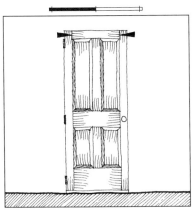

The top rail of a door is the horizontal framing member that runs from *hinge stile* to *lock stile* at the top of the door.

### DORMER

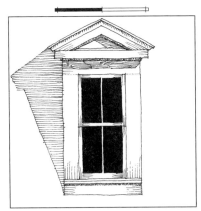

Dormers are small roofed boxes built on top of roofs for the purpose of installing windows or louvers. They are often incorrectly called "doghouses." Dormers are much more energy-efficient and weatherproof than skylights. They have been used for centuries as an elegant way to meet the sky and light the attic.

### DRIP

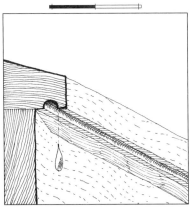

Drips are grooves cut into the bottom of an object such as a window *sill* or *cornice* near the outside edge for the purpose of shedding water. Water that runs back under an object cannot run past the drip and falls away, rather than running back farther to streak the face of the object below.

### EAVE RETURN

The eave return is the section of eave detail that returns along a *gable* wall. It has bedeviled the construction industry for decades. The notorious "pork chop eave" (see page 202) is an icon of cheap tract house construction. The Greek return (shown here in simple form) and its alternatives have solved this problem with much greater elegance.

### (ENTABLATURE) ARCHITRAVE OR EPISTYLUM

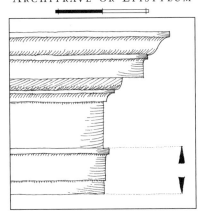

The architrave (AR-kuh-trave) is the lowest and simplest primary division of the *entablature*. Architraves were once heavy timber beams that supported the rest of the *entablature*. Their strong, stocky appearance followed them from ancient wood construction to the classical *orders*.

### (ENTABLATURE) BED MOLDINGS

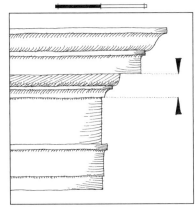

The bed moldings are the lowest primary division of the *cornice*; they occur just below the *corona*. The simplest bed molding is an *ovolo* over a *cavetto* separated by a *fillet*, and it was often used in the Tuscan *order*. More elaborate *orders* usually enriched the basic bed mold with other minor shapes and with *dentils*.

## (ENTABLATURE) BRACKET, CORBEL, OR MODILLION

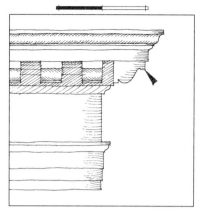

"Bracket," "corbel," and "modillion" are terms that can often be used interchangeably. All occur at regular spacing supporting the *cornice*, just above the top of the *frieze*. If there is a distinction, it is that brackets can be very simple vernacular supporting elements, while corbels and modillions are at least somewhat refined and classical.

## (ENTABLATURE) CYMATIUM

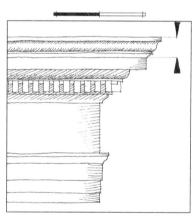

The cymatium (si-MAY-she-um) is the upper primary division of the *cornice*. It is therefore the point where the building meets the sky. It is usually a *cyma recta* (hence the name), but it can also be an *ovolo* or *cavetto*. The common term used for the cymatium is *crown mold*.

## (ENTABLATURE) CORNICE

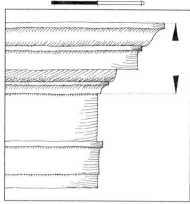

The cornice is the uppermost primary division of the *entablature*. Cornice designs can be quite varied, but they all include at least three basic divisions. The first is a crowning element that meets the sky. It is built on the second, a simpler element that projects well beyond the wall. The lowest division connects the cornice to the *frieze*.

## (ENTABLATURE) DENTIL

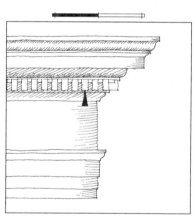

Dentils are small blocks used to enrich the base of the *cornice*. Their name is the result of their resemblance to human teeth. They ordinarily occur within or adjacent to the *bed moldings*.

## (ENTABLATURE) CORONA

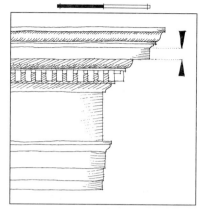

The corona is the central primary division of the *cornice*. It is a simple boxlike shape with a vertical *fascia* and a *soffit* underneath. The joint between the *fascia* and *soffit* normally includes a *drip* to throw water off the building.

## (ENTABLATURE) FASCIA

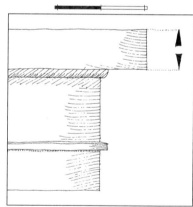

A fascia (FA-she-uh) is generally a plain, vertically faced band. Specifically, the fascia is the vertical surface of the *corona* of the *cornice*. It is usually the last remaining element of the classical *entablature* on very humble buildings (shown here) where the *order* has been greatly reduced. The fascia is often incorrectly called "facer," or "facer-board."

## (ENTABLATURE) FRIEZE

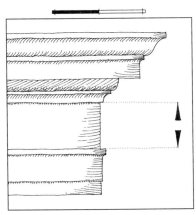

The frieze is the middle primary division of the *entablature*. It is usually composed of a single flat surface upon which sculptural enrichment often occurred until the past century. It may also be elaborated with *triglyphs* and *metopes*, or it may be *pulvinated* (curved outward).

## (ENTABLATURE) GUTTAE, CAMPANAE, OR CAMPANULA

The guttae (GOO-tay) are small shapes that occur immediately under the *taenia* and directly below the *triglyphs*. They may be cylinders, cones, or pyramids. Two guttae occur beneath each glyph of the *triglyph*, for a total of six guttae.

## (ENTABLATURE) METOPE

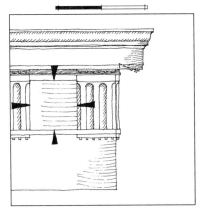

The metope (MET-uh-pee) is the portion of the *frieze* between *triglyphs*. It can be left flat, but was often adorned with very rich relief or elaborate sculptural work until the twentieth century. The metope should be square.

## (ENTABLATURE) MUTULE

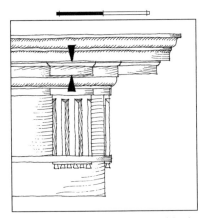

Mutules (MYOO-chool) are blocks that hang over *triglyphs* in the Doric *order*. Greek Doric mutules slope with the roof, while Roman Doric mutules are horizontal. Greek Doric mutules typically have six rows of *guttae* on their *soffit* that align over the *guttae* of the *triglyphs*.

## (ENTABLATURE) PULVINATED FRIEZE

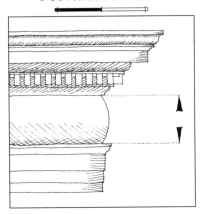

A pulvinated, or pillowed, frieze typically occurred within *orders* no less ornate than the Ionic. Pulvination results in a convex frieze that swells out away from the building.

## (ENTABLATURE) SOFFIT

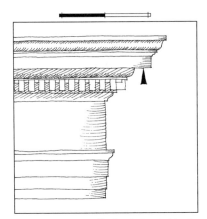

The term "soffit," (SOFF-it) in general, can describe the underside of many traditional building parts. The most common use of the word is to describe the underside of the *corona* of the *cornice*.

## (ENTABLATURE) TAENIA OR TENIA

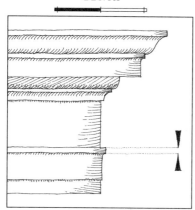

The taenia (TEE-nee-uh) is a somewhat blocky *fillet* that occurs at the top of the *architrave*, separating it from the *frieze*. It is seldom enriched except in the most ornate of *orders*.

## (ENTABLATURE) TRIGLYPH

Triglyphs are symbolic of roof beam ends, and they occur in the *frieze* of the Doric *order*. There are naturally three glyphs in each triglyph. The joints between each glyph either can be fluted (typical of Greek Doric) or "raked out as if by the point of a carpenter's square," per Vitruvius and typical of Roman Doric.

## INTERCOLUMNIATION

Intercolumniation is the measure of the spacing of *columns*. Intercolumniation is measured in *modules*. See *(Order) Module*.

## LANTERN, CUPOLA, OR BELVEDERE

"Lantern," "cupola," and "belvedere" are terms describing small structures that sit atop a roof to let light or air into or out of a building. Lanterns clearly have windows, while cupolas and belvederes may contain louvered vents. Weathervanes, spires, or flagpoles are sometimes incorporated in the design of all three.

## LINTEL OR HYPERTHYRON

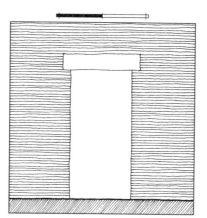

"Lintel" is a general term for a beam that spans an opening. Nearly every traditional architectural vocabulary has celebrated the lintel in some manner, enriching it in a manner consistent with both its structural nature and its function of providing a place for people, light, or air to enter and exit.

## LOGGIA

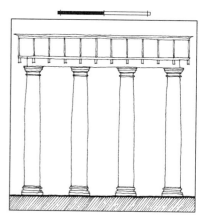

A loggia (LOW-jhe-uh) is an exterior roofed structure that is open to the weather on one or more sides. The roof is usually supported by an *arcade* or *colonnade* on the open sides. A loggia can be free-standing (shown here), but is usually attached to a larger building, in which case it is the same as a *portico* or *porch*.

### (Molding) Apron

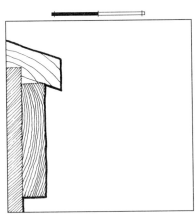

The apron is a flat board placed directly under a window *sill*. This modern term can also be used to describe a flat board beneath a cabinet. Ancient types generally are more elemental, while modern shapes are often made up of several ancient shapes. We define any molding name invented in the past two centuries or so as "modern."

### (Molding) Astragal

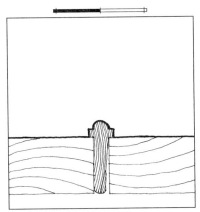

The astragal (ASS-truh-gul) molding is generally a small *half-round* possibly with a *fillet* on one or both sides. Astragals are used most often today to join a pair of double doors as illustrated above.

### (Molding) Backband

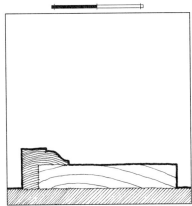

"Backband" is a modern term that describes several molding shapes. Their primary purpose is to enrich flat *casings*. It is a separate piece, allowing the bulk of the *casing* to be made of a flat board while only the backband is molded, thus reducing the material cost of the complete *casing*. The shaped portion of a backband is often a *cyma reversa*.

### (Molding) Base

"Base" or "baseboard" is a blanket term for a molding at the bottom of a wall. It can be composed of numerous combinations of shapes, but generally includes one or more tall flat boards with enrichment at the top and possibly the bottom. The most common modern base is a flat board with a small *cyma reversa* at the top.

### (Molding) Base Cap

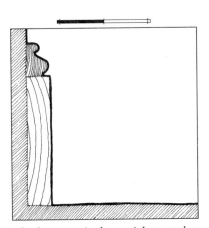

The base cap is the enrichment that occurs at the top of a *base*. It is a separate piece, allowing the bulk of the *base* to be made of flat boards while only the base cap is molded, thus reducing the material cost of the complete base.

### (Molding) Bead

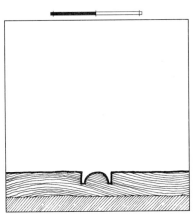

The bead mold can take several related shapes, all of which include at least a *half-round*. Beads are sometimes incised into otherwise flat *panels*.

### (MOLDING) BEAK

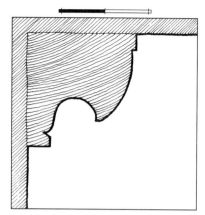

The beak mold is the most complex molding shape: It derives its name from its resemblance to an eagle's beak. It is composed of a variety of radially or elliptically curved shapes. It is an undercut shape, which means that parts of the shape are hidden when it is viewed from the side.

### (MOLDING) BED

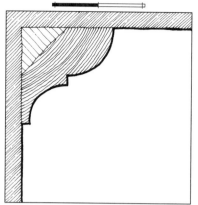

"Bed mold" is a term that describes a number of shapes that occur at the bottom of the *cornice*. The most common bed mold is a *quarter round* over a *cove* with a small *fillet* between the two shapes, as discussed earlier. Bed molds can also be used in other similar situations where one shape overhangs the other.

### (MOLDING) BOLECTION

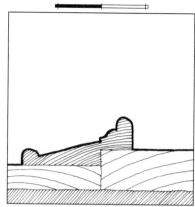

"Bolection (bo-LECK-shun) molding" is a general term that applies to molds that cover joints between materials of different thicknesses, such as door frames and door *panels*. The exposed surface of a bolection molding can take any number of shapes.

### (MOLDING) BRICK

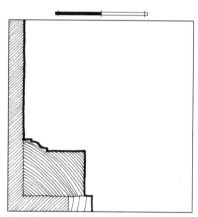

"Brick mold" is a modern term that describes a narrow, chunky shape currently used to trim the exterior of most wood windows. It is usually a block of wood close to 2" square that is nominally enriched with a very shallow *cyma reversa*.

### (MOLDING) CASING

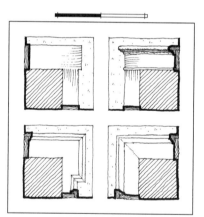

"Casing" is a general term that describes any shapes used to trim a door, window, or cased opening to a wall. Casings can occur on the interior or exterior of a building. Casings range from simple flat boards to very elaborate multipart assemblies.

### (MOLDING) CHAIR RAIL

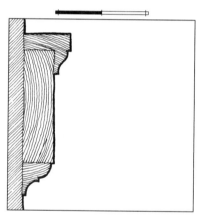

"Chair rail" is a general term that describes any shape that is installed horizontally on a wall, often about 3' above the floor. Chair rails are meant to protect wall surfaces from damage by chairs. Chair rails are usually the top shape of a *wainscot*.

(MOLDING) COVE, CAVETTO, HOLLOW CONGE, OR GORGE

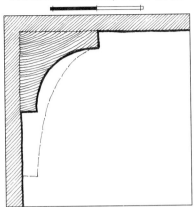

The cove is a circular concave molding and is the opposite of a *quarter round*. A *quarter round* fit into a cove would create a square block. The cavetto (kuh-VETT-oh), hollow conge (KON-zha), or gorge can be identical to a cove, or it can be composed of an elliptical concave curve instead of a circular one.

(MOLDING) CROWN

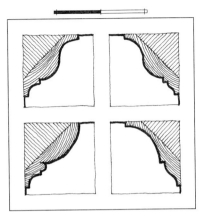

The most common type of crown mold is a *cyma recta* over a *cove (cavetto, hollow conge, or gorge)*. This shape approximates the upper third of a Tuscan *cornice*. Other common crowns include a *cyma recta* over a small *cyma reversa* or *cyma recta* over *dentils*. The cove crown is a *cove (cavetto, hollow conge, or gorge)* over a *cyma reversa*.

(MOLDING) CYMA RECTA OR OGEE

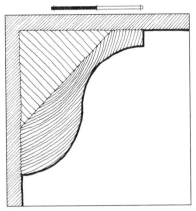

The cyma (SI-muh) recta is made up of a *cove (cavetto, hollow conge, or gorge)* over a *quarter round (ovolo, swelling conge)* meeting smoothly to form an S-curve. The literal meaning of cyma is "wave." The cyma recta is the most common component of *crown* molding.

(MOLDING) CYMA REVERSA OR REVERSE OGEE

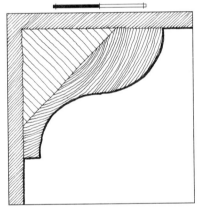

The cyma (SI-muh) reversa is the opposite of the *cyma recta*, made up of a *quarter round (ovolo, swelling conge)* over a *cove (cavetto, hollow conge, or gorge)* meeting smoothly to form an S-curve. The cyma reversa is similar to a *bed mold*, and is often used in similar conditions.

(MOLDING) DRIP CAP

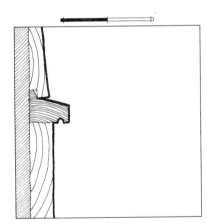

"Drip cap" is a modern term used to describe any shape with a *drip* that is intended to shed water. Drip caps are used most often over doors or windows and usually include an upper leg which extends up behind siding boards and a lower leg which projects well beyond the shape below. The top of the lower leg is sloped to shed water.

(MOLDING) EGG AND DART

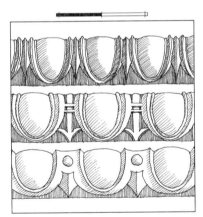

The egg and dart may be the most common molding enrichment ever. It is typically used on the *ovolo*, but it can be used on other shapes as well. It has many variations, but typically consists of a series of oval (egg) shapes separated by thin arrowhead or dart-shaped patterns.

### (MOLDING) FILLET, ANNULET, OR BAND

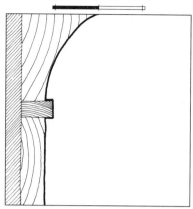

The fillet is a small square or flat shape that enriches a larger shape. It is often used to separate two other shapes. An annulet is a fillet that encircles a column. "Band" is a modern term that can mean the same as "fillet," but sometimes carries the implication of being larger than a fillet.

### (MOLDING) HALF ROUND OR TORUS

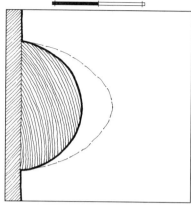

The ___ is exactly what the name implies: a circular convex molding that is exactly one half of a fully round rod. The torus is a half-round that encircles a column *base*. The torus can also be elliptically shaped in rare instances.

### (MOLDING) PICTURE RAIL

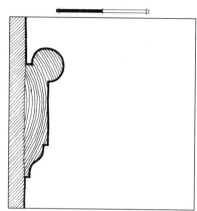

The picture rail is a fairly modern shape that is attached close to the ceiling. It is designed to hold hooks from which pictures are hung below. The most generic shape of picture rail is a three-quarter *bead* over a *fascia* over a *cyma reversa*.

### (MOLDING) PLATE RAIL

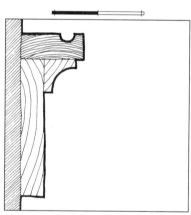

The plate rail is a very recent invention, occurring first in the Craftsman houses of the early twentieth century. It usually occurs at the top of tall Craftsman *wainscots*. It is composed of a wide horizontal board with one or more grooves into which the edges of plates or other objects are placed, allowing them to be displayed against the wall.

### (MOLDING) PLINTH BLOCK

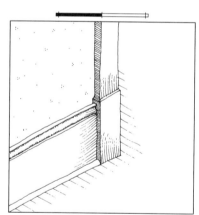

The plinth block molding is distinctly different from a *column* plinth. This shape can be either a plain or a beveled block. It is installed at the bottom of *jamb casings* where the *baseboard* is thicker than the *casing*. The plinth block is thicker than both and is taller than the *baseboard*, giving the *baseboard* a thick surface to die into.

### (MOLDING) QUARTER ROUND, OVOLO, OR SWELLING CONGE

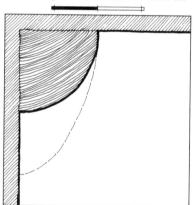

The quarter round is exactly what the name implies: a circular convex molding that is exactly one quarter of a fully round rod. The ovolo (OH-vuh-low) or swelling conge (KON-zha) can be a quarter round, or it can be one quarter of an elliptical rod.

### (MOLDING) QUIRK

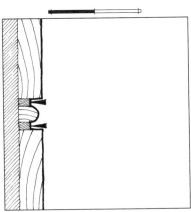

The quirk is an indentation that separates one shape from another. *Beads* incised in *panels* are separated from the face of the *panel* by quirks on either side.

### (MOLDING) QUIRK OGEE

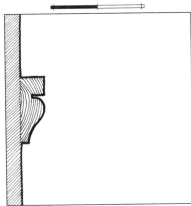

The quirk ogee is a relatively modern shape sometimes used to finish the top corner of a shape. It is composed of a *band* over a *quirk* over a *half round* over a *cove*.

### (MOLDING) SCOTIA

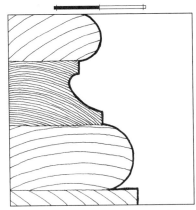

The scotia (SKO-shuh) mold is composed of a *fillet* over a small *cavetto* over a large *cavetto* over another, sometimes larger *fillet*. The scotia is used most often to separate two *tori* of an *Attic column base*.

### (MOLDING) SHOE

The shoe mold is a special sort of elliptical *ovolo* that is taller than it is wide and that is designed to be installed at the bottom of a *baseboard*. "Shoe mold" is a modern term.

### (MOLDING) STOP

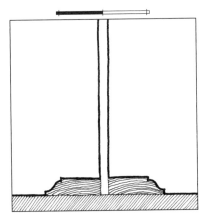

"Stop mold" is a general term that describes any small shape used to fix, or stop, glass into a sash or frame or to stop a sash into a frame.

### MULLION

A mullion (MULL-yen) is a member that joins wall openings such as doors, windows, or cased openings. Mullion *casings* should be flat in most cases and should hardly ever be less than 4" wide (nominal).

### OBELISK

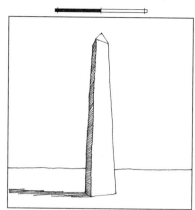

Obelisks (OB-a-lisk) are three- or four-sided shafts that taper slightly from bottom to top and are capped with a peaked shape. The Washington Monument is the world's tallest obelisk. Obelisks are most often used in the streetscape or landscape to mark an important place, although miniature obelisks can be found in furniture design.

### (OPENING) HEAD

The head of an opening is the top member of the opening. It is usually horizontal. The term "head" applies to both the *casing* and the frame.

### (OPENING) JAMB

The jambs of an opening are the side members of the opening. They are usually vertical. The term "jamb" applies to both the *casing* and the frame.

### (OPENING) SILL

The sill of an opening is the bottom member of the opening. It is usually horizontal. The term "sill" applies to both the *casing* and the frame and is most commonly used with window openings. Door sills, when they occur, are usually referred to as "thresholds."

### ORDER

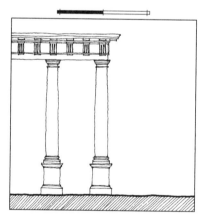

The order is the basic organizing device of classical architecture. Its three primary divisions are the *entablature*, the *column*, and the *pedestal*. The primary orders are Doric (Greek and Roman), Ionic, and Corinthian. Others include the Composite order, which is a combination of Ionic and Corinthian, and the simple Tuscan order.

### (ORDER) COLUMN

The column is the central primary division of the *order*. Columns support the *entablature* and may rest upon *pedestals*. The three primary divisions of the column are the *capital*, the *shaft*, and the *base*. They may be compared to the head, body, and feet of the human form.

## (ORDER) ENTABLATURE

The entablature (in-TAB-luh-chur) is the upper primary division of the *order*. The utilitarian functions of the entablature are to support the roof framing and to throw water away from the building. The three primary divisions of the entablature are the *cornice*, the *frieze,* and the *architrave.*

## (ORDER) MODULE

The module is the primary measuring device of the *order*. The module is the thickness of a *column* just above the *base*. All other parts of an *order* are usually expressed in modules. One of the beauties of the modular system is that it allows correct proportions to be more easily maintained at any scale.

## (ORDER) PEDESTAL

The pedestal is the lowest primary division of the *order*. It is the only optional division and is often not included, especially in humbler buildings where its inclusion would make the other elements seem too small. The three primary divisions of the pedestal are the *cornice*, the *dado*, and the *plinth*.

## (ORNAMENT) ACANTHUS

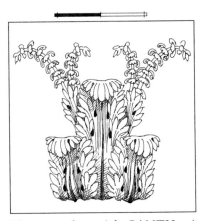

The acanthus (uh-CANTH-us) motif is one of the most pervasive of all traditional architecture. The acanthus plant grows wild in the Mediterranean region, with graceful, looping serrated leaves. Its stylized form can be found on many classical elements, from the Corinthian *capital* to the *foliated scroll.*

## (ORNAMENT) ACROTERION

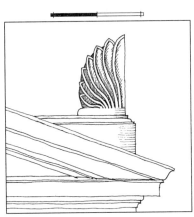

The acroterion (ak-ruh-TER-ee-un) is a pedestal found sometimes at the ends of ridges and/or eaves of the roofs of classical buildings. Acroteria are typically used to support statuary or other sculptural ornaments. Acroteria are part of the long heritage of the celebration of the places where buildings meet the sky.

## (ORNAMENT) CARTOUCHE

A cartouche (car-TOOSH) is a decorative panel normally installed on a vertical surface such as a wall. It is often symmetrical side to side, but hardly ever top to bottom. The ornament may be either inscribed or in relief, and it can be quite elaborate. A cartouche is often circular or elliptical and may have a convex surface.

### (ORNAMENT) CORNUCOPIA

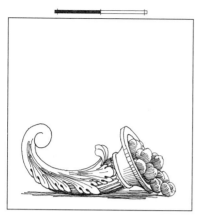

The cornucopia, (corn-yoo-KO-pee-uh) or horn of plenty, is a decorative motif that has been used since antiquity. It is sometimes associated with agricultural themes, since it represents a bountiful harvest.

### (ORNAMENT) FINIAL

"Finial" is a general term that applies to any decorative shape that terminates, or finishes, the top of an object. Finials may occur on anything from fence posts to bedposts. They may be simple turned shapes, or may be sculpted to represent objects as diverse as pineapples and spearheads.

### (ORNAMENT) FOLIATED

A foliated ornament is any shape or device that represents any form of foliage. Many species of plants have inspired foliated ornamentation in every culture throughout the ages, although none has been more commonly used than the Mediterranean *Acanthus* plant.

### (ORNAMENT) GARLAND OR SWAG

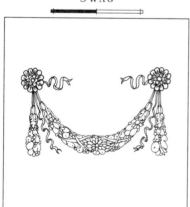

The garland, or swag, is an ornamental motif that generally is draped between two points of attachment. The garland is often *foliated*, while the swag is often more abstract, sometimes representing fabric. The terms, however, are often used interchangeably. "Garland" can also mean a *wreath* shape.

### (ORNAMENT) MEDALLION

The medallion is similar to a *cartouche*, but is usually somewhat more contained while the ornamentation of a *cartouche* may extend beyond the geometric shape of the boundary. Medallions are usually elliptical or round, or sometimes square.

### (ORNAMENT) ROSETTE, PATERAE, OR ROUNDEL

"Rosette," "paterae," and "roundel" are terms that are often used interchangeably, although a rosette is technically a floral ornament that is applied to the simple round paterae or roundel. In any case, they are most often used to elaborate locations where a rod or chain penetrates a ceiling or wall. They are smaller and simpler than *medallions*.

## (ORNAMENT) SCROLL

The scroll can take on a multitude of forms, but the simplest is that of an S-curve that coils into itself. Scroll ornaments can also take the shape of a C-curve, but in any case are based loosely upon the shape of the ancient papyrus scroll partially unrolled. The *foliated* scroll is probably the most popular ornamental device of all time.

## (ORNAMENT) WREATH

Wreath ornaments are exactly what they sound like: ornamental devices based on the shape of the common wreath. They often represent flowering or fruit-bearing plants and are sometimes shown wrapped in decorative ribbons.

## PANEL - BEADED

Large wood surfaces (doors, walls, *pedestals*, etc.) of a more elegant nature are often covered by a system of frames and *panels* designed to overcome the swelling and shrinking limitations of wood. Beaded panels are composed of relatively narrow boards joined with a *tongue and groove* joint with an incised *bead*.

## PANEL - FLAT

Flat panels were originally the most difficult to deal with because the panel must necessarily be so thin to fit in a typical frame. Very thin boards often deform more than thicker ones with time, temperature, and moisture. More recently, flat panels have become more popular because they are built with plywood, which has no such problems.

## PANEL - RAISED

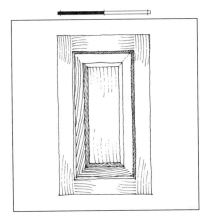

Raised panels were the method of choice for centuries. A raised panel is thin at the edges but thicker, or raised, in the middle. It is the most elaborate and refined panel type in general use today.

## PARGE COAT OR PARGING

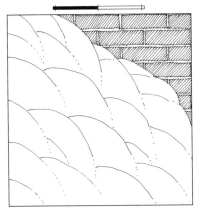

A parge (PARJ) coat is a thin layer of mortar applied to masonry with the intent of hiding the masonry joints. This illustration shows a layer of parging partially applied over a brick wall.

### (PEDESTAL) CORNICE

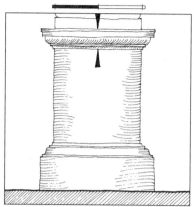

The *pedestal* cornice is the upper primary division of the *pedestal*. The cornice of the *pedestal*, just as the *cornice* of the *entablature*, has three primary divisions of *cymatium*, *corona,* and *bed moldings*, although the *cymatium* may be omitted as shown here.

### (PEDESTAL) DADO OR DIE

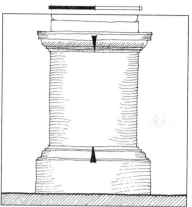

The dado (DAY-doe) or die is the middle primary division of the *pedestal*. It is often plain and unadorned, or it can be enriched with *panel* work, especially if constructed of wood.

### (PEDESTAL) PLINTH

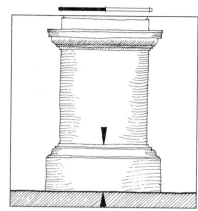

The plinth of the *pedestal* is essentially a large *baseboard* with a very thick *base cap*.

### PEDIMENT - BROKEN

The broken pediment (PED-uh-ment) is almost always used at small scale in conjunction with a door, window, or *aedicule*. It essentially removes the center of the *gable* and turns the *raking cornice* back into the wall at that point.

### PEDIMENT - ROUND

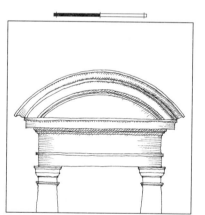

The round pediment (PED-uh-ment) is almost always used at small scale in conjunction with a door, window, or *aedicule*. The *gable* portion of a round pediment is usually laid out as a *bowspring arch*. Round pediments over doors or windows are often alternated with *gabled* ones for decorative relief on long walls.

### PEDIMENT, TYMPANUM

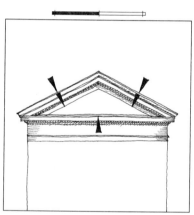

The pediment (PED-uh-ment) includes all parts of the *gable* above the horizontal *cornice*, including the *raking cornice*. Pediments can also be used at a smaller scale over doors and windows and as part of an *aedicule*. They can be *broken* or *round*. The tympanum (TIM-pan-um) is the flat portion of the pediment that occurs below the *raking cornice*.

[38]

### PIER

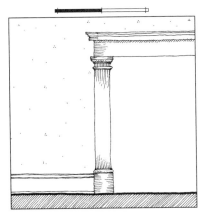

The pier is essentially a masonry *column*. It may be unadorned or may be treated as a *column* or *pilaster*. In such cases, it receives *capital* molding but not usually *base* molding.

### PILASTER

A pilaster (pie-LASS-tur) is a *column* attached to a wall. Pilasters may be round, in which case they are detailed exactly as adjacent free standing *columns*. If the pilasters are square or rectangular in plan, they may be detailed in a simpler manner. Square or rectangular pilasters typically do not have *entasis*, although this is not always the case.

### PORCH OR PORTICO

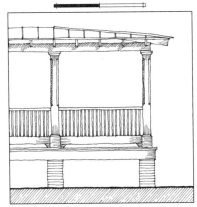

The porch or portico is a type of *loggia* that is always attached to the wall of a building. It is composed of a *colonnade* or *arcade* supporting an *entablature* upon which a roof rests. The roof is typically a *shed* or a *hipped shed* sloping up to the larger roof.

### PORTE COCHERE

The porte cochere (PORT ko-SHER) is typically a *loggia* attached to a building under which a vehicle may drive with the intention of unloading passengers out of the weather. A porte cochere therefore always includes a connecting roof to the main building and a door to the interior.

### POST

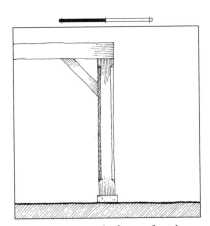

The post is a crude form of a *column*. It is often a simple wood timber. It may contain some elaboration such as *chamfers* at the corners or a very abstracted *capital* or *base*. If the trim is anything close to correct, however, then the element is considered a square *column*, not a post.

### POST AND BEAM, TRABEATION OR TRABEATED

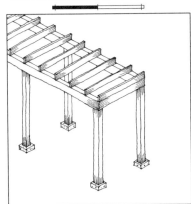

"Post and beam" and "trabeation" (tray-be-AY-shun) both refer to a type of construction that consists of *posts* or *columns* supporting a connecting system of beams above. A roof may rest upon the beams. The post and beam system is arguably the earliest form of construction, being used on everything from barns to temples.

QUOIN

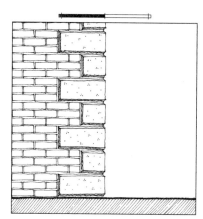

The quoin (KWOIN) is a slightly projecting stone used at the corners of a building. It may also be constructed of brick, wood, or plaster, but is always made to simulate stone. Quoins are often laid in alternating long and short courses. Their purpose is to either emphasize or rusticate the corners of the buildings.

RAKING CORNICE

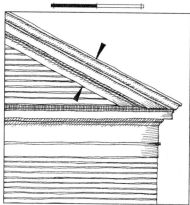

The raking cornice runs at an angle along each slope of a *gable*. The rake rarely includes a full *entablature*, but often includes a *frieze* board that is typically narrower than that of the full *order* below. The *cymatium,* or *crown,* follows the raking cornice, but should always be omitted (as shown) on the horizontal base *cornice* of the *pediment*.

(ROOF) DUTCH GABLE

The Dutch gable is part *hip* and part *gable*. It begins at the eaves as a *hip* roof, but changes to a *gable* about halfway to the ridge. Dutch gables are common in French-influenced areas of the United States such as Louisiana.

(ROOF) GABLE

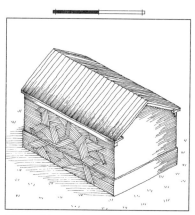

The gable roof is composed of two planes sloping up to a ridge with a gable or *pediment* at each end. The gable roof was the preferred roof shape of classical antiquity.

(ROOF) GAMBREL

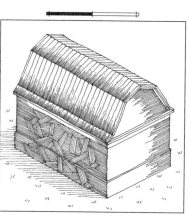

A gambrel (GAM-brul) roof is composed of four planes. The lower two are steeply sloped, while the upper two, which meet at the ridge, are shallower. Small, low-sloped planes are often added at the eaves (shown here) Gambrel roofs are commonly called "barn roofs" since they were often used for barns because they make the hay loft larger.

(ROOF) HALF HIP

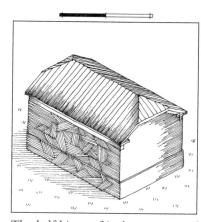

The half hip roof is the opposite of a *Dutch gable*. It begins at the eaves as a *gable* roof, but changes to a *hip* about halfway to the ridge. Half hips were common in medieval England, France, and Germany, where they went by a number of localized names.

(ROOF) HIP

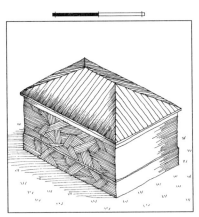

The hip roof is composed of four planes. The two longer planes meet at the ridge, while the shorter planes close off each end of the roof. Special hip types include the pyramidal hip, where all four planes slope up to a single point. The hip roof is by far the most popular roof shape in French architecture.

(ROOF) MANSARD

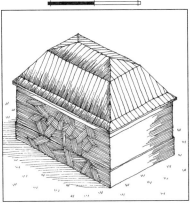

The mansard roof can be thought of as a *hipped gambrel*. It includes a steep plane and a shallow plane on all four sides, with the intent of providing more space on the attic story. A mansard usually includes a small plane of lower slope just above the *cornice*. The mansard was a French invention of the late Renaissance.

(ROOF) SHED

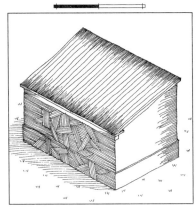

The shed roof is the simplest of all. It is a single plane that slopes from a high wall down to a low wall. Shed roofs typically are used around a larger building to expand the space of the building. In such a case, the high end of the shed rests on the larger roof.

(ROOFING) 5V METAL

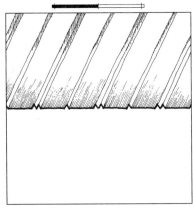

The 5V metal roofing takes its name from its shape. It is a 26" wide panel with two inverted V's on each end and a single inverted V in the center. The two inverted V's on each end overlap the two inverted V's of adjacent panels. The 5V metal was the preferred roofing in the southern United States for many years before the advent of asphalt shingles.

(ROOFING) CLAY TILE

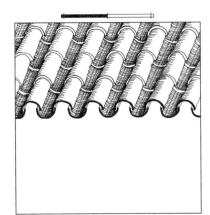

There are several different types of clay tile roofing. Some include convex tiles alternated with concave tiles while others include convex tiles covering joints between flat tiles, with many regional variations. Clay tile roofing, properly installed, can last for centuries.

(ROOFING) CORRUGATED METAL

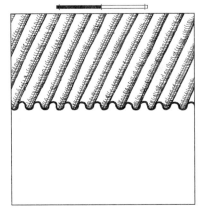

There is only one proper type of corrugated metal roofing. True corrugation is a series of convex half-round shapes alternating with concave half-round shapes. There are no sharp breaks of any kind in corrugated roofing, only one curve smoothly transitioning into another.

### (ROOFING) METAL TILE

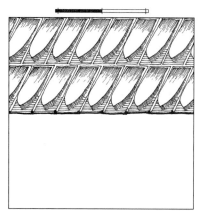

Metal tile roofing often imitates the shape of various styles of *clay tile* roofing. Just as when stone first imitated wood 25 centuries ago, imitation of one material with another superior material is considered proper by many traditional architects. Other types, such as the one illustrated here, imitate no other material.

### (ROOFING) SLATE SHINGLE

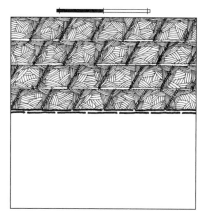

Slate shingle roofing illustrates the opposite condition of imitation to that of metal tile. True slate shingles, and even some of their synthetic imitators, are substantial and can last for centuries. Asphalt shingles, which were originally designed to imitate slate, are far inferior and typically will not even last until the kids graduate from high school.

### (ROOFING) STANDING SEAM METAL

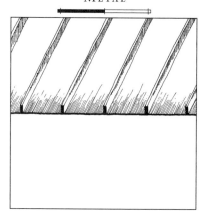

True standing seam metal roofing is one of the best roofing materials available, and it can last for centuries if formed of correct materials such as copper, terne, or Galvalume. Standing seam should always be made of true flat panels with absolutely no pencil-ribs or striations.

### (ROOFING) WOOD SHINGLE

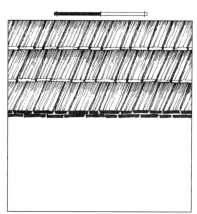

Wood shingle roofs present a dilemma: They are beautiful, but have an extremely short life—usually no longer than that of an asphalt shingle roof and less than even a thatched roof. They are difficult to justify based on anything except aesthetic reasons.

### RUSTICATION

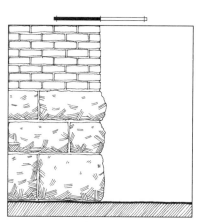

Rustication is the visual roughening of a surface through the use of either highly articulated joints between blocks of stone or extremely rough surface textures. Rustication is typically used at the base of a building with more refined details above.

### (SIDING) BEVEL

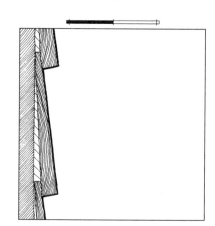

Bevel siding consists simply of boards that are thinner at the top and thicker at the bottom. Bevel siding is often called "lap siding," although this term more properly applies to any siding type where higher boards simply lap over lower boards, including *beveled and rabbeted, drop, plank,* and *shiplap.*

## (SIDING) BEVELED AND RABBETED

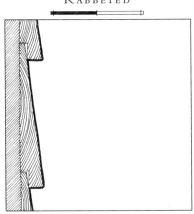

Beveled and rabbeted siding is similar to *bevel* siding except that the back bottom edge of each board is rabbeted to receive the top edge of the board below it. This allows the back of each board to lay flat against the sheathing, making it very resistant to impact damage.

## (SIDING) BOARD AND BATTEN

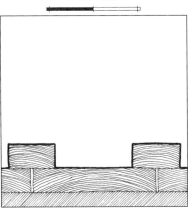

Board and batten siding consists of wide boards running vertically with narrow boards (battens) that cover the joints. Board and batten siding was used almost exclusively for agricultural buildings such as barns in the United States except during the Romantic era, when it was also used for houses.

## (SIDING) DROP

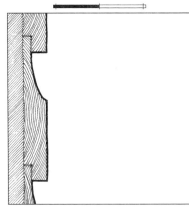

Drop siding is a more elaborate version of *shiplap* siding. It consists of a rectangular board with a rabbet cut out of the front of the top of the board and the back of the bottom of the board to shed water. Additional wood is cut from the board, dropping down in an elliptical fashion from the top rabbet.

## (SIDING) PLANK

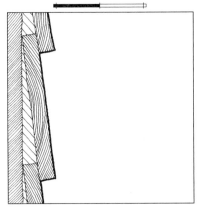

Plank siding is the simplest type. It consists simply of rectangular boards lapping one another. Because neither side is beveled, rabbeted, or otherwise shaped, plank siding is thicker than any other type. This crude profile makes it more appropriate for rustic applications.

## (SIDING) REVERSE BOARD AND BATTEN

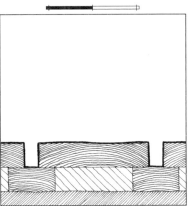

Reverse board and batten is exactly what the name implies. First the battens are attached, then the boards are installed, resulting in a very narrow strip of the batten being visible between the boards.

## (SIDING) SHINGLE

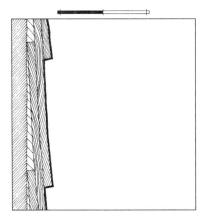

Wood shingle siding is similar to shingle roofing, except that shingle siding is typically thinner and smoother than roofing. Shingle siding lasts much longer than shingle roofing because it is installed on a vertical surface and sheds water more quickly.

### (SIDING) SHIPLAP

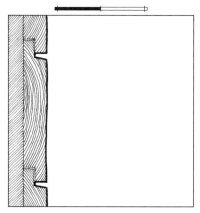

Shiplap siding consists of a rectangular board with a rabbet cut out of the front of the top of the board and the back of the bottom of the board, creating a water-resistant joint when the boards are installed.

### (SIDING) TONGUE AND GROOVE (T&G), BEADED BOARD

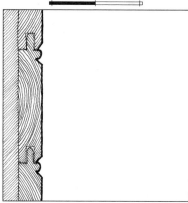

Beaded board tongue and groove siding consists of a flat board with a tongue on one edge and a groove on the other. The front edge of the board adjacent to the groove is *chamfered*, while the front edge adjacent to the tongue is incised with a *bead* and a *chamfer* to create a V-shaped groove with a bead, when installed.

### (SIDING) TONGUE AND GROOVE (T&G), FLAT

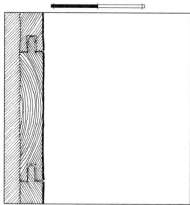

Flat tongue and groove siding consists of a flat board with a tongue on one edge and a groove on the other. Properly installed, it results in a very flat surface with nearly invisible seams. Flat tongue and groove siding was often used for classical elements such as a *frieze* that should be a single smooth surface.

### (SIDING) TONGUE AND GROOVE (T&G), V-GROOVE

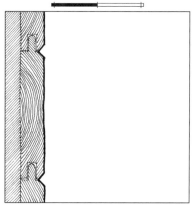

The V-groove (or beveled) tongue and groove siding consists of a flat board with a tongue on one edge and a groove on the other. The front edges of the board adjacent to the tongue and the groove are *chamfered* to create a V-shaped groove when installed. It, like *beaded board* siding, is often used for ceilings or *wainscots*.

### SPANDREL

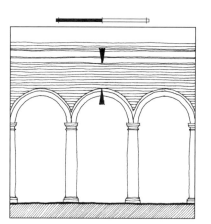

"Spandrel" has other modern meanings, but it was originally used to describe the wall of an *arcade* above the arches and below the *entablature* or *cornice*.

### STAIR NEWEL

The stair newel is the large *post* at the bottom and top of a stair rail. There may also be intermediate newels in a long run of railing.

### STAIR NOSING

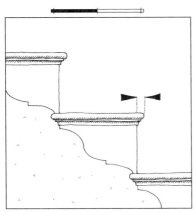

The stair nosing is the trim on the front edge of the stair tread. Stair nosings typically include some sort of bullnosed shape at the top for longer wear.

### VAULT

The term "vault" describes several conditions in which a ceiling is higher in the center than around the edges, including the following examples: The barrel vault is a half-cylinder. The bowspring vault is a smaller segment of a cylinder. The groin vault consists of two intersecting barrel vaults.

### VOLUTE

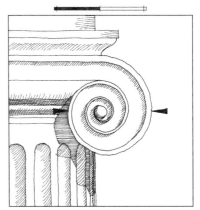

A volute (vuh-LOOT) is a specific kind of *scroll*— one that spirals inward upon itself like a seashell. Volutes are the identifying characteristic of Ionic *column capitals*.

### WAINSCOT

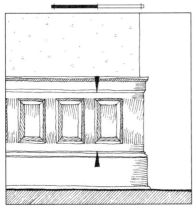

A wainscot (WAIN-scot) is a material applied to the lower section of a wall that is heavier and more durable than the primary wall material. Wainscots are most often built of wood boards or *panels* (often wider than shown here); but they can also be made of stone, brick, or tile. When used with a *chair rail*, they occur between the *chair rail* and the *base*.

### WATER TABLE

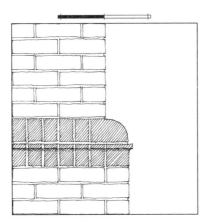

The water table is the joint between the body and the *base* of a building where the wall is built of some sort of masonry or stucco over implied masonry both above and below the joint. To be considered a water table, the *base* of the wall must set out some distance beyond the body of the wall.

### (WINDOW) BAY

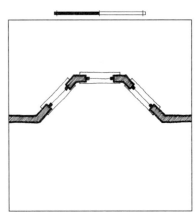

The bay window projects out from the plane of the wall. It contains a central window panel (which may include more than one window) and two side panels (which may include one or more windows). Side window panels may be set perpendicular to the central window panel or may be set at an angle.

## (Window) Bottom Rail

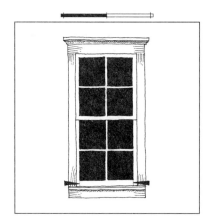

The bottom rail of a window is the horizontal framing member that runs from *stile* to *stile* at the bottom of the lowest *sash*. Bottom rails are sometimes fairly tall, to reinforce the bottom of the *sash* and to provide a location for mounting the operating hardware.

## (Window) Bow

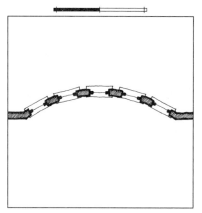

The bow window is similar to the bay window in that it projects out from the plane of the wall in which it is located. But all the windows of the bow are equal in width, and they are set along a curve rather than as a square or polygon.

## (Window) Clerestory

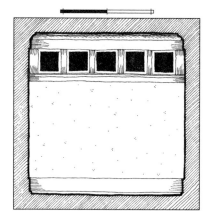

The clerestory (KLEER-stor-ee) (or clear story) window is one that is built high on a wall in a very tall room. They are often composed of window *sashes* that are close to square.

## (Window) Fanlight

The fanlight window is built in the shape of a fan, with a straight bottom and a half-round or half-elliptical top. It is often divided into a number of pie shaped panes by *muntins* radiating from the center of the window. Fanlights are typically used over entry doors, especially those with *sidelights*.

## (Window) Meeting Rail

The meeting rail occurs on double- or triple-hung windows and is actually composed of two parts: the inner meeting rail, which is the *top rail* of the lower *sash*, and the outer meeting rail, which is the *bottom rail* of the upper *sash*.

## (Window) Muntin

The window muntin (MUNT-'n) is a framing member that divides panes of glass. Many windows today use flimsy grilles on one side or the other of the glass to simulate muntins. The only acceptable grillework occurs on both sides of the glass with spacers between double panes, so as to be indiscernible from true muntins.

### (WINDOW) SASH

The window sash is a single slab that may contain one or more panes of glass and is framed with wood or other materials. Sashes move in operable windows, but are fixed in place in fixed windows. Some fixed windows do not include sashes, but are simply glass stopped directly into the frame.

### (WINDOW) SIDELIGHT

The sidelight is typically a narrow window placed on one or both sides of a door. Sidelights may include a *sash*, or the glass may be stopped directly into the frame.

### (WINDOW) SILL

The window sill is the lowest member of the frame. It is usually sloped or beveled to shed water.

### (WINDOW) STILE

Window stiles are the vertical members of the window *sash*. They run from top to bottom of each *sash*.

### (WINDOW) STOOL

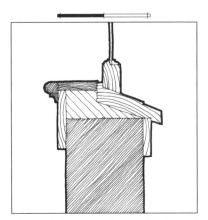

The window stool is a horizontal board installed over the inside of the window *sill*. It is considered to be part of the interior *casing* of the window. It is of course more pronounced on windows located in thicker walls, where it may serve as a flat, table like surface upon which to place objects such as potted plants.

### (WINDOW) TOP RAIL

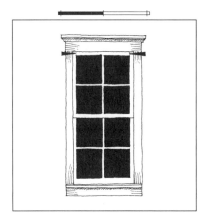

The top rail of a window is the horizontal framing member that runs from *stile* to *stile* at the top of the upper *sash*. The top rail of the lower sash is typically considered part of the meeting rail.

### (WINDOW) TRANSOM

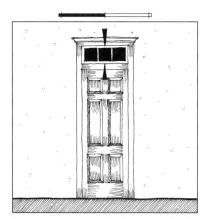

The transom window typically includes a horizontally proportioned *sash* installed over a door. This is a rare instance in which horizontally proportioned panes can be appropriate. Transoms installed over windows are almost always inappropriate; a taller window should be used instead.

### (WOOD JOINT) BISCUIT

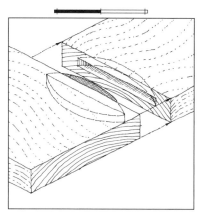

The biscuit joint is a very modern type of joint, and it consists of a thin "biscuit" of wood or other material that is glued into slots cut into the two pieces of wood that it joins.

### (WOOD JOINT) BUTT

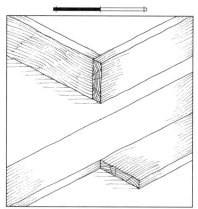

The butt joint is the simplest joint, consisting of two pieces of wood butted together. Corner butts are possibly the oldest joint and are joined with nails and/or glue. Edge butts are much newer and depend on the strength of modern glues for stability.

### (WOOD JOINT) COPED

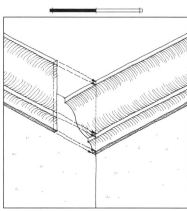

The coped joint is the best method of joining two pieces of molding in an inside corner. The first piece is butted to the wall; then the second is cut with a coping saw to the profile of the first. A good craftsperson can create a very tight coped joint that might not be possible with a miter joint owing to irregularities of the walls.

### (WOOD JOINT) DOVETAIL

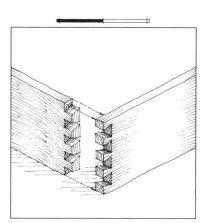

The dovetail joint can take several shapes, most of which include small wedge shaped pieces of wood that resemble the tail of a dove. Dovetail joints are generally considered to be quite attractive, and usually they indicate a higher level of quality owing to their relative difficulty of execution, especially by hand.

### (WOOD JOINT) FINGER

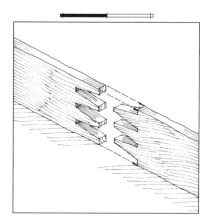

The finger joint sounds just as what it looks: the fingers of two hands meshed together. It is used most often to join boards end to end, but can also be used to join them side to side.

### (WOOD JOINT) LAP

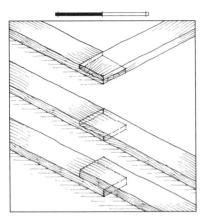

There are several types of lap joints, including the plain lap, the shiplap, or half lap, the end lap, the middle lap, the mitered half lap, and the cross lap. All involve one board lapping over the other. Some are relatively crude, and few are exceptionally strong, making the lap joint a quickly executed but poor choice for many conditions.

### (WOOD JOINT) MITER

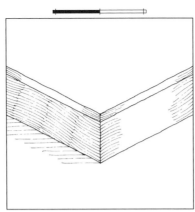

The miter (MIGHT-ur) joint is a very useful outside corner joint because it places the seam at the corner, making it invisible if well crafted. Both pieces of wood are cut back at an equal angle to make the miter.

### (WOOD JOINT) MORTISE AND TENON

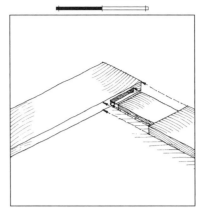

The mortise (MORT-iss) and tenon (TIN-un) joint is made by shaping a mortise, or hole, in one piece to receive a shaped tenon, or projection, of the other. Properly made, mortise and tenon joints are very strong. They are often used in cabinetry and panel work.

### (WOOD JOINT) PEGGED

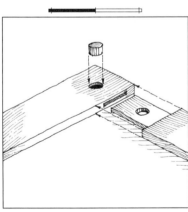

The pegged joint is actually a very strong type of *mortise and tenon* joint in which a round hole is drilled through the mortise and the tenon and a peg is inserted that makes it impossible for the tenon to slip out of the mortise. Pegged joints are often used with heavy timber construction, but also in cabinetry.

### (WOOD JOINT) SCARF

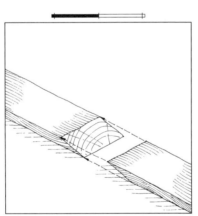

The scarf joint is created by cutting the ends of two boards at an acute angle so that the glued surface area is much greater than that of a *butt* joint, and so that the back-cut piece and the front-cut piece fit to prevent horizontal movement. This is the preferred end joint for two pieces of trim on a long wall.

### (WOOD JOINT) TONGUE AND GROOVE (T&G)

The tongue and groove joint is similar to the spline joint, except that a groove is cut in only one board. A spline-like tongue is shaped on the other board, which fits into the groove of the first. This is a simpler and stronger joint because there are only two parts rather than three, making this a very commonly used joint.

# Chapter 4
~
# The Classical Orders

## General Principles

THE classical *orders* of Greek and Roman antiquity form much of the genetic material of traditional architecture. Languages as disparate as the Romanesque and the many dialects of the Victorian bear the marks of their ancient predecessors. Any study of Western architecture must include knowledge of the classical *orders* as one of its cornerstones. The Lexicon (Chapter 3) defines many of the elements of the classical *orders*. This chapter puts them together. Terms defined in the Lexicon are *italicized* here.

The modern world has some difficulty understanding the chronological nature of the *orders*. Today, we seem to expect a Style of the Month, or at least a Style of the Year. In the past two centuries or so, one style gave way to another, and another, and another. Sometimes, one style evolved from another in a relatively orderly manner, such as when Jeffersonian Classicism gave way to the Greek Revival. In other instances, the succeeding style was a rejection of the one that came before, such as when the "morally superior, Christian" Gothic Revival superseded the "pagan" Greek Revival. Early Modernists, in their messianic fervor, played the ultimate trump card by rejecting everything that had come before.

Classical antiquity, however, proceeded according to an entirely different set of rules. It is true that the development of the *orders* occurred over a period of several centuries. But each new *order* did not supersede the next. Rather, each took its place in a pantheon of architectural devices that could all be used at the same place and time. Often, the *orders* differentiated between building types. Simple utility buildings might be Doric while the local temple might be Corinthian or Composite, depending on the god. Some buildings were large enough or complex enough to use several *orders* as an ordering device within the same facade. The Colosseum in Rome was Greek Doric on the ground level, Ionic above, and Corinthian above that, proceeding from massiveness at the base through successively taller and more attenuated stories as the building stretched to meet the sky.

Another common misconception is that the classical *orders* were rigid and narrow. It is easy to see how early Renaissance architects could have believed so because so few written works on classical architecture have survived from antiquity. Vitruvius' work is by far the most significant and was accepted as canonical early in the Renaissance. That notion should have been long since dispelled by the huge body of archaeological work that has been done over the past three centuries. The *orders*, far from being restrictive kits of parts, are actually general categories that are useful in classifying an extremely rich body of work. Unfortunately, Modernists have spun the myth of stiff, stodgy classicism to their own advantage for nearly a century. Today, the general public has a less accurate view of classical architecture than at any other time since at least 1650 or so.

There were strong commonalities of proportion, to be sure, but the wealth of diversity of detail is beyond the scope of this book to describe. The examples that follow are intended to illustrate only the general proportions and characteristics of each *order*.

The classical *orders* do, however, share certain common terms and proportional techniques. The *orders* are post-and-beam structures by nature. They engage walls in many ways, to be sure, but the *column* and the beam define them.

The *orders* also embody the three-part head/body/foot or cap/shaft/base composition found first in the human body and then throughout the construction traditions of humanity. For example, each *order* is made up of *entablature*, *column*, and *pedestal*. The *entablature* is made up of *cornice*, *frieze*, and *architrave*; and the *column* is made up of *capital*, *shaft*, and *base*. At a smaller scale, the *capital* is composed of *abacus*, *necking*, and *astragal*.

*Post* is the correct term for a very simple square support with little or no *capital* or *base*. *Posts* are often tied to beams with *brackets* or braces of some sort. *Posts* are typically used in buildings that are simple or rustic. *Column* is the correct term for a vertical support member that is more articulated. *Columns* may be either square or round, but they all have at least a fairly articulated cap, or *capital*. *Columns* typically are found in buildings that are of nobler nature. *Columns* of the classical *orders* are the highest form of the supporting element. *Columns* almost inevitably engage walls at some point in a building. A *column* that engages a wall is known as a *pilaster*.

The *entablature* is the member that spans between the tops of the *columns*. Classical *entablatures* are made up of three major parts. The *cornice* is the top part that engages the roof. The *cornice* projects from the face of the *entablature* to help throw water off the building. A *cornice* may be used alone to join a wall to a roof, but not to span between *columns*. This is often attempted, but always results in a building that doesn't appear to be structurally sound. Some version of a complete *entablature* must be used so that there appears to be a beam supporting the *cornice*. That beam is ordinarily made up a *frieze* and an *architrave*.

The *frieze* occurs below the *cornice* and is usually flat. It is often used as a canvas for sculptural enrichment. Indeed, it is probably the most common location on the entire classical building for figurative adornment. The *frieze* is often the tallest part of the *entablature*. The *architrave* is the lowest part of the *entablature*. It may include various simple moldings, but never sculptural enrichment since its visual function is purely structural. In other words, it needs to appear simple and strong in order to carry the entire load above it.

An incredible wealth of proportional rules and techniques are used in the creation of classical architecture. The *module* is the single overriding unit by which all the *orders* are measured. The *module* is the diameter of a *column* just above the *base*. All other parts of an *order* are usually expressed in *modules*. Note that some Renaissance authorities defined the *module* as the radius, not the diameter, of the *column*, but this interpretation is not commonly used today. The major classifications of *orders* illustrated on the following pages are listed in the chronological order of their appearance.

# GREEK DORIC

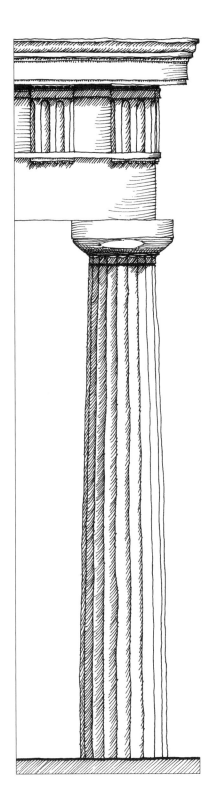

THE Greek Doric takes its name from the Dorian Greeks. It is the most ancient of *orders*, and it spanned the era between civic buildings built of wood and those built of stone. Much of the vocabulary of the *order* was therefore directly descended from the more ancient timber construction.

It could be described as a very experimental *order*, because the canons of classical proportions had not yet been fully developed. Some of the early Greek Doric temples were extremely stocky, with *columns* that were only four *modules* tall. Later Greek Doric *columns* were a bit more slender.

The *columns* of the Parthenon are 5½ diameters tall. Note, however, that although the proportions were being refined during the early centuries of this *order*, the components and their relationships were already well defined and changed very little after the transition from wood to stone.

The centuries of refinement elevated this *order* to a level of sophistication never seen again in the history of human construction. The optical corrections of classical *entasis* have rarely been attempted in two millennia. *Entasis* was an extremely subtle device that corrected the optical illusion of hollowness in an extended straight line – resulting in the appearance of the *columns* sagging inward.

The *columns* of the Parthenon are 34 feet high and 6 feet 3 inches in diameter at the bottom, and have a total convexity of 3.4 inches. Unlike the Roman *orders*, the Greek Doric *entasis* began at the foot of the *column*. The optical corrections weren't just applied to the *columns*, either – the entire Parthenon is composed of slight curves and inclines that ensure the whole building is seen as truly horizontal and vertical lines.

Greek Doric did not remain the only classical *order*, of course. The architects of antiquity assimilated all the *orders* as they created a coherent system of architecture that used each *order* to express a certain characteristic of a building or building part, as previously noted. The Greek Doric, owing to its massive nature, came to be known as the *order* based on the proportions of a very stocky man, such as an athlete. It is used most often for buildings that are more utilitarian or authoritarian, such as military buildings or prisons. It is also used on the lowest story of multistory buildings because of the visual strength of its proportions.

# TUSCAN

THE origins of the Tuscan *order* in the hands of the Etruscans in northern Italy are a bit more obscure than those of the Greek Doric. Some consider the Tuscan *order* to be a provincial version of Greek Doric, influenced by spotty contact with Greek colonies in the south of Italy. As a matter of fact, several authorities consider it to be not an *order* at all, but rather a rude indigenous version of the Doric. Vitruvius included a description of the Tuscan in his writings of the first century B.C., but this was sometimes seen as an act of deference to an inferior local style. We have included it here because the refined Renaissance versions of the *order* based on Vitruvius' descriptions are often quite elemental, illustrating some of the basic figurative goals of the classical ideal more clearly than higher, more ornate *orders*. The Tuscan *order* is quite instructive in this regard.

Early Tuscan buildings were probably built of wood; none have survived, of course. Archaeological evidence suggests that the first Tuscan temples were probably low, wide-eaved buildings that bore little resemblance to the more vertically proportioned temples of the Greeks. The *columns* of these buildings are the only elements that strongly resemble the Renaissance Tuscan *order*, primarily because both are so simple. Tuscan *columns* are invariably smooth, non-*fluted* elements with only the most unadorned of *capitals* and *bases*. The *entablature* is equally elemental, making this the most economical of *orders* and suitable for buildings of humble or utilitarian use. The Tuscan *order*, just as the Greek Doric before it, is associated with the proportions of a man. Vitruvius set the Tuscan *column* at 6 diameters tall, as did Serlio, but most Renaissance architects set it at 7 diameters tall. Scamozzi set it at $7\frac{1}{2}$ diameters.

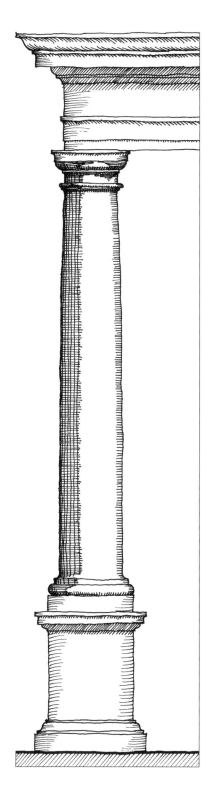

[53]

# ROMAN DORIC

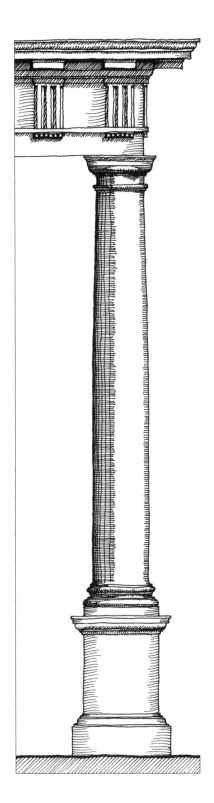

THE Roman Doric *order* developed in large part as a result of the Roman conquest of the Greek colonies in southern Italy. The Romans modified the Greek Ionic and Corinthian *orders* to a degree, but their modifications to the Doric were much more pronounced, qualifying it as a distinct *order* in the opinion of many. As a matter of fact, most casual observers find few similarities between the Greek Doric and the Roman Doric at first glance. The *columns* are much more slender, typically reaching a height of 8 diameters rather than the 4 to $5\frac{1}{2}$ diameters of the Greek Doric. A *base* has been added to the *column*, and some of the more tyrannical Greek refinements have been ignored. The *triglyphs*, for example, no longer are shifted to meet at the corner of a building, but rather center over each *column* regardless of its location. The *entablature* is more idealized, with the *mutules* no longer sloped but rather detailed as shallow *brackets*. The *cornice* design varies more than in the Greek Doric, often including enrichments such as *dentils*. The proportions of the *entablature*, however, were settled by this *order* at one-fourth the height of the *column*. This proportion can be found in numerous examples of all later *orders*.

The Roman Doric is still considered to be based upon the proportions of a man, but clearly a more refined man than that of either the Tuscan or especially the Greek Doric *order*. The Roman Doric *order* is often used for buildings of a commercial or administrative nature, such as office buildings, shops, or sometimes the less refined buildings of academic institutions. It is interesting to note that Renaissance Europe knew very little of ancient Greece until the middle of the eighteenth century, so the Roman Doric *order* was the only Doric known to Renaissance architects and theorists such as Serlio, Vignola, Palladio, and Scamozzi.

# IONIC

THE Ionic *order* originated along the western shores of Turkey and in the adjacent islands. Ionia was populated by Greeks who had emigrated from the mainland three or four centuries before the development of the *order*. The area was well suited for commerce and became extremely prosperous as a result. The Ionic *order* clearly developed after the Greek Doric, but almost certainly with full knowledge of the Doric. It is therefore the first *order* consciously developed as a counterpoint to the Doric.

Vitruvius writes that the Ionic *order* originated as a reflection of a woman. It was the most slender *order* yet developed, with a *column* height often set at 9 diameters. The *volutes* of the *column capital* have symbolized the curls of a woman's hair since the canonization of the *order*. Some contemporary buildings were even more literal, using sculptures of women, called caryatids, in place of *columns*. *Column capitals* were not the only departure of the Ionic. *Column bases* were more varied than within the later Roman Doric *order*, and the *entablatures* employed a significant increase in variations. It is interesting to note that *column bases* were first introduced with the Ionic *order*. Their tremendous variety parallels the proportional experimentation of the Greek Doric in process if not in time. *Triglyphs* virtually disappear from the Ionic *order*, often replaced by *dentils* at the bottom of the *cornice*. The relative elegance of the *order* and its association with female form as opposed to the severity and vigor of the Doric have always lent it to uses that are calmer or more sedentary.

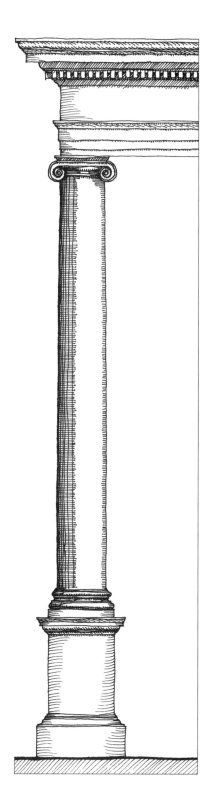

[55]

# CORINTHIAN

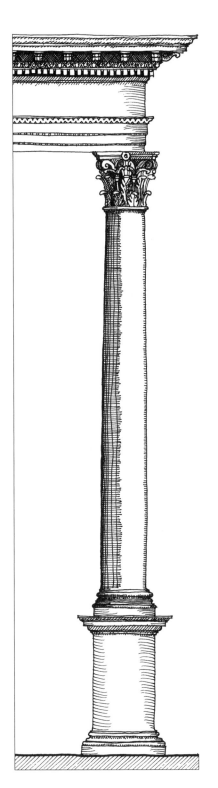

THE Corinthian *order* originated in the Greek city of Corinth around 400 B.C., accompanied by one of the most memorable stories to survive from antiquity. Vitruvius tells of a young Corinthian maiden who died unmarried. Her nurse placed all her earthly possessions in a basket, placed them on her tomb, and put a square roofing tile on the basket to keep the rain out. Over time, an *acanthus* plant grew up around the base of the basket, curling up to the roofing tile. The renowned Athenian sculptor Callimachus happened by the tomb one day and was touched by the sight. He went on to create a new *column capital* based on the basket, *acanthus*, and tile, which became the foundation of the Corinthian *order*. The truth of the legend is now lost to the ages, but if the Ionic has the proportions of a woman, then the Corinthian *column* clearly has the more slender proportions of a young maiden at a height of up to 10 diameters. The *acanthus*, too, was commonly used in funeral rituals and grave site decoration, so the story certainly is plausible.

It is interesting to note that the Corinthian was originally an entirely interior *order*, protected from the elements by more massive *orders* such as the Doric. It was not used on the exterior of a significant building until 174 B.C., which was very late in the development of the classical canon. The Corinthian *entablature* is essentially Ionic in nature, with distinctions developed only by the Romans. The Corinthian *column shaft*, *base*, and *pedestal* may be identical to the Ionic. Roman development of the *entablature* made it more highly adorned than Ionic *entablatures*. Elaborately carved *corbels* or *modillions* reflect the severe Doric *mutules*, while surfaces are much more likely to be elaborated with moldings or sculpture. The more decorative nature of the Corinthian led to its becoming the *order* of choice in the Roman era for buildings of great importance or beauty.

# COMPOSITE

THE Composite *order* is a purely Roman phenomenon, with the first known examples dating from the first century A.D. It is both the slenderest and the most ornate of the *orders* with *columns* that are typically 10 diameters in height. The clearest distinction of the Composite *order* is the *column capital*, which is a combination of the Ionic and the Corinthian *capitals*. It was developed after Vitruvius' day, so no written descriptions of the *order* survived from antiquity. Despite the lack of written evidence, surviving examples make clear the notion that the ancients regarded it as a distinct *order*.

The Composite *order* was used most often in antiquity for triumphal arches and other such buildings to which were ascribed the greatest degree of significance and glory. The connection with the glory of military victory is significant, so much so that some have speculated that the origin of the female Winged Victory figure began with the female origins of the Ionic and Corinthian *orders*, which contributed to the creation of the Composite. Medieval architects used crude variants of the *order* frequently in church buildings as a symbol of the victory of Christ. The Composite has been used most frequently since that time by Baroque architects, which is consistent with the Baroque inclination to vocabularies that were extremely ornate. Its use since that time has been limited, especially in recent centuries, as architectural taste for extreme opulence has waned.

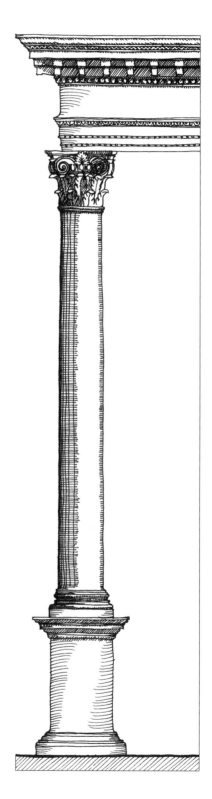

[57]

# CHAPTER 5

# BASIC PRINCIPLES

THE basic principles of traditional architectural languages resemble the rules of grammar of spoken languages. No quantity of fancy words is of any profit if the speaker does not know how to put them together according to the basic rules of grammar. Similarly, if the basic principles of traditional construction are violated, no amount of good detailing can rectify the situation. In order to lay this foundation, this chapter discusses the following basic principles:

## MASSING

## PROPORTION

## ARRANGEMENT

## PHOTO NOTES

PHOTOS USED ON THE FOLLOWING PAGES ARE NOT MEANT TO PORTRAY A PARTICULAR PLACE, BUT RATHER A PARTICULAR IDEA.

There are close to 1,000 photographs on the pages that follow, taken in locations across the eastern U.S. Half of them are on the "Do" pages, while the other half are on the "Don't" pages. Photos on the "Don't" pages have generally been cropped tightly enough to make it unclear exactly where the photo was taken. The intent of this book is not to criticize a homeowner or a contractor, but rather to criticize mistakes that we have all made for years. So if you think you see your house on a "Do" page, congratulations! But if you think you see it on a "Don't" page, the chances that it's really your house are slim because these same mistakes have been made thousands of times over the last half-century.

## CONFIGURATION NOTES

ALL THE CONFIGURATIONS NOTED HERE ARE SUBJECT TO REVISION ACCORDING TO GOOD LOCAL PRECEDENT, WHICH TYPICALLY MEANS BUILDINGS BUILT BEFORE 1925 THAT ARE GOOD EXAMPLES OF THEIR STYLES.

Why 1925? Prior to the 1920's, different styles were promoted almost exclusively by their champions, who believed that their style was superior to those of their predecessors. The styles often were based on some of the same precedents as their predecessors, but the new generation of "style champions" set their work apart with refinements particularly appropriate for the needs of the day. By 1925, however, the Modern movement had siphoned off most of the talent in the architecture profession, leaving traditional architecture in the hands of style merchants who didn't care what style they sold. In most cases, these merchants were the builders and their designers.

Read the house plan books of the era, and you will notice a subtle but important change in tone. Rather than arguing passionately for a particular style, these books most often make the case for the value of their plans based on their economy rather than on their style. It seems a bit strange today, but some house plan books from the mid-1920's didn't even list the square footage of the house, but rather listed the cubic footage. Lower cubic footage was considered better, since that meant that there was less air to heat. And you will also notice that they usually encompassed a wide range of styles. "Would you care for a Mission Style? How about a Colonial? Or maybe you'd rather have an Arts & Crafts house? Pick a style, any style; we've got them all..." seems to have been the prevailing message.

This was all happening in the years leading up to the Great Depression. Once the Depression began, the focus on value kicked into overdrive. And if value is the only thing left to sell, then what's the purpose of all the Mission Style detailing, or the Colonial detailing, or the Arts & Crafts detailing? The Great Decline of Architecture that began in the mid-1920's accelerated furiously after 1929. The only good body of work built during the Depression years were the simplest vernacular houses of the mid-1930's that had to be creative in order to be cheap enough to be affordable. The only good body of work during the war years was the simplest military architecture of necessity. However, the end of the war left us left with nothing but the icon of architectural soullessness: the brick rancher.

So although some good traditional work certainly was being done up to World War II and a tiny remnant of talented traditional architects persevered all through the dark decades of the 1950's, 1960's, and 1970's, most of the buildings built since 1925 should be discounted as good examples of a traditional style. Well-executed buildings before this date are the best source of appropriate local precedent.

## I
### SIMPLICITY OF MASSING

THE ROOT OF NEARLY ALL TRADITIONAL ARCHITECTURAL MASSING IS SIMPLICITY. GO BACK TO THE BUILDINGS THAT ARE THE FOUNDATION OF ALMOST ANY STYLE, AND YOU WILL FIND A SIMPLE VOLUME, OR AN ASSEMBLY OF SIMPLE VOLUMES.

The reason for this pattern is the fact that most traditional architecture is based in necessity and economy. The seed buildings from which most styles grew or developed were usually simple, utilitarian buildings that nonetheless resonated strongly with the culture, the climate, and the available materials of the places where they were built. Such buildings were often built by hand and were usually constructed by their owners and their extended families. This meant that elaborate shapes or extra complications could cost days of additional hard manual labor. These simple, resonant seed buildings were then discovered and appreciated by trained designers who distilled and formalized them into a particular style. The simple massing of the style, however, usually remained in the formalized version.

The Shingle Style of the late nineteenth century is a great example of this pattern. One

*Don't use complicated forms. Too many gables, dormers, and roof breaks waste thousands. Throwing away this kind of money on "street appeal" isn't necessary in neighborhoods where the streets themselves have appeal. This type of house usually spends so much money on the front that no budget remains for detailing on sides or rear, where the owners spend all their outdoor time.*

*Don't: Spanish McMansions: too many hips.*

*Don't: English McMansions: too many gables.*

*Do keep massing simple. Composing a house of one or a few simple boxes saves tremendous amounts of money for more effective things like proper porch detailing, back porches, garden walls, frontage fences, pergolas, and a number of other things that help the owners enjoy inhabiting all of their property.*

*Do: Simple box with single porch gable clearly saves money.*

*Do: Simple two-story box with wrap-around one-story porch.*

man, Stanford White, formalized this style and while it produced some of the grandest homes of the Gilded Age, it was nonetheless based on the simple shingled boxes of Nantucket and Cape Cod. Even a style such as this, which was capable of some of the most elaborate structures ever seen in the United States, usually has a simple main building mass at its core. Other styles, such as the Federal, remain nothing more than simple boxes, no matter how large the building becomes.

No matter what the style, therefore, traditional architecture is usually characterized by simple masses to which other simple masses are added according to the needs of the building. And in every good example, this translates to building shapes that are rational and sensible.

SEE 2~HIERARCHY OF MASSING.

## 2
# HIERARCHY OF MASSING

ALMOST ALL TRADITIONAL ARCHITECTURAL LANGUAGES EMBODY A CLEAR HIERARCHY OF MASSING WHEN BUILDINGS ARE LARGE ENOUGH TO BE COMPOSED OF MORE THAN A SINGLE VOLUME.

The most important or most public functions should be located in the largest, most prominent part of the building, which is usually called the "main body." Less prominent or less public functions occur in wings, which are sometimes called "back buildings." Other utilitarian or totally private functions occur in "outbuildings," which were once called "dependencies."

The clearest examples of this pattern occur in the buildings of Andrea Palladio and his legion of admirers in the centuries since the beginning of his career. The iconic version of Palladio's so-called "winged device" was a large main building and two side buildings connected to the main building by "hyphen buildings," or connectors. Everything from Thomas Jefferson's Monticello to the U.S. Capitol to thousands (or possibly millions) of humbler buildings around the world have been built according to this pattern.

*Don't clump everything equally under one enormous roof. Many McMansions with a confusing assembly of gables show the guests at first glance neither the entry nor the principal rooms of the house. All buildings should pass the First Glance Test, but many McMansions such as those below fail miserably.*

*Car entries are clearly the most important thing here; how about the people?*

*This house fails the First Glance Test for entries, and appears to have two main bodies.*

[62]

*Do mass a house so that it passes the First Glance Test. Massing of a house should clearly show two things at first glance: the location of the main body of the house and the location of the entry for people, which ought to be more important and more noble than the car entry. The houses below illustrate this pattern clearly.*

There are many less formal examples of this pattern. A clear vernacular example is the American farmstead. The main body is often a two-story structure, surrounded by smaller structures that may be a cottage for Grandma, the smokehouse, the dairy, guest quarters, or a carriage house, or may serve any number of other functions. These functions are usually arranged by their relative formality or utility rather than by their location on the spectrum of public to private, since farms seldom had neighbors nearby. Here, the porch or the covered breezeway often served as the "hyphen" to connect some or most of the various elements.

SEE 1~SIMPLICITY OF MASSING.

*This house leaves no doubt concerning the location of the main entrance.*

*The hierarchy of main body and side wings is obvious.*

## 3
# SIMPLICITY OF PROPORTION

MOST GREAT ARCHITECTURE IS
BUILT AROUND A COLLECTION
OF SIMPLE PROPORTIONS FOUND
IN NATURE AND MUSIC THAT
INCLUDE THE RATIONAL (1:1,
2:1, 3:2, 4:3, ETC.) AND THE
IRRATIONAL (THE SQUARE ROOT
OF 2 AND THE GOLDEN MEAN).

Simple proportions are usually found in more classical buildings because architects realize that these proportions "resonate with the universe," in one man's words. Simple proportions, when found in vernacular buildings, are usually there for less lofty reasons, such as the fact that it's just easier and less expensive to build things when the dimensions aren't complicated. Things are also more likely to line up with each other when the proportions are regular. Structural necessities sometimes mandate simple proportions, such as the need for a circular dome to be located over a square room or a room of another shape but in a 1:1 proportion.

But whatever the reasons, simple rational or irrational proportions resonate throughout nature. In music, 2:1 is the proportion of the wavelengths of an octave; 3:2 is the proportion of the fourth note, while 4:3 is the proportion of the note. 1:1 is the proportion

*Don't use arbitrary proportions. This drawing illustrates arbitrary proportions in a floor plan. No wall length has any particular relationship to any other wall length, nor do the door locations have any particular proportional relationship to the walls. The same principles apply to elevations, as illustrated below.*

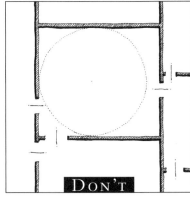

*Are there any simple proportions in this house at all?*

*Or in this one?*

[64]

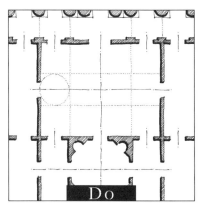

*Do create simple, harmonious proportions. Repeated rhythms stack the deck in your favor in the creation of simple, harmonious proportions, as illustrated both in the floor plan to the left and the elevations below.*

*1:1, 3:2, and 5:2 proportions are obvious here.*

of a circle, which corresponds to objects ranging from the human eye to the earth itself (and the sun, and the moon, of course). The Golden Mean (the square root of 5 minus 1 divided by 2, or about 0.618) is found in everything in nature from the shape of a nautilus shell to the curve of a ram's horn. Clearly, it makes sense to build things that are in harmony with proportions that come so naturally to the physical world.

SEE 1~SIMPLICITY OF MASSING; 4~SYMMETRY OF THE FACE; AND 5~REGULAR ARRANGEMENT OF COLUMNS AND OPENINGS.

*Lower porch columns are placed on 1:1; upper columns are 4:3*

# 4
## SYMMETRY OF THE FACE

ALMOST ALL TRADITIONAL
ARCHITECTURE REFLECTS THE
BILATERAL SYMMETRY OF THE
HUMAN FACE IN SOME WAY AT
THE ENTRY OF THE BUILDING.
MOST MACHINE-BASED
ARCHITECTURE IS FACELESS.

*Don't make the face, or entry, of a building irregular. Modernist buildings usually go to great lengths to bear no resemblance to the human face.*

*Don't: Some traditional materials, but laid out with no reflection of human form.*

*Don't: This goes further: look carefully at the window patterns (and where's the door?).*

The human body can stand at attention, symmetrical in every feature about the vertical central axis of the body, just as the more formal traditional buildings do. The human body can also take uncounted relaxed poses, some with the limbs slung seemingly everywhere, and more relaxed buildings can do the same. The insides of a human body are asymmetrical, because they are simply doing their job, just as the floor plan of a building is more likely to be asymmetrical because of the many functions that the different rooms must perform. But no matter what the rest of the body does, unless a person is trying to distort his or her face to frighten a young child or make an older child laugh, the human face is always bilaterally symmetrical. You can't throw your left eye or your nose over the back of a sofa as you might do your arm. Yet this is what many buildings appear to do.

Again, traditional architecture takes its cues from the

Do

*Do reflect the symmetry of the human face at the entry of a building. Entry compositions do not have to specifically look like a human face to be laid out according to some of the same principles, although some buildings do have a door like a mouth and windows above like eyes (not shown here).*

human body. The face of the building is the place where you enter. The area surrounding the entry of buildings of almost every traditional language of architecture has elements that reflect the symmetry of the human face, no matter how composed or how relaxed the rest of the building is. Without these symmetrical elements, the building would seem to be faceless, which is exactly what machine-based architecture usually works so hard to create.

SEE 2~HIERARCHY OF MASSING.

*Do: Two story symmetrical porch composes the entire front elevation.*

*Do: Great example of symmetrical entry in an otherwise asymmetrical facade.*

## 5
## REGULAR ARRANGEMENT OF COLUMNS AND OPENINGS

TRADITIONAL ARCHITECTURE, WHETHER AT THE CLASSICAL (COMPOSED) OR VERNACULAR (RELAXED) END OF THE SPECTRUM, ALMOST ALWAYS PLACES COLUMNS AND OPENINGS IN A MANNER THAT WHILE SOMETIMES NOT SIMPLY REGULAR, IS NONETHELESS EXTREMELY RATIONAL.

Many of the patterns of traditional architecture such as this one appear, on the surface, to be based purely on formal aesthetic notions. But often there are underlying utilitarian principles based on efficient use of time or of material or on some other basic need such as comfort or safety. Here, the utilitarian reason for the regular placement of columns is this: If the column spacing varies, the beam that the columns support must be designed for the widest span between columns. It makes little sense to change beam sizes from span to span, so the largest required beam size is often used throughout the entire colonnade. This means that the beam is probably oversized everywhere except at the long span, wasting time, materials, and therefore money.

Window openings are not quite so utilitarian. A slight

*Don't place openings and columns randomly. The "form follows function" dictum has been used for years as an excuse not to compose elevations except according to the basic functional needs of the interior rooms. In all except the most skilled hands, the results usually resemble these.*

*Don't: The drawing above looks like a joke, but this really happens all over America.*

*Don't: This might seem better at first glance, but why not go ahead and get it right?*

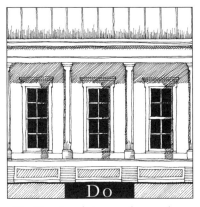

Do: Openings between columns above.

Do: Entry at center of columns.

Do: Ideal column/opening arrangement.

*Do place columns and openings according to a rational system. Openings centered between regularly spaced columns are one obvious strategy, but the important thing is simply to have a system of composing the elevations that is more than the usual randomness.*

Do: Regular windows.

Do: Relaxed but composed.

Do: Entry to one side but composed.

amount of layout time might be saved with a regular arrangement of windows, but the time saved would usually be negligible. The primary reason here for the regularity of door and window openings, which has been seen countless times in both great and humble buildings since the beginning of construction, appears to be humanity's deep need to try to make sense out of the surroundings. Individual humans tend to take disorder in their worlds and try to order it. This explains not only the regularity of window openings, but also why the average person usually turns away from the new styles of architecture that look more like train wrecks than buildings.

SEE 1~SIMPLICITY OF MASSING.

## 6
# CAP, SHAFT, AND BASE

NEARLY EVERY ELEMENT OF
TRADITIONAL ARCHITECTURE
REFLECTS THE
HEAD/BODY/FEET
(OR CAP/SHAFT/BASE)
ARRANGEMENT OF THE HUMAN
BODY.

The arrangement of the human form is such a clear influence on the shape of traditional buildings that everything from the shape of the entire building to the shapes of the smallest details contains reflections of this pattern. For example, the building is usually composed of a visible roof, wall, and foundation. If the roof is not visible, then entablature at the top of the building is usually highly expressed, to create the cap. Within the classical order, there is the entablature (cap), the body (shaft), and the pedestal (base). Within the entablature, there is the cornice, the frieze, and the architrave. Within the cornice, there is the cymatium, the corona, and the bed. Within the column, there is the capital, the shaft, and the base. Within the capital... you get the picture. Even elements as simple as baseboards contain the base cap, the base, and the shoe.

Few patterns have been as powerful for as long as this one has in the entire history

*Don't build decapitated buildings or buildings that are cut off at the knees. Buildings with no head or base bear no resemblance to the human body and usually create places that do not resonate with most people.*

*Don't: Headless and baseless column.*

*Don't: Headless building.*

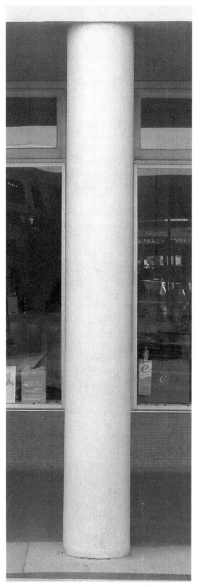

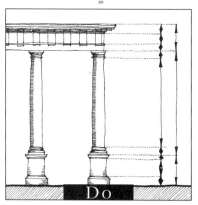

*Do arrange buildings and their elements to follow the pattern of cap (head), shaft (body) and base (feet). This ordering of cap, shaft, and base has resonated with humanity since the dawn of time.*

*Do: Building with cap, shaft, and base.*

*Do: Porch with cap, shaft, and base.*

of architecture. This pattern descends directly from the theme of architecture for people. It has spawned thousands of patterns, but requires nothing but the human form for support. No architecture except for machine-based architecture has ever opposed it, and its omission has produced three generations of headless and baseless buildings to which most people do not respond.

SEE BUILDINGS FOR PEOPLE (PAGE 10); AND 4~SYMMETRY OF THE FACE.

UNITED STATES CUSTOM HOUSE

## 7

## SITE ARRANGEMENT

MOST TRADITIONAL
ARCHITECTURE IS ARRANGED
ON THE SITE TO CREATE
EITHER INTERNAL COURTYARD
SPACES OR EXTERNAL STREET
SPACES. ONLY THE NOBLEST
CLASSICAL BUILDINGS SHOULD
SIT BACK ON THE CENTER
OF THEIR LOTS BY VIRTUE OF
THEIR IMPORTANCE IN THE
COMMUNITY.

This pattern makes sense in several ways, and that is why it has existed almost since the dawn of civilization. It also deals with the heart of the nature of the city, which is to create the most public and the most private places next to each other. The primary spaces of the city include the square, plaza, or park; the street; and the private courtyard.

Civic buildings are placed either around a public square or at the center of a public square for a number of reasons. First, it makes them more prominent according to their function within the community. Second, placing a building a distance from the street allows more people to see it at once and for a longer time as they pass by. Both aspects are appropriate for important buildings. Finally, placement on a square or in a square provides a convenient place for people to congregate before, during, or after functions at the civic building.

*Don't site buildings so as to create useless leftover land around them. Buildings plopped in the center of their site combined with a front-facing garage is a recipe for a very ordinary street with no appeal. When the street has no appeal, the buildings must spend thousands to have street appeal.*

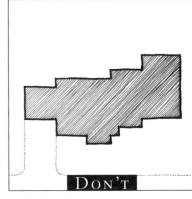

DON'T

*Don't: Houses sitting back to display their cars.*

*Don't: Even the prettiest garages disrupt streetscape with a huge slab of concrete.*

[72]

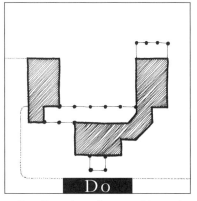

*Do site buildings to create courtyards and usable street spaces. Courtyard houses provide outdoor privacy of the highest order. Rear lanes, if they are available, provide access to the garage that leaves the streets free to be beautiful. If lanes or alleys are unavailable, a single-lane driveway to a garage (ideally side-facing as illustrated here) set far back on the lot does far less damage to the beauty of the street than a double-wide driveway.*

*Do: Rear view of courtyard house (garage is right wing; floor plan is shown above).*

*Do: Garage tucked behind house is scarcely visible.*

Most of the fabric of cities, however, was traditionally built not on squares, but rather on streets. Streets were the usual condition; and plazas, squares, and parks were the special conditions. To function properly as a public room and not just as a corridor for cars, streets must have a wall on either side that is tall enough to make the street feel as an enclosed room does. The primary civic responsibility of non-civic buildings, therefore, is to pull up as close, as tight, and as tall to the street as is appropriate to their location in the city. On a main street, they should stand shoulder to shoulder and pull right up to the sidewalk, whereas in lower-density, primarily residential areas, they can obviously be set back and separate themselves by yards.

The enclosure of space on private land has almost become a lost art. Once, people would not have considered building a house without a partially enclosed courtyard or garden somewhere in the design to provide private outdoor space. Even in the country, the American farmyard followed this same pattern, with outbuildings or dependencies forming a ring around a rear yard.

SEE 2~HIERARCHY OF MASSING.

[73]

# CHAPTER 6
~
# DETAILS

THE errors of detail in construction today are more numerous than errors of any other kind. As a matter of fact, bad details are the most common defining element of poor construction. This chapter deals with general detail rules from the inside (the materials they are made with) and from the outside (the Transect zone in which the building occurs.) The subsequent chapters group patterns according to building components beginning at the ground and working up and then out: walls; doors and windows; porch columns and beams; eaves; roofs; dormers; attachments, such as chimneys, awnings, and signs; and sitework. These major categories of details are included as follows:

## MATERIAL NOTES

A number of products are available today that have exceeded the originals in performance and have equaled them in appearance. Also a number of natural materials have declined in recent years; the foremost of these is probably wood that is genetically engineered for fast growth, but that is thereby doomed to being a mushy, fast-rotting mess. So it is becoming ever more important to find materials that perform well while achieving the desired look. The following two rules establish common-sense standards for deciding which of the new materials are acceptable and which are to be avoided.

ARM'S LENGTH RULE: SUBSTITUTE MATERIALS MAY BE USED FOR MATERIALS NOTED HERE, BUT THEIR APPEARANCE MUST BE INDISTINGUISHABLE FROM THE ORIGINAL AT ARM'S LENGTH OR LESS, AND THEIR PERFORMANCE MUST EXCEED THAT OF THE ORIGINAL IF THEY ARE TO BE USED BELOW THE SECOND FLOOR.

The Arm's Length Rule is based on the fact that people often touch a building, but almost never look at a part of a building with a magnifying glass. The Arm's Length Rule is therefore practical, but not quite scientific. Touch is very important because few things are as unsatisfying as touching something that should feel solid and heavy, only to find that it is hollow and plastic.

EYES ONLY RULE: SUBSTITUTE MATERIALS USED AT OR ABOVE THE SECOND FLOOR MUST BE INDISTINGUISHABLE FROM THE ORIGINAL AT A DISTANCE OF 10 FEET.

The Eyes Only Rule recognizes that some materials could never pass the test of the Arm's Length Rule yet are acceptable when they are a certain distance in the air. The Eyes Only Rule also allows some materials that would not stand up to the abuse of a teenager at ground level, but that otherwise perform admirably at heights no teenager can reach. These clearly include materials that do not feel like the original, but also those materials whose fine-grained detail is not exactly like the original's but is close enough to be indiscernible from a distance of 10 feet.

## THE TRANSECT

THE TRANSECT IS AN IDEA THAT ORGANIZES PLACES FROM THE MOST RURAL TO THE MOST URBAN. SOME OF THE PATTERNS IN THIS BOOK CHANGE ACCORDING TO THEIR LOCATION ON THE TRANSECT.

The idea of the Transect originated in the 1900's as an ecological tool used to describe a series of natural habitats. A typical example is the Transect that runs from ocean to beach to dune line, on to palmetto grove and oak forest. The Transect allows scientists to study each habitat and observe the elements of each. The idea has been found to apply equally well to the human habitat. The Transect is the organizing device of the items in this book that vary from rural to urban conditions. The Transect of human habitat is divided into six Context T-Zones for administrative purposes. Each zone is defined by very specific rules, which may be characterized as follows:

## CONTEXT ZONE T1: NATURAL

The T1 Natural Zone includes the wilderness and lands such as local, state, and national parks. It is actually a place that is just a bit dangerous to humans; something could bite you, for example. The only buildings likely to be found are farmhouses, ranch houses, rangers' cabins, and campground structures. This is the quietest place you can find, and it's the place where the stars shine the brightest.

## CONTEXT ZONE T2: RURAL

The T2 Rural Zone may be characterized as farmlands and countryside. This zone isn't quite as dangerous, as long as you stay out of the pasture where the big bull lives. Man begins to shape this zone, but he uses natural or rustic materials to do it, like columns of fruit trees marching like soldiers over the hills of the orchard or the lonely lines of barbed wire strung along cedar posts at the edge of a field. Buildings most likely to be found here are farmhouses, barns, and their outbuildings. You may hear a distant tractor plowing the fields by day, or the cows mooing as they come home in the evening. The blips of the fireflies over the fresh-mown fields are still the most numerous lights, but you may occasionally see a light in the window of a farmhouse as you go by, at least until bedtime.

## CONTEXT ZONE T3: SUBURBAN

The T3 Suburban Zone may be characterized as either hamlets or the outskirts of towns and villages. It is the place where the street grid begins to give way to nature. Here, lots are usually larger, streets begin to curve with the contour of the land, and fences, if you have them, look more like their country cousins. Streetlights and sidewalks are scarce and only occur on major roads. This Zone isn't exactly the 'burbs as we have known them for 40 years, but rather the places they should have been.

## CONTEXT ZONE T4: GENERAL URBAN

The T4 General Urban Zone is the place where settlements finally start coalescing into strongly identifiable neighborhoods within easy walking distance to a village or town center. This is the place where the houses pull up close enough to the street that you can sit on your porch and talk to your neighbor who has stopped to lean over your fence with the latest news. Here, the neighborhood is compact enough that kids can safely walk or ride their bikes down tree-lined sidewalks to the ice cream store down on the corner, and return home before they finish the cone.

## CONTEXT ZONE T5: URBAN CENTER

The T5 Urban Center Zone is Main Street America. There were sometimes townhouses at the edge of Main Street and there was always a good selection of apartments over the Street itself, and over the square. Young couples just getting started would often live in an apartment over Main Street, but they weren't alone. The Main Street neighborhood included merchants living over their shops and old folks who didn't want to have to saddle up to get to all the necessities. You could see lights on in the windows over the square every evening, and could hear mothers calling their kids to come in and do their homework long after the old men out in front of the general store had folded up their checkerboard and gone home for the day.

## CONTEXT ZONE T6: URBAN CORE

The T6 Urban Core Zone only occurs in cities. It is the busiest, most exciting part of a region. It has the tallest buildings, busiest streets, and most variety. It's the place where you should find one-of-a-kind functions like City Hall, but it's also the place with all the galleries and the biggest selection of restaurants. The Urban Core is the place where the only trees are lined up in planters beside the street, and where the river running through town is contained in grand stone embankments. That may sound dismal to nature-lovers, but the Urban Core is so intriguing that thousands or even millions stay there for months on end, leaving nature in the wilderness to grow in peace.

# CHAPTER 7
~
# WALLS

## 8
## NUMBER OF
## MATERIALS

**NO MORE THAN TWO WALL MATERIALS SHOULD BE VISIBLE ON ANY EXTERIOR WALL, NOT COUNTING THE FOUNDATION WALL OR PIERS.**

This item derives from the Apparent Structure theme of traditional architecture and the patterns of simplicity. Construction was once much more difficult and expensive than it is now, so any sensible vernacular builder tried to use simple construction systems to create the buildings. They may have enriched the buildings with ornament, but the basic construction system was almost always simple. The classical languages took their hints from their vernacular predecessors so the classical buildings therefore used simple construction systems. Because of this, most walls were built of one material or maybe two, not counting the foundation and trimwork.

Today, however, the public realm is often so poor that people feel compelled to clutter the walls of buildings with as many materials and shapes as possible, in the hope of creating "street appeal" since the street itself has no appeal at all. Unfortunately, the result is often just the opposite, creating buildings with fragments

*Don't use too many wall materials. Even if the design of the wall is beautifully composed, too many materials ruin it by the sheer power of distraction. The two homes below exhibit a certain level of skill of composition, for example, but the number of materials is overpowering. In most cases, the use of an excessive number of materials is an attempt to cover up a lack of design ability.*

DON'T

*Don't: Brick walls, siding gable, stucco bay, wood trim… what have we missed?*

*Don't: This one trumps the one above with stone, brick, 2 types of siding and shingles.*

*Do use one or two primary wall material. The use of few materials focuses attention on the composition of the design and may be a sign of a confident (and competent) designer.*

*Do: Use of only one wall material, which in this case is the same as the trim material.*

*Do: Two closely related materials (shingle siding and lap siding) are not objectionable.*

of two or three distinct styles on nearly every wall.

Some of the worst offenders today are the "French Country" stock house plans. Most of these plans have a bit of Norman, a touch of Lutyens, a dash of Collegiate Gothic, and a healthy portion of Tudor. Season to (lack of) taste with "English Village," or maybe a pinch of "German Village," and you have one of the foulest architectural stews imaginable. It is probably not even possible for a tornado to throw together this many styles in the French countryside (if there were tornadoes in France). A true French country house, on the other hand, can be quite beautiful.

The materials are mixed in as liberally as the styles, of course. It is not unusual to find dry-stacked stone, brick, stucco, siding, and fake half-timbering all on the same elevation. Let's see... What other wall materials are there? If you don't count dressed stone, these houses pretty much cover the spectrum. The only conceivable response of future generations to these excesses must be, "What were they thinking?"

SEE APPARENT STRUCTURE (PAGE 11); 9~SIDING MATERIALS; 10~STONE VENEER WALL MATERIAL; 11~BRICK; 12~STUCCO; AND 13~TRIM.

## 9
# SIDING MATERIALS

THERE ARE A NUMBER OF
SIDING MATERIALS AVAILABLE
TODAY, AND THEY RANGE
ALL OVER THE COST/BENEFIT
MAP. SOME OF THEM ARE AS
FOLLOWS:

## LOWLAND CYPRESS

Lowland cypress is called one of the "eternal woods" because of its rot resistance. The others are redwood and cedar. Lowland cypress is the most rot-resistant of the three. Cypress logs sometimes lay half submerged for centuries without rotting. Upland cypress is available in some areas, but it has no more rot resistance than pine, so it should be avoided. Lowland cypress was once extremely expensive because it grows in swamps and is therefore very difficult to harvest. Recently, however, lumber companies have discovered that they can airlift cypress trees out with helicopters, greatly reducing the cost of the material. The lumber companies often harvest just the dead trees, eliminating the need to cut trees in a difficult wetland setting. Lowland cypress is without doubt the best material for exterior siding, trim, windows, and doors.

## REDWOOD

Redwood is next on the longevity scale. Unfortunately, it is softer and in many cases is becoming more expensive than lowland cypress. There are also concerns about cutting in old-growth redwood forests in the northwestern United States that may limit the availability of this wood in the future.

## CEDAR

Cedar is the softest of the "eternal woods." It is also the least expensive. Unfortunately, its longevity can vary. In some instances cedar siding has deteriorated in as little as a decade in certain areas of the United States. Cedar should be used only when a better material is clearly beyond the budget of a job.

## CEMENTITIOUS SIDING

Cementitious siding is a fiber-reinforced cement-based product that should be the first choice of siding materials on any project where cypress is not economically feasible. Cementitious siding cuts as wood, nails as wood, paints as wood, looks like wood does, but doesn't peel like wood does. If you have ever tried to remove paint from concrete, you will understand how well paint sticks to cementitious siding. It is not one of the mythical "maintenance-free materials," but it needs to be repainted much less often than wood of any type. It is quite economical and is indiscernible from rabbeted beveled siding, even at arm's length from the wall. The manufacturer of the most popular cementitious siding product, Hardi-Plank, now has a $3/4$" thick trim material on the market that may replace wood trim in widths from $1^{1}/_{2}$" (1X2) to $11^{1}/_{4}$" (1X12), although the edges currently are a bit rough.

## PINE

Untreated pine siding and exterior trim simply should not exist. The material we call pine today is far different from pine wood a century ago and is much more susceptible to rot. Use of this wood in wet locations will pretty much guarantee that the owner will be replacing those components in less than a decade.

## POPLAR

Poplar makes great paint-grade interior trim, but simply should not be used on the exterior for the same reasons as noted above for pine.

## MASONITE

Masonite is a synthetic wood-based product that was popular as a siding material a few years ago. It is one of the least expensive siding materials available. Unfortunately, it didn't hold paint very well and was known to deteriorate quickly in some areas. It has largely been replaced by Hardi-Plank siding, which costs about the same as Masonite but is a much better material for the reasons noted previously.

## ALUMINUM

Aluminum siding was the first material that was touted as being maintenance-free several few years ago. Unfortunately, many believed the sales pitch and have found out otherwise. The thickness of the aluminum is usually quite insubstantial, meaning that a well-placed baseball or football, a rock from a lawn mower, or a thousand other things that kids think of can dent a siding panel. Once damaged, the panel cannot be repaired short of hiring an auto body expert. And it is virtually impossible to match the pre-finish of siding that has been weathering for several years with another piece right off the assembly line. These are some of the practical reasons for not using aluminum siding. One other huge factor is that aluminum siding and its trim pieces bear little resemblance to wood siding. In other words, it looks cheap and ugly next to wood siding.

## VINYL

Vinyl siding has all the problems of aluminum siding plus several more of its own; yet vinyl siding has become highly popular in recent years due to its relatively low cost. The only advantage vinyl has over aluminum is that it is less likely to dent. It is, however, much softer than aluminum so physical damage is easier to inflict. String trimmers (weed whackers) are known enemies of vinyl siding, as is the average family dog. Vinyl also melts at temperatures much lower than those generated in an innocent backyard barbecue. The aesthetic damage done by vinyl siding is enormous. Most vinyl siding will gleam in all the glory of fakeness when the sun hits it just right. Even on cloudy days, vinyl siding can be discerned from a great distance due primarily to the horribly detailed trim pieces, but also to the telltale curve of the surface and design of the connectors. Vinyl siding has become the standard-bearer for cheap, insubstantial construction and should be avoided wherever possible.

SEE 19~WALL MATERIAL JOINTS; 37~CASING PRINCIPLES; 38~HEAD CASING PRINCIPLES; 44~SILL CASING; AND 46~BEAM MATERIALS.

---

## 10
# STONE VENEER WALL MATERIAL

### NATURAL STONE SHOULD BE LAID WITH THE STONES HORIZONTAL.

Stone veneer walls present challenges in addition to the ones listed under 16~Masonry Veneer Walls because the mason has the added choices of stone size, shape, and orientation. Far too many stone veneer walls in the past 40 years have created the illusion of stone wallpaper by turning the broad face of the stone to the outside of the wall. No structural stone wall would ever be laid this way because such a wall would not be nearly as strong as one that was properly constructed.

Structural stone is always laid in a pattern resembling the pattern of stone in the earth, which is horizontally oriented strata with the broad face up, not out. This is an unusual instance in which there are potentially more correct patterns than incorrect ones. Some are referred to as "dry-stack," while others are simply called "stacked stone." Unfortunately, most masons have still chosen the fewer incorrect patterns.

Note that this is one case in which the wrong detail is undeniably cheaper than the right one. The reason is

Don't turn the broad face of the stone to the outside because this makes a weaker wall. The pattern shown here is perfectly acceptable for stone flooring, but not for stone walls. Using patterns similar to this on a wall is as incorrect as covering a wall with linoleum or covering a floor with wallpaper.

*Don't: The arch is correct, but the walls are structurally no better than stone wallpaper.*

*Don't: Ultra-exaggerated flagstone flooring pattern on the wall.*

*Don't: Non-structural pattern combines with non-structural window headers to create something that cannot possibly be a real stone wall.*

*Don't: Is it possible to disgrace stone more than this? Not only is the stone laid like flooring on a wall, but it is also panelized, which makes it seem lighter than the wood frame members.*

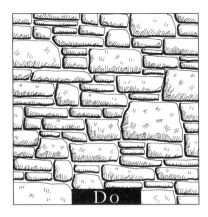

*Do lay stone veneer to resemble structural stone walls. This pattern is appropriate for walls because the stones are coursed even while naturally shaped, and the long dimension is turned horizontally.*

simple: There are fewer pieces of stone in the wall when the broad face is turned out. Nonetheless, the person who wants a stone wall should be willing to pay for it to be done right. Even though stone veneer is not structural, it registers subconsciously as a structural wall. Stone veneer that does not appear structural may give the viewer a vague sense of unease. If the person wants something akin to wallpaper, it is much less expensive to hang a roll or two of stone-patterned linoleum on the outside of the building.

SEE 16~MASONRY VENEER WALLS; 18~FRAME WALL/ MASONRY BASE ALIGNMENT; 19~WALL MATERIAL JOINTS; 39~MASONRY LINTEL PRINCIPLES; 40~ARCH PRINCIPLES; 41~JACK ARCHES; 42~ARCH/EAVE ALIGNMENT; AND 43~KEYSTONES.

*Do: Stacked stone foundation.*

*Do: Stacked stone wall.*

*Do: This might at first seem as random as the flooring patterns, but look closely. This is a real stone wall where the stone, while irregular, is coursed.*

*Do: Rectilinear stacked stone wall pattern.*

## 11
# BRICK

BRICK SHOULD LOOK AS IF IT COULD HAVE BEEN PRODUCED LOCALLY IN 1895. BRICK MAY BE PAINTED IF APPROPRIATE TO THE STYLE AND TO LOCAL PRECEDENT.

Today, you can buy brick stamped with glove prints, brick stamped with raccoon paw prints, and brick stamped with maple leaves. You can buy brick colored to look like walnut wood, brick colored to look like vanilla ice cream, brick colored to look like chocolate, and even brick colored to look like..., well, just about anything except the ocean or grass, unless you want glazed brick, in which case anything is possible.

The range of brick choices available today is a great illustration of how modern construction has become too easy. Construction, throughout most of history, was a difficult endeavor at best, leaving us with the great historical construction contradiction: Once construction reached a certain basic threshold of construction capability, the least technologically advanced periods (classical Greek antiquity and the Gothic era) generally produced the most highly developed architecture while the most technologically advanced era (our own) generally pro-duces some of the least developed architecture.

How is this possible? It is likely that during the greatest eras, because construction was difficult, it was also honored. Today, it is very easy and of little consequence to many. So what does this have to do with brick? Throughout most of history up until the late nineteenth century, brick construction followed the same path. Brick was typically constructed locally of locally available materials at great effort, often being fired on-site for large houses. In any case, it was a difficult material to produce and was treated with great respect,

Don't use brick of the wrong shape or surface. 1: To fix head joints, every long queen-size brick at corners must be cut. 2: Pitiful attempt at faking a whitewashed finish is one of the worst errors of brick design today. 3: Fake texture, queen-size corner problem left uncorrected creates uneven head joints. 4: Rake joint creates shadow line and unnatural appearance. 5: One of the oldest really bad bricks, this one screams "I was wire-cut, not hand-made!"

1

2

3

4

5

*Do use simple brick designs in standard or modular sizes. 1: Thin joints, creative brick detail. 2: The elegance of white-painted brick is timeless. 3: Simple, plain, classically attractive brick with no significant color variation. 4: Flemish bond, common on fine American buildings a century ago, alternates headers and stretchers. 5: Simple brick showing simple joints and header course used to tie the wall together.*

1

2

4

3

5

being used in a noble fashion on the finest buildings. The only more desired material was cut stone.

Today, brick is cheaper than it has been in absolute terms in decades, if not ever; yet it is used only as a veneer on other materials, and it is a cheap substitute at best. If budgets no longer allow for brick to be used to construct walls because construction is too easy, then we should at least have enough respect for this venerable material to not dress it in a clown's suit of paw prints and unnatural colors. Look at local buildings constructed before 1895. In nearly every instance, the color range

was very similar because of the characteristics of the local clay and shale.

The texture, too, was similar. Handmade bricks were shaped in wood molds before being dried and then fired in the kiln. This means that the surface was relatively smooth, if slightly irregular because of deformation that occurred while it was being pulled out of the mold. Today, brick is extruded as so much extra toothpaste. Unfortunately, many brick styles actually accentuate this extrusion process by allowing rough material in the brick to scrape across the edge of the mold, creating vertical streaks on the brick, which screams, "I was extruded!"

Brick ideally should be wood-molded to attest to its noble heritage as a handmade material, but that is not often economically feasible. However, at the very least, brick should be sand-faced and formed of a mix that minimizes the extrusion streaks. It should, as a bonus, be slightly deformed to approximate handmade brick. Mortar joint designs should be simple and the mortar surface compressed by tooling. This is possible with either a concave or a grapevine joint. It is possible, in these ways, to show respect to a once-noble material.

## 12
## STUCCO

STUCCO SHOULD BE SMOOTH
SAND-FINISHED. SYNTHETIC
STUCCO, IF USED, ABSOLUTELY
MUST ADHERE TO CERTAIN
BASIC RULES.

A smooth sand finish is the natural finish of stucco. Most installers of natural stucco know this, so there is not a problem. The problem arises most often with synthetic stucco, or the Exterior Insulation and Finish System (EIFS). Most EIFS manufacturers provide a few other finish choices, all of which are rougher-textured than natural stucco. Some of these finishes include large aggregate that is swirled around with the applicator's trowel to create a "wormy" appearance. The objective is to distract the eye from flaws in the finish. These finishes clearly are simply an excuse to do a sloppy job, and they should never be accepted on this basis alone.

There are several other enormously important issues with EIFS. If they are dealt with properly, a good installation should result, but if they are done improperly, serious flaws can result. These issues are as follows:

Possibly the worst detail in the history of human construction was once found in installation manuals from a number of EIFS manufacturers. This detail called for the EIFS wall finish to be run down the wall to a few inches below the surface of the ground. The problem here is twofold. First, it creates a conduit for moisture to wick up into the building and rot or rust the framing. That's obviously bad enough, but it gets much worse in areas susceptible to termites. Here, termites can travel into the building undetected. In numerous instances the termite damage was so bad that the building was in danger of collapse by the time the damage was discovered. EIFS should never be used within about 3' of the ground.

Second, a very pervasive error is the use of paper-faced sheathing. Probably 90 percent or more of EIFS installations over the past 20 years have been performed with paper-faced sheathing. Unfortunately, moisture will even-

*Don't: Highly textured finish is designed to cover up a bad framing job.*

*Don't: Another type of highly textured finish.*

tually get into the system from a number of potential sources, causing the paper to rot. When this happens, probably 10 to 15 years after installation, the EIFS is guaranteed to fall off the wall. Anything less than fiberglass-faced sheathing is absolutely unacceptable for a proper EIFS installation.

There has been a popular misconception that EIFS acts as flashing. This simply is not true. All openings in EIFS walls must be flashed just as they would be with any other wall material. Without head and sill flashing, water will get into the wall with predictable results: rotting or rusting of the wall framing.

A related error is un-flashed upward-facing EIFS surfaces. EIFS surfaces should face only horizontally or downward. Any upward facing surfaces, even if at an angle, encourage water to sit on them, which results in water penetration. All upward-facing surfaces must be flashed with metal flashing. To visualize this, consider an EIFS ball. Exactly half of the ball (the upper half) should be flashed with metal.

Finally, EIFS does not meet the arm's length test, either in touch or in abuse. Just ask any teenager with a pencil or other instrument. Or ask any intruder with a pocketknife. EIFS, for these reasons, should not be used below the second level of any building.

If that is so, then what can it be used for? The best use of the material is for cornices or entablatures. There are several reasons for this. First, there is no danger of an entablature inadvertently being run down into the ground. There are no penetrations on an entablature that need flashing. Entablatures generally are built outward as they go upward, meaning that all surfaces except the well-protected top surface of the taenia face either horizontally or downward. And insulation board is arguably the easiest material available today out of which to form elaborate shapes such as the curves and offsets of an entablature. EIFS, used in this manner, should be a long-lived, low-maintenance material that meets a need that wood cannot.

*Do: This finish is called "smooth sand." Nothing rougher should be accepted.*

*Do: Smooth finishes accentuate the design, not the surface.*

## 13
## TRIM

EXTERIOR TRIM SHOULD BE
INDISTINGUISHABLE FROM
WOOD WHEN PAINTED,
AND SHOULD BE SIZED
APPROPRIATELY TO ITS
LOCATION.

Many American buildings were once trimmed with pine, which used to be a dense, fine-grained material that resisted weathering fairly well. Those days are long gone; the genetically engineered pine of today quickly becomes a mushy mess when exposed to the weather, much to the dismay of those who have trimmed the exteriors of buildings with it over the last three or four decades. The only two remaining woods affordable by mere mortals that resist weathering enough to be used as exterior trimwork are lowland cypress and redwood. And neither of these is particularly inexpensive. Pressure-treated pine is affordable and durable, but it has so many problems with twisting, cupping, and warping that it barely merits a mention here. If pine is used at all on finish work, the grade should be significantly better than the commonly used number 2.

So if wood itself isn't acting much as wood anymore, then what are the choices? One of the more promising contenders is fiber-reinforced cementitious trim, a material which is also used for siding. The release of the material was delayed to work out a number of technical issues, including the smoothness of the edge of the board. The product as currently sold is a bit rough on the edges, but with a coat of paint, it simply appears to be a slightly rough board. It would never pass for cabinet-grade material, but could easily be mistaken for mid-grade wood trim when painted. Because it is built of a fiber-reinforced cementitious material it will never rot or be susceptible to termites, since the insects don't favor concrete for dinner.

There are other promising materials appearing on the market, including several that are PVC-based. This general product type is quite interesting, because while more expensive than the cementitious-based products, PVC-based products and their cousins are not confined to being simple flat boards like cementitious trim. PVC trim is easily extruded into any shape desired. The only drawback is the fact that the setup cost for a non-standard shape is quite high, making custom shapes

*Don't: Above: See how aluminum roof trim ripples? Lower Left and Right: J-trim is vinyl's Achilles Heel, leaving no doubt that siding is slipping behind thin plastic.*

unaffordable on all except the highest-budget jobs.

If large-scale custom shapes are unavoidable, consider synthetic stucco (EIFS). There are serious problems with this material if it is used improperly, but those errors are now fairly well understood and avoidable. EIFS has a number of significant advantages when used as trim (especially entablatures or cornices) that no other affordable materials now can offer. EIFS does not rot as wood; properly detailed, it should last for many decades. Because the underlying shape of EIFS is

created with expanded polystyrene or similar foam-based materials, custom shapes at any size are easily shaped with a full-size template and a hot wire cutter. People have long felt that EIFS detailing is necessarily crude and imprecise, but recent examples demonstrate that this simply is not true. Lack of crispness generally is the fault of the designer, not the applicator. There is no reason that EIFS should be any less crisp than the stucco cornices of Charleston, South Carolina, for example. The most important single limitation of EIFS as trim is that,

because it will never resemble wood at any reasonable distance, it should never be used where the trim must appear to be wood. Stucco cornices could reasonably be used on brick, stone, or stucco buildings, but should never be used on wood siding buildings. Neither should EIFS.

Appropriate trim sizes vary significantly from style to style, with few principles that apply across the board. The single most important principle to remember when you are choosing trim sizes is simply not to confuse a trim piece with another component by virtue of its size and proportion. For example, contractors will select extraordinarily wide corner boards, assuming that these boards appear richer than thin corner boards. Unfortunately, as the proportion of a corner board approaches 1:16 or especially 1:12, it begins to look like a pilaster. But because it has no capital or base trim, it looks like a very cheap pilaster rather than a very expensive corner board.

*Do: Above: Siding butts solid to wood trim. Lower Left: Simple wood boards can be used in many creative ways. Lower Right: Same principle at the roof's edge.*

See 9~Siding Materials; 12~Stucco; 19~Wall Material Joints; 26~Brick Mold; 37~Casing Principles; 38~Head Casing Principles; 51~Entablature Principles; 62~Trim under Cornice; and 66~Eave Overhang and Enclosure.

## 14
## COLORS

COLORS FOR ALL EXTERIOR
MATERIALS (SIDING, TRIM,
BRICK, STONE, MORTAR,
STUCCO, ETC.) SHOULD BE
SELECTED APPROPRIATE TO THE
BUILDING STYLE AND TO LOCAL
PRECEDENT.

The case for the importance of adhering to patterns of local color cannot be stated strongly enough. Some of the more important factors are as follows:

### CLIMATE

Colors in a region often are a result of its climate. A predominately misty or rainy environment usually results in an entirely different palette of materials than one that is sunny all the time. Even the sunshine itself may vary. Cold, thin sunshine in the northern reaches of a nation also often suggests a very different range of colors from that of hot southern regions. Places where the light is most precious often have very light buildings. Places with scorching heat also often have entirely white buildings to reflect the heat. Places in the middle climates are the ones most likely to employ darker colors.

### SOIL

Regional color may originate with the colors of the soil. An especially powerful example is the desert southwest of the United States. Santa Fe was once built almost entirely of adobe (whether real or simulated is unimportant to this discussion). Until recently, you could drive by Santa Fe on the interstate and never know you were next to a city. The buildings literally disappeared from a distance into the warm, muted desert hues of the land, almost as if in camouflage. It is especially disappointing to be able to drive by today and pick out a number of buildings that are now colored inappropriately.

### VEGETATION

A regional palette may also derive from the vegetation of the area. Many wooded mountainous areas, including the Smoky Mountains of the eastern United States and the Rocky Mountains in the west have developed vernacular architectures built primarily of weathered wood or paints composed of woodland greens or maybe browns. These buildings, too, often blend into the local environment. A bright red brick building would look quite strange here in most cases.

### NATURAL BUILDING MATERIALS

Sometimes, local color may not be painted at all, but rather may result from the unpigmented use of natural materials. The stone buildings of northern French villages are one such example, as are the stone towers of northern Italian hill-towns. It is impossible for the colors of these buildings to fail to match the colors of the surroundings.

### URBAN SURFACES

Even large cities create their own local color. Look at how much urban architecture in metropolitan areas mirrors the natural grays or metallic colors of the paving, grates, utilities, and curbs of the basic urban environment. Gray limestone (or possibly granite) buildings were once considered the standard for urban buildings. Even the Modernists typically got this one right, although they often swerved far to the metallic end of the urban spectrum.

## ECONOMICS

But color is not always the result of the local natural environment. Cultural choices that have nothing to do with the local landscape play a part in many instances. A classic example is that of Victorian architecture in various parts of the United States. The Victorian "painted ladies" of San Francisco are world renowned for their exuberance of color. The Victorian styles, to be sure, were generally some of the most vibrant created in the western hemisphere in centuries, so this seems to be a natural part of the style. But look carefully at the Victorians in other parts of the country. Nowhere does the vigor of the colors exceed that of the painted ladies; Victorians in most areas are noticeably more restrained, depending on the region. The South contains the starkest contrast. The Civil War was concluding as most of the Victorian styles were approaching their peak, and the entire region was thrown into extremely hard times for decades afterward. Nearly all buildings built in the South during this era were of humble origins unless the owner was unusually wealthy. Southern Victorians, as a result, were almost always painted white, and the gingerbread was typically very restrained. In many cases, the origin of the house shape was Victorian, but there was no gingerbread at all. People from other regions might not even recognize the houses as being Victorian.

## CULTURAL HISTORY

Southern bungalows are another example of a style whose colors changed at the borders of a region. The result is similar to the southern Victorians, but for different reasons. Textbook American Arts & Crafts bungalows originated in California and carried with them a warm, pastel West Coast palette. Southern bungalows, however, were a different story. The South had begun to recover from the Civil War by this time, but still clung to an affinity for the golden era of the region: the first half of the nineteenth century when the Greek Revival movement held sway. The colors of choice for Greek Revival buildings were usually white paint or limestone for the body of the building and dark green for the shutters. A century later, the South was painting its bungalows white not out of necessity, as their Victorians had been 20 years before, but because of the collective memory of an earlier time.

## STYLE

The least important influence on the color palette, therefore, is often the style, or at least the textbook definition of a style. If they are understood as a starting point, the sanctioned colors can be helpful, but they should almost never be used universally without regard to local precedent.

SEE 9~SIDING MATERIALS; 10~STONE VENEER WALL MATERIAL; 11~BRICK; AND 12~STUCCO.

## 15
## WALL HEIGHT

EIGHT-FOOT-TALL WALLS
SHOULD NEVER BE USED
EXCEPT IN RARE CASES WHEN
THEY ARE APPROPRIATE TO THE
ARCHITECTURAL LANGUAGE.

The 8' wall height may well be the original sin of modern construction. Principal rooms of even the humblest houses had relatively tall ceilings until the mid-1920's. Previously, the primary proponents of any style had been architects or designers, but that all changed just after World War I. It is possible, even as good as the plans were, that the Sears Catalog houses may have set the stage by turning houses into products, just like a pair of khakis or that wheelbarrow on page 872.

In any case, we all know that marketing is about perceived value. The 8' ceiling fad was intensely marketed as one of the most important "value features" of the "modern house" because it reduced heating bills. Never mind that these houses were very hard to cool in the summer, especially before the days of air conditioning and proper insulation.

The biggest damage, however, was due to the effect of 8' walls on the style of the house. It is nearly impossible to detail a traditional house properly with 8' tall walls with rafters

*Don't use 8' walls. 8' walls condemn your window choices to not much more than the two shown here, neither of which is appropriate, as drawn, to any beautiful architectural language known to humanity.*

*Don't: Colonial or English Arts & Crafts? Without proper wall height, it's hard to say.*

*Don't: Here's why Spanish colonists never conceived of Spanish Colonial with 8' walls.*

*Do use walls that are at least 9' in height on the main level. Preferably, they should be taller for most styles. Walls properly sized to the architectural language of the building are enormously important to the success of the design.*

*Do: Proper height, especially on the first floor, allows proper door and window detailing.*

*Do: This porch fits between first and second floor windows because of proper wall height.*

above. Within a decade of this "innovation" most builders quit making any attempt at traditional exterior detailing resulting in the visual bankruptcy of post–World War II tract housing.

Variations of ceiling heights throughout a building can be good, including some ceilings set at 8' or even lower. This can be accomplished in several ways (including furrdowns) that do not necessarily affect the principal plate height of the house. It is virtually imperative to have at least a 9' plate line in order to even approach proper traditional detailing. The 10' or higher plate lines, at least on the main level of the main body of the house, make this a much easier task.

There are other common methods that can be used to increase the perceived height of the wall. If the roof is being truss-framed, the heel height can easily be increased 16" or more. If the heel is laid out flush with the wall with only a top chord overhang at the top of the truss, then the wall material can run up the heel and it will be perceived as part of the wall. If floor decking for storage is anticipated, then a kneewall can be built on top of the floor system that extends the wall height as far as desired.

## 16
## MASONRY VENEER WALLS

MASONRY VENEER WALLS SHOULD BE DETAILED EXACTLY AS MASONRY BEARING WALLS, ESPECIALLY AT OPENINGS.

Masonry walls once were built of solid masonry. It's true that the facing of the wall was often made of a much nobler material than the core, but the wall was solid masonry from face to face. The weight and volume of the wall materials put certain constraints on the wall design.

Short openings, for example, could be spanned with straight lintels, but the lintels had to be of a certain height to span the opening. Once lintels got too long to be made of a single piece of stone, they had to be constructed of a series of stone wedges with a single large keystone at the center. The whole assembly was called the jack arch. There was a point, however, where the flat jack arch simply could not span an opening in a cost efficient manner. So other types of arches were developed to span the largest openings.

The height of the wall imposed other restraints. Tall walls had to be thicker at the bottom, or else they would fall over. The wall could generally be thinner if buttresses were used at regular intervals to support the wall.

Masonry veneer walls came into common use about a century ago because of cost concerns. One thin wythe of brick veneer plus a stud wall is obviously much cheaper than a four- or five-wythe brick wall. Most traditional architects would, without question, prefer to build solid masonry walls rather than masonry veneer walls. The realities of construction cost budgets, however, are such that solid masonry walls will be out of the question on all but the most richly appointed structures for the foreseeable future.

The problem with masonry veneers arises when the archi-

*Don't detail masonry veneer walls unconvincingly. 1: This house commits all major brick veneer infractions, leaving no doubt that its brick is just wallpaper. 2: Nice entry ruined by adjacent lintel-free window. 3: Otherwise nicely detailed, but wood beam supporting brick wall above leaves no question concerning whether this is a real brick wall or not. 4: Simple elevation has some positive aspects, but lintel-free windows expose its veneer.*

1

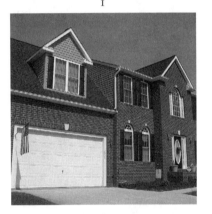

2

3

4

Do

*Do detail masonry veneer walls as if they were structural masonry walls. All of the examples below celebrate the act of building with brick. Arches are properly proportioned and detailed. Eave and belt details are authentic. All of these buildings could also be built of brick veneer if detailed as carefully as these examples were.*

tect forgets to detail them as if they were structural masonry walls. Arches become impossibly thin, often nothing more than a single rowlock. Lintels become a single soldier course that would obviously drop out of the opening if not supported by a steel angle. Worse yet, the lintel often disappears entirely, requiring the brick to run straight across the opening as if gravity did not exist. We all know that it does exist, however, so we are left with only one logical conclusion: This isn't brick at all, but rather is some very convincing wallpaper.

One can clearly see the superiority of the traditional

solution. First, the details of the wall tell a story that is consistent with the material of the wall. There is no confusion among viewers concerning the nature of the wall. True, the actual load is being carried by the frame wall, but the story is being told and the job is being done. There is an added benefit to proper detailing in that the arch or lintel can actually carry the load of the masonry veneer above, eliminating the need for the cost of the steel lintel.

SEE 10~STONE VENEER WALL MATERIALS; 11~BRICK; 17~BRICK COURSING AT WALL OPENINGS; 19~WALL MATERIAL JOINTS; 24~BRICK JACK ARCH; 39~MASONRY LINTEL PRINCIPLES; 40~ARCH PRINCIPLES; 41~JACK ARCHES; 42~ARCH/EAVE ALIGNMENT; AND 43~KEYSTONES.

# 17
# BRICK COURSING AT WALL OPENINGS

BRICK SHOULD COURSE EXACTLY TO BOTH THE TOP AND THE BOTTOM OF ALL WALL OPENINGS.

At one time, exterior masonry bearing walls were built first, and doors and windows were custom-built to fit the openings. If one opening were a little larger or a little smaller, then the carpenter would simply build the door or window to fit. Now, however, the manufacturer generally predetermines opening sizes. The head heights of the openings are also generally pre-set, and all doors and windows are set in place before brickwork begins. Seldom does this result in a head or sill height that aligns with standard brick coursing. The result is one of the most careless-looking details in traditional construction today: slivers of brick above and below the window opening. This condition only serves to heighten the illusion of brick as wallpaper. It looks as though the mason simply took scissors and cut the brick wallpaper wherever it happened to hit the window, with no regard for the location of the joints.

This problem may begin with the construction sequence, but architects who don't take the time to give the problem any

thought exacerbate it. There are several methods at the architect's disposal that could solve the problem. One option is to vary the width of the head (and jamb) casings so that the top of the head casing hits the brick joint. This changes the look of the finished opening slightly, but leaves the heads of the doors and windows at the exact right height. This is our first choice. Another option is to move the head height up or down slightly to meet the mortar joint. This option doesn't change the casing width, but may mean that the head height of exterior openings doesn't quite match the head height of interior

*Don't lay brick slivers around openings in walls. All of the examples below show brick slivers around window openings which are one of the symptoms of a building that has been built without careful thought. Brick houses built without slivers today are rare, but the problem is easy to solve (see the description of the procedure in the text), especially if the designer draws the detail correctly in the beginning.*

*Do course brick properly at openings. All great architecture (and even the simple, good buildings such as the ones below) course brick properly at the openings. Even if the designer does not take the time to figure it out (as he or she should) on the drawings, the builder can still solve the problem by setting the window head to brick coursing and using a filler strip (shown with stars in drawing above) above the masonry sill.*

doors. The difference will never be more than 1 3/8".

The sill condition is much easier to adjust as long as the casing doesn't miter around all four sides of the opening. Generally, sills in traditional construction were notably different from heads and jambs for water-shedding reasons. If this is the case, then simply insert a filler strip between the bottom of the window and the top of the brick (or stone) sill. This filler should be painted to match the color of the window casing.

All the options above begin with the architect. It is imperative that the contractor know that the coursing and casings have been resolved on paper; otherwise, a single change by the contractor may ruin the entire situation. There is one other option that can be done in the field. A good mason can vary the width of the mortar joint slightly to either expand or compress the brick within a particular band of the wall. In doing so, the mason can make the joints hit the top and bottom of the window. This option works best in near-miss conditions where the joint widths do not have to vary significantly.

SEE 10~STONE VENEER WALL MATERIAL; 11~BRICK; 16~MASONRY VENEER WALLS; 24~BRICK JACK ARCH; 41~JACK ARCHES; 42~ARCH/ EAVE ALIGNMENT; AND 43~KEYSTONES.

## 18
### FRAME WALL/ MASONRY BASE ALIGNMENT

THE FACE OF STUD OF FRAME WALLS SHOULD ALIGN WITH FACE OF MASONRY OF FOUNDATION WALLS BELOW.

This condition occurs whenever a wood frame wall sits atop a brick foundation wall. Architects and builders once aligned the outside face of the foundation wall, floor framing, and stud wall above. What could be simpler?

Well, nearly everyone gets confused about this detail today. Any builder knows that the face of floor and the face of stud wall should align with the face of foundation wall, but they consider the foundation wall to be just the concrete block wall. Brick is never anything more than a nonstructural veneer to an average builder (or architect, for that matter). So the builder typically aligns the face of block, face of floor framing, and face of stud. Then the brick veneer is set out 5" or so from the face of the block, forming a horizontal ledge all around the house at the bottom of the siding. This ledge is normally capped with a brick rowlock.

What's the problem? There are several, actually. First, the detail is downright unsightly and looks just like the typi-

Don't create a horizontal ledge between a wood frame wall and a masonry base. This detail has several serious problems beyond being seriously ugly. It leaks and can rot the floor system, and it sits wood siding and trim on a horizontal masonry surface, exposing them to high rot risk. It is also seldom built without exposing brick cores in the unsightly manner shown. The examples below further illustrate the problems of this detail.

DON'T

*Bad joint when meeting upper brick veneer.*

*Ledge at second floor has all the problems of the first.*

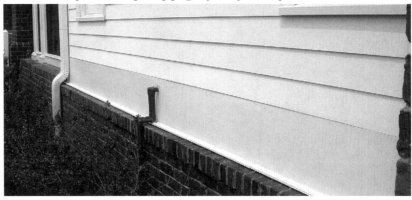
*Vertical placement requires piping in floor system to penetrate skirt board.*

Do

*Do align the faces of stud walls and masonry bases. Below are several examples of proper frame wall/masonry base joints executed with several foundation materials. This detail was always done correctly before the advent of masonry veneer construction.*

cal brick wainscot details that were so popular on split-levels of the 1960's. Second, because it forms a horizontal ledge, it creates a location where water can collect, infiltrate, and rot the floor system. Third, it actually costs more than doing it right since a properly detailed wall would have no need for the rowlock course.

What's the solution? Opening one's mind to the possibility that brick can actually be a structural material changes the whole picture. The brick should be laid as a part of the foundation wall structure. To do this, first it should be pulled tight to the block wall. Allow 4" from the outside face of the block to the outside face of the brick, which creates a $3/8$" space between brick and block. This space should be filled with mortar. Next, use horizontal truss-type joint reinforcement every other block course, beginning at the top of the bottom block course. Finally, use a 2X12 sill plate, set it flush with the outside of the brick, and then align the face of the floor system with the outside face of brick. This is simpler, cheaper, and more sensible than the normal way of detailing this condition.

SEE 16~MASONRY VENEER WALLS.

*Stucco foundation wall.*

*Rough coursed stone foundation wall.*

*Brick foundation wall.*

*Faux stone (stucco) foundation wall.*

*Stucco foundation wall.*

*Precast stone foundation wall.*

## 19
## WALL MATERIAL JOINTS

HEAVIER MATERIALS SHOULD BE LOCATED BELOW HORIZONTAL JOINTS. VERTICAL JOINTS BETWEEN DIFFERENT MATERIALS SHOULD OCCUR ONLY AT INSIDE CORNERS EXCEPT IN RARE INSTANCES THAT ARE APPROPRIATE TO THE STYLE.

There are a number of acceptable ways to join different wall materials, and at least one very unacceptable way to do so. Horizontal joints are probably the most common. Heavier, more basic or more unadorned materials should generally be below the joint. Traditional buildings generally become lighter and more adorned as they approach the sky.

Vertical joints between materials should generally occur at inside corners. This occurred naturally when additions to buildings were built of a different material. It is common in some areas to see original houses of wood, for example, with additions of brick because the family became more prosperous over the years. Other scenarios exist, of course; but whatever the story was, the material change always occurred on an inside corner so that the main body was all of one mate-

*Don't create vertical joints at outside corners between materials of different weight. The following is a rogue's gallery of improper wall material joints. In every case, dissimilar materials (brick veneer and siding) meeting at an outside corner makes the heavier material look light and fake.*

*Do join materials in an authentic manner. 1: Vertical joints at pilasters. 2: Vertical joints at inside corners between wings. 3: Vertical joints where two storefronts abut. 4: Same weight material, but more refined (stone versus brick) wraps corner, toothing into less refined material. 5: More refined bay material (stone versus brick) of same type (masonry) breaks at interior corner. 6: Lighter (wood shingles) over heavier material (brick) at horizontal joint.*

1

2

3

4

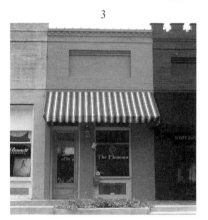

5

6

rial and the wing was of an entirely different material.

Material changes at outside corners, however, are unnatural. It is difficult to imagine a situation where this would be acceptable. This occurs most often when a more expensive material such as brick is used on the front of a building and a less expensive material such as vinyl siding is used elsewhere. Such a joint practically screams that the owner of the building is trying to build something beyond his or her means. An alternate explanation would be that the owner could afford to do it right, but was just cheap to do so. Either option is obviously very unflattering to the owner and gives the entire building an aura of fakeness. It would have been much better to do the entire building elegantly out of siding than to build something that makes it look phony.

SEE 9~SIDING MATERIALS; 10~STONE VENEER WALL MATERIAL; 11~BRICK; AND 12~STUCCO.

# CHAPTER 8
## ~
# DOORS AND WINDOWS

### DOOR AND WINDOW MATERIALS

# Door and Window Configurations

## 20
## DOOR MATERIALS

RESIDENTIAL DOORS
SHOULD BE BUILT OF WOOD.
COMMERCIAL DOORS MAY
ALSO BE HOLLOW STEEL FRAME
OR EXTRUDED ALUMINUM.
IN NO CASE EXCEPT FOR
RESIDENTIAL GARAGE DOORS
SHOULD METAL DOORS BE
STAMPED TO RESEMBLE WOOD
DOORS, UNLESS THEY ARE
INDISCERNIBLE FROM WOOD AT
ARM'S LENGTH.

Doors are one of the few items in a building that people touch on a regular basis, and are the first building elements that they see from a distance of less than arm's length as they are entering the building. The door, therefore, sets the tone of the entire building for a visitor, and it should not be treated poorly. Fake materials, especially at an entry door, taint the person's entire remaining experience in a building. A few doors are available today that are indiscernible from doors built of real materials at arm's length, but they are by far the exception.

Synthetic materials for exterior doors have gained favor in recent years because they supposedly last longer than wood. There is some truth to this, but consider the following: Most traditional architecture provides some sort of cover, whether it be a full porch or simply the projecting overhang of an aedicule at a stoop, combined possibly with a recessed door, to protect the door from the worst of the sun and the rain and to protect either the guest or the owner as this person either waits for someone to answer the door or looks for her or his keys. Wood doors under porches of

proper depth may last for centuries, wearing out from use before they deteriorate from weather.

Synthetic materials, while they may technically weather better than wood, clearly have their own problems. Dings, scratches, or gouges in a wood door are easily filled, sanded,

*Don't: The tell-tale sign of the plastic door is visible from great distances: the light plastic window grilles are almost impossible to hide. Most people can spot these driving by at high speed. Closer encounters are even worse, with their plastic feel and inability to wear gracefully, making for a less than ideal way of greeting your guests at the door.*

*Don't: Stamped metal doors are somewhat more subtle. Their shallow panels are the giveaway. From arm's length, however, there are other symptoms, including the way they feel so cold to the touch. Very expensive ones have foam injections to keep them from clinking like hollow metal, but the cheap ones do not.*

and painted. But try fixing a dent in a metal door; it's difficult, unless you happen to own an auto body shop. And if the metal door happens to have an embossed fake wood grain, you might as well just drive down to the local building supply store and buy a new one. The one place where metal doors possibly make sense is on a commercial building in a setting where there is no attempt at elegance. Such doors are often built as just a frame of metal around one or two large panes of glass, rather than trying to mimic wood paneled doors.

The fibrous materials actually fare worse, and not only because they are softer. Some of them are built with a very thin veneer of real wood over structural and filler materials, with the real wood veneer treated for weather resistance. But whether there is any real wood on the door or not, all it takes is one gouge through the outer surface layer to reveal the filler inside.

SEE 28~DOOR AND WINDOW TYPES; 29~DOOR AND WINDOW STYLE VERSUS BUILDING STYLE; AND 33~GARAGE DOOR SIZES.

*Do: Wood doors can be built to an unlimited number of panel patterns. They also are easier to trim because their frames are usually wood, not metal, and therefore fit more easily into the overall design of the woodwork.*

*Do: Real wood doors can also accept glass of any design. Their panels are also usually thicker and more substantial than those found in doors built of other materials.*

## 21
# WINDOW MATERIALS

RESIDENTIAL WINDOWS SHOULD BE BUILT OF WOOD. VINYL-COATED WOOD, ALUMINUM-COATED WOOD, AND SOLID PVC WINDOWS MAY ALSO BE USED, BUT ONLY IF THEY ARE INDISCERNIBLE FROM WOOD AT ARM'S LENGTH. COMMERCIAL WINDOWS MAY ALSO BE EXTRUDED ALUMINUM OR HOLLOW STEEL FRAME.

Many people sing the praises of clad windows, and partially with good reason, because the wood available today for building windows may be characterized as a fast-growing, pulpy mess when compared to the wood used a century ago. Simply put, it does not hold up to the weather as the old wood did. Century-old windows still exist, while it is not uncommon to replace new wood windows after just a decade or two.

Clad windows, however, have their own set of problems. Just as in the case of synthetic door materials (or synthetic materials of any sort, for that matter), when clad windows are damaged, they generally cannot be repaired. Either you live with the dent or the ding or the gouge, or you buy an entire new window sash if you're lucky. If it's not damage to the sash, however, then the window has to be ripped out of the wall

and an entirely new window unit installed, complete with exterior and interior patching work. Of course, if your exterior finish materials are synthetic also, you could be replacing an entire wall of vinyl siding, because the new siding from the factory doesn't match the color of the siding

on the wall that has been baking in the sun for a few years. It should come as no surprise that, as the supposed "no-maintenance houses" continue to age, they look worse and worse because the ripple effect of what would have been a small Saturday morning repair with a house built

*Don't automatically choose non-wood windows; they may have a number of problems.*
*1: The surface-mount plastic window is exceptionally flat in every detail. Perhaps there is no other modern building component that is more of a cartoon of the object it is meant to represent than the surface-mount plastic window. The fact that the edge of the window is meant to conceal the ends of vinyl siding strips only makes matters worse.*
*2: All-aluminum windows often are overly harsh in their profile. If the manufacturers were to look carefully at good wood windows, it would be possible to build a good metal window because almost any shape that can be drawn can be extruded. A few metal window manufacturers actually do this; there is no reason that all of them should not.*
*3: Is it possible to manufacture a double-hung window of scrawnier components?*
*4: PVC windows, on the other hand, tend to have components that are often much thicker than they should be.*

1

2

3

4

of natural materials becomes instead a construction project that requires a home equity loan.

Clad windows have purely aesthetic problems, too. Nearly every vinyl or aluminum clad window on the market is built with a bulbous projection from the front of

the frame that can be up to 2" wide and may project more than 2" from the face of the wall. It may be considered a "tumor" of sorts, because it is an unnatural growth on the window frame that simply shouldn't be there. Cheaply built houses sometimes allow siding or brick to abut the

backside of the vinyl tumor. One can abut a window casing to the back of the tumor, but it is categorically impossible to properly case a window that has a vinyl tumor on the frame.

So what is the solution to this dilemma? The portion of the window that needs the greatest protection from the weather is the sash, simply because the sash has more exposed area and because it is the portion of the window that is in motion. Pushing and pulling a sash to open or close the window opens up seams in wood windows, allowing water to enter. The frame, on the other hand, has only a very small area exposed to the weather. From the outside, as little as a $1/4$" reveal strip may be exposed on the frame. There are some window companies that now sell windows with clad sashes and wood frames, allowing windows to be cased properly again while being protected against the weather. This is generally the best option available on the market at this time for those who need the protection of clad windows but want them to be properly detailed and cased.

*Do consider wood windows, or at least windows with wood frames.*
*1: Wood windows, or clad windows in wood frames, allow the windows to be fully incorporated into architectural assemblies such as these. This is not impossible with windows built of other materials if the manufacturers will work on their edge details. Presently, however, there are very few metal or plastic windows that could be used to replace the wood windows in this design without detracting from the design.*
*2: One of the greatest errors of current window design is the "vinyl tumor" that projects nearly 2" out from most window frames. This window assembly would look much different (specifically, much worse) if the windows had vinyl tumors.*
*3: Classic square wood window.*
*4: Just as in the first example, this corner window design would be much degraded by the use of most current plastic or metal windows. The manufacturers must do better.*

1
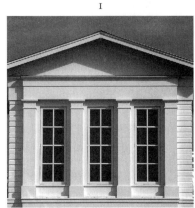
2
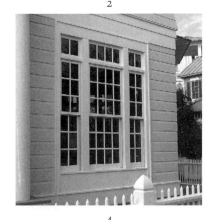
3

4

SEE 9~SIDING MATERIALS; 28~DOOR AND WINDOW TYPES; AND 29~DOOR AND WINDOW STYLE VERSUS BUILDING STYLE.

## 22
## STOREFRONT
## MATERIALS

### STOREFRONTS SHOULD BE BUILT OF WOOD, CUSTOM METALWORK, EXTRUDED ALUMINUM, OR HOLLOW STEEL FRAME.

Elegant shops and restaurants should always have wood storefronts, because neither aluminum nor hollow metal frames will ever be capable of the elegance of detail that can be achieved with wood. Metal storefronts can work on buildings that need to appear crude or gritty, but their framing members are large enough and blocky enough that they simply are not capable of creating fine details. Custom metalwork storefronts, on the other hand, use components small enough to achieve a fine level of detail. Custom metalwork storefronts are usually out of the budget range of most projects; but if they are contemplated, they should be patterned after good examples of their style, of course.

Regardless of the material used, storefronts should be detailed to include only framing members, with no standard wall surface coating whatsoever. For example, if the building is built of wood with siding, there should be no siding whatsoever within the storefront design, but rather only glass, window frames,

*Don't ignore the context and purpose of the storefront when choosing storefront materials. Extruded aluminum storefronts such as the two examples below violate every rule of storefronts, including the following:*

RULE 1: *2" aluminum natural (silver) or bronze (dark brown) storefront has been enormously over-used. Avoid it like the plague.*

RULE 2: *If you use thin storefront framing members, have some other part of the design that is thick to contrast it against.*

RULE 3: *Provide, somewhere within the storefront design, a glass panel smaller than 17 square feet (which is the size of glass in a thinly framed glass and metal door).*

RULE 4: *Use storefront colors that are compatible with the neighborhood. Raw metal usually isn't. Nor is bronze-brown, in most cases.*

*Do use properly detailed wood or metal as appropriate to the context*
*and purpose of the storefront.*

*1: This storefront is composed entirely of cast metal pieces, yet it is delightful.*

*2: This storefront is also mostly composed of metal except with wood windows.*

*3: Simple, classic wood storefront with large glass panels below, divided light transoms*
*above and sheltering awnings at the entry.*

*4: Elegantly simple wood storefront.*

*5: Every piece of this storefront except the window sashes themselves is repetitive and*
*was mass-produced (probably cast iron) but is delightful. Storefronts need not be custom*
*wood to be beautiful.*

*6: Minimal metal and glass storefronts make sense when used adjacent to beautiful,*
*ornate pieces such as this.*

1

2

3

4

5

6

and casing. There are several reasons for this, including the fact that because it is a special part of the building, the storefront should not incorporate ordinary wall materials, but should be treated in a more refined fashion.

The material below the storefront, if it does not extend to the sidewalk, should also be more refined than the standard wall material. This means that it should be capable of a finer grain of detail than the wall material. Usually, it should be some sort of panel or base consistent with the style of the building. The bottom edge of storefront glass should never be higher than 24" above the sidewalk; lower heights are generally preferable, because they create more display space. Storefront glass should always be clear; if glare is an issue because of solar orientation, retractable awnings are often both a sensible and a charming solution. The top of the awning should be installed just below the storefront beam, which should probably be designed to include a band sign.

SEE 13~TRIM; 25~BAY JAMB MATERIAL; 37~CASING PRINCIPLES; 44~SILL CASING; 50~COLUMN TO ENTABLATURE; 90~AWNING MATERIALS; 94~ATTACHED SIGNS; AND 99~AWNING CONFIGURATIONS.

[109]

## 23
## SHUTTER
## MATERIALS

SHUTTERS SHOULD BE BUILT
OF CEDAR OR REDWOOD.
SOLID PVC SHUTTERS ARE
ALSO ACCEPTABLE IF THEY ARE
INDISCERNIBLE FROM WOOD AT
ARM'S LENGTH.

Tract house builders have used fake, tacked-on shutters for so long that Americans are almost desensitized to the beauty of true operable shutters. The vast majority of the fakes are not even installed with shutter hardware, but are simply tacked on the wall with four nails or screws. But even if they were installed with shutter hardware, they still would be easy to spot because of the fact that they simply don't have the "meat" that is required of a shutter that actually has to operate. The old adage "If it's worth doing, it's worth doing well" applies as much to shutters as to any other single building component. There is no inherent disgrace in a building with no shutters. Indeed, nearly any building would be more attractive if the builder were to simply save the money that would otherwise be spent on fake shutters and spend it on slightly better window casings instead.

Real shutters, especially those with operable louvers, must have enough strength

*Don't use fake, tacked-on shutters for "effect." The effect is sure to be unpleasant.*
*The shutters below loudly proclaim their plastic-ness.*
*The following are all symptoms of the fake shutter disease:*
SYMPTOM 1: *Dented frames where shutters are screwed into the wall*
*and the installer doesn't stop the screw gun until it's too late.*
SYMPTOM 2: *Those cute little plastic buttons, like on the shutter below, that the more*
*expensive fake shutters use to try to hide the screws (which don't exist on real shutters).*
SYMPTOM 3: *Shutters that are not exactly half the width of the window.*
SYMPTOM 4: *Round-top shutters that do not match the window radius.*
SYMPTOM 5: *Over-exaggerated fake woodgrain, such as in the bottom picture.*
SYMPTOM 6: *Lack of normal shutter hardware, which includes hinges and dogs (latches).*

*Do use functioning shutters in materials that pass the test of the Arm's Length Rule. The four sets of shutters below represent the four basic types of real shutters, all of which are built of wood or of materials indiscernible from wood at arm's length.*

*Flat board shutters: this shutter gains its strength by the use of vertical boards on the outside and horizontal boards on the inside.*

*Paneled shutters, shown here on the upper level of a building, were often used on the street level for security, even if louvered shutters were used above.*

*Square-top louvered shutters are the most common type. They let in light even when they are closed.*

*Curved-top shutters may be either bowspring arched or full Roman arched according to the shape of the window. These are louvered, but they may also be board or paneled shutters.*

to operate repeatedly and to withstand an occasional wind-storm when someone forgets to fasten them to the wall with shutter dogs. This requires a thickness close to that of an interior door and frame members at least as wide as those of a window sash. Natural shutter materials should be either cedar or redwood. Other materials such as pine are simply unsuitable for exterior use for reasons discussed earlier in 9~Siding Material and 13~Trim. There are a few synthetic shutters available which are indiscernible from wood shutters, even while you are holding them. Most are currently constructed of cellular PVC with solid color impregnated throughout and internal steel reinforcement. They operate just as real shutters, and the louvered models adjust just like any operable wood louver does. Shutters may be paneled, boarded, or louvered. Solid paneled or boarded shutters were once used on the first level of buildings for security with the louvered panels used at upper levels.

SEE 9~SIDING MATERIAL; 13~TRIM; AND 35~SHUTTER PRINCIPLES AND DETAILS.

## 24
# BRICK JACK ARCH

**BRICK JACK ARCHES SHOULD BE BUILT OF GAUGED BRICK.**

The reason for this is directly descended from the Apparent Structure theme of traditional architecture (page 11.) As discussed in 16~Masonry Veneer Walls, masonry openings should be detailed exactly as they would be if the walls were load-bearing masonry whether the masonry walls are actually carrying the load or are just brick veneer. The only way a brick jack arch can support itself is for each of the bricks of the jack arch to be tapered to be a little wider at the top and narrower at the bottom, creating a series of wedges that converge on a single radius point. The wedge action of the bricks is what supports the wall above.

There are many incorrect ways of doing brick jack arches. One of the most common is simply to lean the bricks to either side at the same angle and use a misshapen keystone in the middle. Another is to omit the keystone and replace it with a triangle of brick in various patterns that vary from job to job. But no matter what the method, all of the incorrect jack arches are characterized by one feature: If steel lintels did not support

*Don't cheat by building a non-supporting fake jack arch. There are many incorrect ways of building jack arches, four of which are illustrated in this drawing. All share the common characteristic of being unable to support themselves without the help of steel structural members in the wall.*

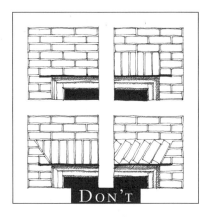

*Don't: This fake jack arch gets the angle at the ends right, but uses rectangular (non-gauged) brick. It would collapse if not for the steel used to support it.*

*Don't: This is a conventional soldier header with cut brick triangles at each end in a weak attempt to resemble a jack arch.*

*Don't: This fake jack arch might seem to deserve a commendation for creativity, but it, too, would also probably collapse if not for the steel. Masonry does not support itself without wedges, and very few members of this header are wedged.*

Do

*Do use a proper jack arch capable of supporting the brick in the wall above. Proper brick jack arches may vary in width, depth, and occasionally angle, but little else. The principles of proper jack arches have been understood since Roman times and are unlikely to change, since they are based on the properties of brick and the law of gravity.*

them, they would not support themselves.

The beauty of building a brick jack arch correctly is that no steel support is needed; it holds itself up, once the mortar is set, doing the job that brick jack arches have done for centuries. There are two ways of achieving a proper brick jack arch: They can be ordered as custom shapes from the brick manufacturer, or they can be customized on-site if the mason has an employee who is skillful with a masonry saw. The most economical method is determined by local market conditions.

SEE APPARENT STRUCTURE
(PAGE 11); 16~MASONRY
VENEER WALLS; 17~BRICK
COURSING AT WALL OPENINGS;
39~MASONRY LINTEL
PRINCIPLES; AND 41~JACK
ARCHES.

*Do: These are taller than structurally necessary, but perfectly legitimate. Several languages (styles) of architecture such as Romanesque Revival exaggerate lintel depths for artistic effect.*

*Do: These jack arches are as thin as is acceptable, but they work perfectly well for simpler languages.*

*Do: These jack arches are of medium height, but are still tall enough to require more than one brick. Bricks should be staggered as shown in such instances.*

## 25
# BAY JAMB MATERIAL

**BAY WINDOW JAMBS SHOULD BE TRIMMED WITH A SINGLE VERTICAL JAMB CASING THAT EXTENDS FROM THE WINDOW SASH TO THE CORNER OF THE BAY.**

Bays, because they project from the wall of a building, should be seen primarily as framing members so that they have visual support. If they appear simply as a bumped-out wall with no visible stiffening, then either the house appears to be constructed of a too-light material such as cardboard, or the bay looks unnaturally weak. Bays with single, strong casing boards at the corners look much more substantial than those that look like standard windows set in a standard wall with siding.

The second reason for using a single jamb casing for bays is because of the fact that bays exist because of their windows. Usually, the windows extend almost from corner to corner. The common method is to use scrawny corner boards at the corners, 2" or narrower brick mold for window casing, and narrow slivers of siding between the two. This is significantly more time-consuming and therefore costly than the proper method, which is to use a single vertical jamb casing that is wide enough

*Don't use small slivers of wall surface material to finish the space between window and corner.*
*1 and 6: brick slivers. This clearly illustrates that brick bays of any sort are impossible to detail correctly unless the bay is enough larger than the windows to allow a large expanse of brick to either side of all windows.*
*2 through 5: siding slivers.*

DON'T

1

2

3

4

5

6

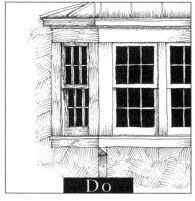

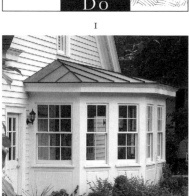

*Do use proper bay jambs casings that are solid from window to corner.*
*1 through 3: Classic bay jamb casing. Note that ganged windows use min. 4" mullion casing between them. 4: Corner trim is possible for some styles. 5: Casing is OK as pilasters with the addition of capital trim. 6: This bay is large enough to allow siding on either side of the window. Siding height/width proportion is assisted by the lack of corner boards and the narrowness of the siding.*

to extend from the edge of the sash to the corner of the bay. One board replaces two boards plus up to a dozen little pieces of siding; there should be no question concerning which method costs more.

The last reason is similar to some of the issues with storefront materials: The bay is a special part of a building, so it should be treated in a more refined fashion than ordinary walls. This means that the materials used to finish the bay should be capable of a finer degree of detail than the wall material. The typical wall material of the rest of the building is usually inappropriate here because the finest degree of detail possible with siding is the width of one board and the finest degree of detail possible with brick is the width of one brick. Trim boards, however, are capable of details as narrow as $3/4$" and shaped trim is capable of an even finer degree of detail.

SEE 13~TRIM; 21~WINDOW MATERIALS; 22~STOREFRONT MATERIALS; 26~BRICK MOLD; 29~DOOR AND WINDOW STYLE VERSUS BUILDING STYLE; 31~WINDOW PROPORTIONS; 32~WINDOW PANE PROPORTIONS; 34~BAY WINDOW SUPPORT; 37~CASING PRINCIPLES; 38~HEAD CASING PRINCIPLES; AND 44~SILL CASING.

## 26
# BRICK MOLD

BRICK MOLD SHOULD USUALLY
BE MUCH WIDER THAN THE
2" SHAPE THAT IS COMMONLY
USED.

This is a style-specific issue. There is one common style in the United States in which door or window surrounds as narrow as 2" are acceptable, and that is the Federal style. The Federal style followed closely in both time and sympathies the Adam style that was developed in England around 1800 by the brothers Robert and James Adam. Their work took place at a time of discontent with the proportions of canonical Renaissance classicism, which was fueled in part by archaeological work that demonstrated that the classicism of antiquity was much more varied than had been previously believed. The Adam brothers chose to evolve the classical Renaissance language in an extremely thin, attenuated manner. Members that were previously of a particular dimension might end up twice as slender in an Adam building. Narrow window surrounds not much wider than 2" are therefore acceptable on Federal or Adam style buildings.

Their use on other buildings, however, looks as silly as using a toothpick for a baseball bat:

*Don't use brick mold except on brick walls, and even then only when appropriate to the building style. Brick openings should have a masonry (brick or stone) header above to visually carry the weight of the wall. Brick mold can work on brick walls, because it does not need to appear to carry the wall. Wood door or window casing, however, should appear to carry the weight of the wall, which is a task brick mold can never hope to do because it is far too thin.*

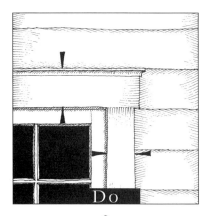

1

2

3

4

5

*Do use brick mold wider than 2" in all except Federal buildings. Brick mold is merely casing that covers the gap between the window sash and the brick opening. It should therefore be the same width at both the head and the jamb of the window. The window sill, however, has a different job, which is to get water from the window out of the wall. It should therefore be different from the shape of the brick mold.*

*1: Brick mold on Federal or Adam style buildings looks fine at 2" wide.*

*2: Head casing in a wood siding wall should be wider and possibly more expressive when the jamb casing is the narrowest allowable width, which is 4" nominal.*

*3: Wider casing on a wood wall can act as both jamb and head.*

*4: Head casing should obviously follow the contour of an arch, but may be straight where it meets the window.*

*5: Wider brick mold in non-Federal building.*

The proportions are entirely wrong, and they simply don't work. What are the right proportions? That depends on the style, of course. It is clear, however, that door or window casings on anything other than a Federal or Adam Style building should be no less than the width of a 1x4. 1x6 casing or larger is appropriate for many styles. Casing on walls with siding may be simple flat boards, while casing around doors or windows in brick walls must have some sort of backband or brick mold (the old style made to do this job which is both narrower and thinner) to close the gap between the casing and the brick veneer.

SEE 13~TRIM; 21~WINDOW MATERIALS; 29~DOOR AND WINDOW STYLE VERSUS BUILDING STYLE; 37~CASING PRINCIPLES; 38~HEAD CASING PRINCIPLES; AND 44~SILL CASING.

## 27
# WINDOW MUNTINS

MUNTINS SHOULD DIVIDE
PANES INTO TRUE DIVIDED
LIGHTS. THE ONLY ACCEPTABLE
WINDOW GRILLES ARE THOSE
THAT ARE ADHERED TO BOTH
SIDES OF THE GLASS WITH A
SPACER IN BETWEEN TO BE
INDISCERNIBLE FROM TRUE
MUNTINS.

Almost everyone knows someone else whose dog at one point has jumped up against a new window, only to break out the fake window grilles and leave them as a shattered mess in the floor. Or maybe it was a broom handle that fell against the window that did it, or maybe it was one of the kids. In any case, removable window grilles have taken their place in the Hall of Shame of cheap construction, alongside the worst examples of vinyl siding and the infamous "pork chop eave."

As a matter of fact, window grilles (fake muntins) have given divided light windows such a bad name that many people have asked why they need divided lights at all. Isn't it better (and cheaper) to have single-pane windows than to have something that looks so fake? The answer is that there are a number of reasons to do divided light windows well.

First, it has been suggested (and is likely) that the result-ing play of light and shadow across the retina of the eye is physically more pleasurable than the harsher, glaring light of an undivided window. Second, divided light windows are inextricably linked in the minds of almost everyone with various human-based languages of architecture. Any attempt to build in these styles with single-pane windows is likely to be viewed as a cheap substitute for the real thing. Finally, properly built divided lights actually strengthen the window sash.

So if there are valid reasons for using divided lights, what are the best ways to build them? The dilemma occurred during

*Don't use fake muntins that fail the test of the Arm's Length Rule. Contoured grilles (top drawing) and internal flat bar grilles (bottom drawing) are two unacceptable replacements for window muntins. Fake muntins are visible from great distances when caught between shade and shadow as in the photos below.*

*Do use muntins that are indistinguishable from real muntins. True window muntins (top drawing above) are indiscernible from some simulated muntins if the exterior and interior shapes of the muntin are correct and if there is a spacer bar between the glass panes as shown. With no spacer, one could see between the two pieces when standing near the window. Look at the difference between the muntins below and the fakes on the previous page.*

the energy crises of the 1970's, when single-glazed windows suddenly became unacceptable because of their energy losses. Single-pane glass fit nicely in traditional muntins, but double-pane glass is more than twice as heavy due to the gaskets around the edge of the "glass sandwich," and therefore it requires a much heavier muntin, which looks very clunky and is also very expensive. True divided-light double- (or triple-) glazed windows are therefore prohibitively expensive and awkward-looking.

The reasonable option goes by several different names depending on which window manufacturer is talking, but it is often described as the Simulated Authentic Divided Light window. It consists of a double- or triple-glazed sash with authentically detailed muntins adhered to each side of the glass sandwich. It is acceptable for exterior muntins of clad windows to be extrusions of aluminum or other non-weathering materials, as long as the profile is correct. The final (and absolutely necessary) element is the spacer between the layers of glass that occurs at every muntin. The spacer not only makes it impossible to tell whether the muntins go clear through the glass or not when you are standing close to the window, but also strengthens the window. Anything less looks cheap and fake upon close inspection.

SEE 21~WINDOW MATERIALS; 31~WINDOW PROPORTIONS, AND 32~WINDOW PANE PROPORTIONS.

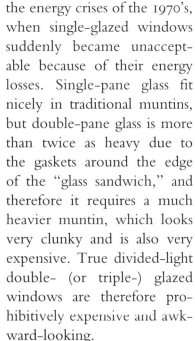

## 28
# DOOR AND WINDOW TYPES

**ALL DOORS SHOULD BE SIDE-HINGED EXCEPT FOR GARAGE DOORS, WHICH MAY BE SECTIONAL. OPERABLE WINDOWS SHOULD BE SINGLE-HUNG, DOUBLE-HUNG, TRIPLE-HUNG, OR CASEMENTS.**

America's 30-year honeymoon with sliding glass doors now appears to be over. Sliding glass doors fit in well with the machine-based architecture of the 1960's that tried its best to eliminate all vestiges of the human form. A door is the one part of a building that most sensibly should reflect the vertical proportion of the human body since humans walk through it, which is why the horizontal proportion of most sliding glass doors appealed so much to practitioners of machine-based architecture. Unfortunately, it did not take very long for people to discover that sliding glass doors failed humans in other ways as well. They are huge energy wasters, as was made obvious when the first energy crisis hit. They are poor security risks, as many people unfortunately discovered first-hand. And once doors jump their tracks, the cheaper ones never work properly again. Most of the United States has found its way back to the traditional swinging door, which still solves all those problems, just as it has been doing for centuries.

Garage doors, because they are the one door in a building that typically is for automobiles rather than humans, may be a different type. Double swinging garage doors are beautiful, to be sure, but their size requires them to be so heavy, and their operators so powerful in order to withstand the wind, that they are affordable only on the most expensive of buildings. Sectional doors are usually the best type of garage door, and they are in the most common use at this time, making them the most affordable.

*Don't use impractical door or window types, too many types in one building, or too many of a special shape.*
*1: Too many circles. Also, these are detailed so that they would collapse if not supported by hidden steel lintels.*
*2: Sliding glass doors.*
*3: Too many shapes and sizes.*
*4: Sliding windows (sometimes simply called sliders).*
*5: Hoppers or awnings? It is impossible to tell unless they are open.*

1

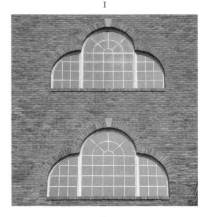

2

3

4

5

*Do use sensible door and window types.*
*1: These double French casements open fully without a center bar to obstruct the opening. These are the miniature versions of French doors.*
*2: Swinging single door with fixed rectangular side lights and transom.*
*3: Arched swinging double garage door.*
*4: Swinging double door with fixed rectangular side lights and elliptical arched transom above.*
*5: Double-hung window.*

1

2

4

There are three possible types of windows: fixed, hinged, and sliding. There are three primary types of hinged windows: top-hinged (awning), bottom-hinged (hopper), and side-hinged (casement). The jalousie is an exotic type similar to the hinged windows, but it hardly merits a mention because it is such a terrible energy-waster and security risk. Of the others, both the awning and the hopper are best suited to poorly proportioned horizontal sashes. Vertical awning or hopper sashes either project far into the interior (hopper) or far to the exterior (awning) when open, creating a hazard for anyone

3

5

walking near the wall. The side-hinged geometry of the casement, however, is much better suited for vertically proportioned windows.

There are two basic types of sliding windows. Vertically sliding windows include the single-hung, double-hung, and triple-hung. Horizontally sliding windows are basically miniature sliding glass doors, with all their disadvantages. They also have the additional disadvantage of having the sliding surfaces of the sashes on the top and bottom. The problem is not the top, but the bottom, because water naturally drains to the bottom. The sash track has to hold the sash in so that it does not fall out, but that naturally holds water in, too. The problem can theoretically be solved, but it is never a good idea to have water, snow, and ice collecting in the same place that a sash must slide, which is the final reason why vertically sliding windows are the only acceptable sliding types.

SEE 21~WINDOW MATERIALS; 31~WINDOW PROPORTIONS; AND 33~GARAGE DOOR SIZES.

## 29
## DOOR AND WINDOW STYLE VERSUS BUILDING STYLE

THE STYLE OF THE FRONT DOOR SHOULD MATCH THE STYLE OF THE BUILDING, AS SHOULD THE STYLE OF THE WINDOWS.

Doors and windows that do not use the same architectural language as the building to which they are attached tell a very confusing story. The necessity of including this item is an indictment of the prevailing lack of aesthetic sensibility today. A century of styles that no one except an architect could love has desensitized the average person to the finer points of stylistic consistency. Today, there is essentially one front door for all high-end buildings and one window for all residential buildings.

Everyone knows what the front door looks like; it's the door on display at the end of the door aisle at your local Home Depot, or Lowe's, or wherever. It is vaguely Victorian in nature. The wood is dark, even if it's only a stain. The glass absolutely must be leaded, and it's probably beveled, or at least some of it is. And it's almost certainly divided into two 3' tall vertical panes, which probably have some sort of curve at the top. The bottom half of

the door is paneled wood. You know; you've seen it, on Georgian houses, and on Greek Revival houses, and even on bungalows.

This door is being sold as a symbol of elegance and class, and as a way to set you apart from the masses that supposedly buy four-

*Don't use doors or windows incompatible with the building style. 1: Victorian door and side lights on vaguely classical McMansion. 2: Victorian door and side lights on vaguely Georgian McMansion. 3: Possibly an Oriental moon gate door on a vaguely classical house. 4: Same problem as #1, but with even more gusto. 5: Even more affordable houses have the same Victorian door disease. 6: Victorian door on vaguely Mediterranean house.*

1

2

3

4

5

6

panel front doors with Colonial fanlights. Unfortunately, almost everyone else bought that line, too, so this door has become today's equivalent of the Colonial door. You could set yourself much more apart if you were to buy a door that is consistent with the style of the house.

The six-over-six double-hung window has become every bit as over used as the leaded glass Victorian front door. It is true that the six-over-six is the appropriate window for a number of popular house styles— but not for all of them.

Traditional architectural languages have employed a wide variety of window types and light patterns over the centuries. Unfortunately, today's construction industry is increasingly formula-driven, and the six-over-six is certainly part of the formula. Close comparisons can be drawn between today's houses and the Chrysler K-Cars of the early 1980's. Interestingly, the formula is both the strength and the flaw of both the cars and the houses: Underneath the superficial differences, there are telltale signs that they are all built on the same frame. There is probably no greater display of sameness than the six-over-six double-hung window.

SEE 28~DOOR AND WINDOW TYPES AND 29~DOOR AND WINDOW STYLE VERSUS BUILDING STYLE.

1

2

3
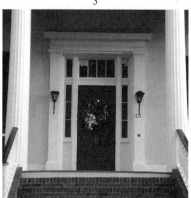

4

5

6

## 30
# ENTRY SURROUNDS

ENTRY SURROUNDS ARE A
MAJOR PART OF THE FACE
OF THE BUILDING, AND
THEY SHOULD BE DETAILED
CAREFULLY ACCORDING TO THE
STYLE OF THE BUILDING AS ONE
OF ITS MOST EXPRESSIVE PARTS.

Entry surrounds, like store-fronts and bays, are some of the most important parts of buildings, so they should include none of the ordinary wall materials of the building. All materials within the borders of the entry surround should be more refined than those of ordinary walls. If there is a place within the style of the building for more elaborate details, this is it. The face of a building should get the greatest care and attention to detail, just as each person's face usually gets the greatest care and grooming of any part of the body.

The entry surround is often detailed as an aedicule that contains the entire order of the building, including the proper columns and full entablature. An aedicule on a highly classical building may even be built to a higher order than the rest of the building, to signify the importance of the entry. Even the very vernacular languages often compress the full order of the house into the aedicule. If the aedicule is set in a brick wall, it should almost always

overlap the brick rather than be set within it, so that any arches or lintels required to support the brick above are hidden by the aedicule.

Elements within the aedicule generally include the front door, possibly a transom, possibly sidelights, and casing. Casing should gener-

*Don't: Shapes, brick slivers, etc.*

*Don't: Proportions, eave details, etc.*

*Don't: Arch supports, proportions, etc.*

*Don't: Arch, column placement, etc.*

*Don't: Wonder why it's reduced?*

*Don't: Proportion, mullions, support, etc.*

[124]

*Do: Grandeur can occur in one story.*

*Do: Framing elliptical transom.*

*Do: Three-bay with Adam detailing.*

ally connect all other members with single boards that run from one member to the other, similar to the manner in which a bay jamb runs from window to corner. It is crucial that no casing within the aedicule be narrower than a 1x4. It is common practice to mull the door frame directly

*Do: Simple entry, but pleasant.*

*Do: Single-bay porch.*

*Do: Federal recessed stoop.*

to the sidelight frame and case both with a 1x2, but this looks horribly flimsy, and the entry surround is the worst possible place in a house to do this. Any form of siding within the aedicule should be avoided, unless the door is recessed farther than 12", in which case siding may be used, but only if it is of a more refined sort than that used elsewhere on the house. In no case can lap siding be used; the minimum acceptable siding is V-groove tongue and groove (T&G), although smooth-face tongue and groove is preferable.

SEE 4~SYMMETRY OF THE FACE; 13~TRIM; 20~DOOR MATERIALS; 21~WINDOW MATERIALS; 22~STOREFRONT MATERIALS; 25~BAY JAMB MATERIAL; 26~BRICK MOLD; 27~WINDOW MUNTINS; 28~DOOR AND WINDOW TYPES; 29~DOOR AND WINDOW STYLE VERSUS BUILDING STYLE; 37~CASING PRINCIPLES; 38~HEAD CASING PRINCIPLES; 40~ARCH PRINCIPLES; 43~KEYSTONES; 45~COLUMN MATERIALS AND PROPORTIONS; 46~BEAM MATERIALS; 50~COLUMN TO ENTABLATURE; AND 51~ENTABLATURE PRINCIPLES.

## 31
## WINDOW
## PROPORTIONS

### WINDOWS SHOULD BE
### VERTICALLY PROPORTIONED OR
### SQUARE.

Windows have been called the eyes of a building. There are actually a number of correlations between window proportions and the human form in traditional architectural languages. Square, round, or semicircular windows are sometimes used high on a wall or on a roof. These are similar both in proportion and in location within the building to the human eye.

Most traditional architectural languages employ windows with the proportion of either the human face or the entire human body. Generally, the more relaxed or informal languages and building types seem to gravitate more toward windows of a human face proportion (3:2). The more formal types and languages seem to favor windows proportioned more as the entire human body is (2:1 to 3:1 or sometimes a little taller). One may conclude that face-proportioned windows represent a closer, face-to-face type of conversation, whereas full-body windows represent a more formal, distant conversation.

*Don't use horizontal windows which do not reflect the proportion of the human body. 1: This Depression-era building retains some semblance of the order that was taken for granted earlier: at least the proportions of two of the windows are vertical and the window heads are aligned. 2: Fast-forward a half-century, and the breakdown is complete. Even the window types disagree with each other. The confusion of proportions here is only the beginning.*

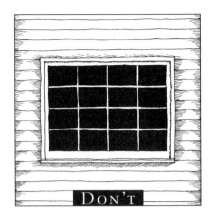

DON'T

1

2

Do

1

*Do choose vertically proportioned or square windows which reflect several aspects of the proportion of the human body.*
*1: Windows stand tall and stately in this Beaux-Arts mansion. But a building need not be a mansion to learn the rules of gracious window arrangement and proportion.*
*2: Traditional windows often are shorter on upper levels, sometimes close to the proportion of a human face.*

2

3

4

*3, 4: These dormers show two depictions of the proportion of an eye. The top is square when not viewed from below. Both square and circle (eye) share 1:1 proportion. The bottom one is actually called an "eyebrow dormer."*

Main-level windows are often the tallest in a building, and normally they open into the most formal rooms, whereas upper-level windows opening into less formal rooms are often shorter. Buildings with several levels sometimes run the gamut from the proportion of the body on the main level to the face on upper levels to the eye at the roofline.

Modern architecture tried to rid the world of thousands of years of architectural conventions, and window proportions were no exception. Windows of any human proportion became undesirable. The only acceptable vertically proportioned windows were narrow slits. The big winner in the window derby, however, was the horizontal ribbon window, which architects loved to unroll endlessly around a building.

Unfortunately, most people never quit looking at things the old way. This insistence on being different for the sake of being different ended with two logical interpretations: The thin slits look like a painfully anorexic person, whereas the horizontal strip windows resemble the proportion of someone who is dead.

SEE 32~WINDOW PANE
PROPORTIONS AND
84~DORMER BODY
PROPORTION.

## 32
## WINDOW PANE
## PROPORTIONS

WINDOW PANES SHOULD BE
VERTICALLY PROPORTIONED
OR SQUARE. VERTICALLY
PROPORTIONED WINDOW
PANES SHOULD BE SIMILARLY
PROPORTIONED THROUGHOUT
AN ENTIRE BUILDING.

The reasons for vertically proportioned or square panes are similar to those for window proportions: The pane should reflect the proportions of either a human face or a human eye (round = 1:1 = square). There is an additional utilitarian reason. Equal-size windows divided into equal-size panes of either 2:1 (vertical) or 1:2 (horizontal) proportion have roughly twice as many horizontal muntins when the panes are horizontally oriented. Water runs off vertical muntins easily, whereas horizontal muntins create ledges that slow water flow and may actually collect water. This may not be a major issue if the muntins are made of a weather-resistant material other than wood, but it clearly is a consideration with wood windows.

Few things look more haphazard than radically different window pane proportions within the same building. Having only a few window sizes throughout a building helps to limit this problem,

*Don't use horizontal window panes or vary pane proportions dramatically within a building. There is no utilitarian reason why window panes cannot be vertical; it's simply a matter of choosing a different pattern.*

DON'T

*Don't: Horizontal panes on one, square panes on the other. What's the third?*

*Don't: Everything about this window is horizontally distorted.*

*Don't: It clearly would have been just as easy to have run the muntins vertically in this window.*

*Do use vertical or square window panes and limit them to a few similar proportions. The window in the Do drawing contains one fewer pane in each sash than the one in the Don't drawing. It also contains half the number of horizontal muntins, which are usually the first to leak. Designing a building so that all window pane proportions are similar takes a little effort from the designer, and does not inherently increase the construction budget.*

*Do: Square panes in square sashes reflect the proportion of the human eye.*

*Do: Simple vertically proportioned panes approximate the proportion of the human face.*

*Do: More elaborate pane designs may contain panes of varying proportion if carefully thought out by the designer.*

but it is not usually possible to have only one window size. Buildings on the classical end of the traditional spectrum of architecture should be the most composed and refined, of course, so window pane proportions in these buildings should be the most similar. A reasonable and achievable standard for classical buildings is a maximum variation (not counting any square panes) of 12 percent in pane size. In other words, the shortest pane proportion should be 88 percent of the tallest pane proportion.

Buildings at the vernacular end of the traditional architecture spectrum, however, are often more relaxed, so window pane proportions may vary more. A reasonable and achievable standard for these windows is a maximum variation (again, not counting square panes) of 20 percent in pane size. Buildings elsewhere on the traditional spectrum of architecture should be adjusted between these two extremes based on the buildings' location on the spectrum.

SEE 31~WINDOW PROPORTIONS.

## 33
# GARAGE DOOR SIZES

**GARAGE DOORS SHOULD BE NO WIDER THAN 9'.**

The double-wide garage door developed at about the same time as the sliding glass door, apparently in response to machine-based architecture's craze for all things horizontal. The fact is, however, that they do not work nearly as well as two single doors on several counts.

First, double-wide doors are most commonly 16' wide, whereas single doors are often 9' wide. A 6'-wide vehicle pulling into a 9'-wide door obviously has 1.5' of clear space on each side. If there is 1.5' of wall between the two single doors, then there will be 4.5' of space between two vehicles parked in adjoining spaces, which is plenty of room for everyone to open car doors without banging into the adjacent vehicles. Double-wide doors, however, are a different story. If each of the drivers of the 6'-wide vehicles allows the same 1.5' between vehicle and car when pulling into the garage, then there will be only 1' left between the vehicles, which clearly is not enough room to open doors at all. So each driver must hug the edges of the door much closer to leave any

*Don't lock yourself into a box with double-wide garage doors. 1: The rest of this house uses arches as an important part of the architecture, but the pathetic attempt at an arch on the garage door highlights the proportional problems that occur when the door gets too wide.*
*2: The designer of this door has resorted to abstract decorative patterns over the door because any conventional header design would look wildly out of proportion if based on the door width.*

1

2

Do

*Do use single-bay garage doors for design flexibility and practicality. Single garage doors are narrow enough to incorporate either an elliptical arch (1) or a bowspring arch (2) of proper proportion. They are also narrow enough to be able to use the gold standard of garage doors: the swinging door. This is something that the double-wide door simply cannot accomplish.*

1

2

reasonable amount of room to get out of the doors on the inside of the garage, increasing the risk of vehicle damage both on the outside from scraping the garage and on the inside from vehicle doors. Single doors should be clearly preferable over double-wide doors on this issue alone.

There is more, however. Double-wide doors are more likely to sag over time, simply because their panels are nearly twice as long. They also require larger door operator motors to operate them, since they are heavier. Finally, if a double-wide operator fails, there is no way to get out of the garage without manually disengaging the door and raising it by hand, whereas two single-door operators are unlikely to both fail at the same moment. This may not seem to be like an important issue if the person in the garage when the operator fails is tall enough to reach the disengagement mechanism and strong enough to operate the door; but it could be an issue for someone who is either small or frail.

SEE 20~DOOR MATERIALS AND 28~DOOR AND WINDOW TYPES.

## 34
## BAY WINDOW
## SUPPORT

BAY WINDOWS EITHER SHOULD
EXTEND TO THE GROUND
OR SHOULD BE SUPPORTED
BY VISIBLE BRACKETS OF
APPROPRIATE SIZE.

This pattern springs directly from the Apparent Structure theme of traditional architecture. It is clearly possible to support a bay with cantilevered joists or beams that are not visible when the building is completed. Anyone looking at such a bay, however, should probably conclude either that it is so light that it requires no substantial support, or that it is unstable. Neither option, obviously, is desirable.

The two appropriate solutions are either to extend the bay to the ground with an appropriate masonry foundation wall or to support it with visible brackets. If brackets support the bay, they should be consistent with the style of the building. In no case, however, should the brackets be less than 3½" in any dimension. Anything less does not appear to be structural, which would defeat the purpose of having the brackets. The only exceptions to this rule occur occasionally in certain Victorian variants where the detailing is very light and lacy. In these cases, brackets may be as little as 2" thick. Any such

*Don't build bay windows with no visible means of support. None of the bay windows below follow this principle, making them appear either too light or unstable.*

DON'T

Do

*Do build bay windows that are visually supported. All of these bays either go to the ground or have support brackets of some sort.*
*1: Integral scrolled base*
*2: Angle brackets*
*3: Collection of scrolled corbels*
*4: Angle bay with ground support*
*5: Square bay with ground support*
*6: Square brackets*

detail, however, should be soundly based on good local examples of the style.

There is one complication to the bracketed bay that occurs only at first level bays. If the floor level at the bay is not sufficiently high above outside finished grade, then there will not be enough space for proper brackets, since any wood members should have at least 6" of clearance above earth or mulch to reduce the risk of rot. Bays sitting close to the ground should therefore be given a solid masonry foundation.

SEE APPARENT STRUCTURE
(PAGE 11); AND 55~BALCONY
DESIGN.

1

2

3

4

5

6

## 35
### SHUTTER PRINCIPLES AND DETAILS

SHUTTERS SHOULD BE EXACTLY ONE-HALF THE WIDTH OF THE SASH THEY ARE COVERING. ALL SHUTTERS SHOULD BE INSTALLED WITH HINGES AND DOGS. SHUTTERS SHOULD BE LOUVERED, PANELED, OR CONSTRUCTED OF BOARDS AS APPROPRIATE TO THE STYLE OF THE BUILDING.

Shutters, as noted earlier in 23~Shutter materials, are better not used than used improperly, since fake paste-on shutters are one of the hallmarks of ordinary or substandard construction. There are several principles involved in using shutters properly.

First, shutters must shut; otherwise, they aren't really shutters, are they? This means that shutters must be hinged so that they may shut. Hinges work best if they are installed directly onto the window casing, for two reasons. First, hinges mounted to the casing do not have to have the same offset (and therefore greater cantilever and stress) as hinges mounted to either the brick or the siding outside the casing. Second, window casing usually is installed directly over at least a stud and a liner, meaning that hinges mounted here are attached much more solidly than elsewhere.

Second, shutters still cannot shut fully if they do not cover the window opening. Fake shutters for years have been manufactured to a width of 14", regardless of the width of the window. This only highlights the fact that they are fake. Such shutters are worse than just a waste of

*Don't: Too narrow, too short, etc.*

*Don't: Too narrow, etc.*

*Don't: Too narrow, far too short, etc.*

*Don't: Too narrow, wrong radius, etc.*

*Do: Proper louvered shutters.*

*Do: Proper arched board shutters.*

money, because they fairly scream their uselessness to the viewer. Real shutters should be exactly half the width of the sash, plus about ½", which allows the shutters to seat on the edge of the window casing.

Third, shutters will not last very long if they flop in every

*Do: Proper paneled shutters.*

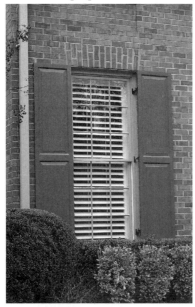

*Do: Proper board and frame shutters.*

breeze. Some types of shutter hinges have a gravity stop that requires a user to lift slightly when closing the shutter. These hinges, however, will not stop a shutter from flopping if the wind is high enough, because the wind simply lifts the shutter, just as a user would. Shutter dogs are the best answer. A shutter dog is a device mounted to the wall that may be pivoted to prevent the shutter from moving when in the open position. Shutter dogs, however, have their own problems, at least to the stylistic purist. The type used almost exclusively today is a stamped S-dog, which means that it is stamped out of sheet metal in the shape of an S. This type, however, was only used in the Victorian era and later, because the stamping technology did not exist before that time. Earlier shutter dogs were wrought, with a finger loop that projected away from the wall. Any style before the Victorian styles should technically use wrought dogs.

Finally, properly installed fixed-louver shutters are turned to drain water toward the wall when open (when it doesn't matter ... it's an exterior wall, after all) so that they can drain water away from the window when shut.

SEE 23~SHUTTER MATERIALS.

## 36
## PALLADIAN
## WINDOW
## PROPORTIONS

━━━━◆━━━◇━━━

PALLADIAN WINDOWS SHOULD
CONFORM TO CERTAIN
PRINCIPLES OF PROPORTION
AND DETAIL.

━━━━◆━━━◇━━━

Palladian windows are generally composed of a cen-
tral circle-head window with
flanking smaller windows,
similar to the winged device
popularized by Renaissance
architect Andrea Palladio,
which consisted of a large
central building flanked by
and connected to two smaller
volumes. Palladian windows
are almost always surrounded
by a full classical order, with
an arch above the circle-head
window. There are count-
less ways of doing Palladian
windows incorrectly— so
many, in fact, that the incorrect methods will not be dealt
with here. There are a wide
variety of correct designs, too,
most of which share the following characteristics:

The sidelights are almost
always four panes high, and
they can be executed either as
a double-hung window that is
two panes high in each sash or
as a fixed single sash.

The central window is
almost always five panes high
below the circle head portion.
Because the pane height is
identical to the sidelight pane
height, there is a space equal

to one pane height above the
sidelights and below the circle-head that is dedicated to a
full entablature.

The central window may
be three, or occasionally four
or five, panes wide. The sidelights may be one or occasionally two panes wide. In
all cases, the pane width in
the sidelights should match
the pane width of the central
window.

The order of the columns
and the entablature should
match or exceed the high-
est order found elsewhere in
the building. In other words,
if the order of the rest of
the house is Ionic, then the
Palladian window should be
Ionic, Corinthian, or possibly Composite. Palladian
windows are almost always a
central focus of the building,
and they therefore should be
treated with the utmost dignity. If the entry surround is
a full-featured aedicule, then
the Palladian window sur-
round often matches the order
of the aedicule.

The Palladian window sur-
round includes four pilasters:
Two flank the outsides of
the sidelights, while the other
two occur between the sidelights and the central window.
These pilasters are mounted
directly against the window
casing. The pilasters are more
often square, but may also be

half-round in the most elegant
examples.

The springline of the arch
should occur at the top of
the cornice of the entablature. The extrados of the arch
should not occur outside the
base width of the inner pilasters. In other words, if the
central window sash is 32"
wide, the casing at the base of
the pilaster is 2" wide (each
side) and each of the pilasters
is 8" in diameter, then the
diameter of the extrados of
the arch should be no more
than 32" + 2" + 2" + 8" +
8" = 52".

Finally, if the Palladian window is set in a brick wall, it is
enormously important that the
entire surround be set outside
the face of brick so that the
pilasters, entablature, and arch
will overlap the brick, which
should be run straight behind
them in running bond with
no border brick of any sort.
A common error is to set all
the elements of the Palladian
window behind the face of
brick, requiring a header of
some sort at the top of the
opening. Unfortunately, it is
physically impossible to design
a brick veneer header at the
upper borders of a Palladian
window that would be self-
supporting. Years ago, when
brick walls were solid and
structural, there would be a
brick pier behind each of the
inner pilasters that supported

*Do design Palladian windows according to time-tested principles and precedent. This drawing and these photos illustrate three of the many good Palladian window designs that employ these principles.*

a structural brick arch in the center and jack arches over each sidelight, all of which were covered by the entablature and arches. But when the brick veneer hangs outside the Palladian elements, there is absolutely no way to support it that appears structural; nearly all the options look exceptionally silly.

SEE 13~TRIM; 21~WINDOW MATERIALS; 26~BRICK MOLD; 27~WINDOW MUNTINS; 28~DOOR AND WINDOW TYPES; 29~DOOR AND WINDOW STYLE VERSUS BUILDING STYLE; 30~ENTRY SURROUNDS; 31~WINDOW PROPORTIONS; 32~WINDOW PANE PROPORTIONS; 40~ARCH PRINCIPLES; 42~ARCH/EAVE ALIGNMENT; 43~KEYSTONES; 44~SILL CASING; 45~COLUMN MATERIALS AND PROPORTIONS; 46~BEAM MATERIALS; 50~COLUMN TO ENTABLATURE, AND 51~ENTABLATURE PRINCIPLES.

*This Palladian opens to a balcony.*

*Simple, blocky design due to small size.*

## 37
## Casing Principles

Door and window casing on all except brick walls should never be narrower than 3½". Mullion casing should never be narrower than 3½" regardless of location. Brick should never be visible between a door or window and its casing.

Casings narrower than a 1x4 simply appear too narrow and flimsy. Jamb casings should be an abstraction of columns supporting an abstraction of a beam, which is the head casing. Anything narrower than a 1x4 simply looks too weak to carry the load. The only exception is the window casing of a Federal window or door in a brick wall; but in such an instance, the brick lintel is obviously carrying the load, not the casing.

Doors mulled to windows or two or more windows mulled together are almost always sent to the job site with the frames mulled directly together and cased with a 1x2. This detail almost always looks exceptionally cheap and insubstantial. Mullion casings should hardly ever be less than a 1x4, which requires that the manufacturer add a spacer between the window and the door or window. This is one pattern that clearly adds cost to the building, but it is well worth the very small additional charge.

A common casing error, when anything more elaborate than a simple casing is added to a brick wall, is to attach the elaborate surround to the face of the brick, where it should be, but then to neglect to connect the surround to the door or window casing with extenders. This results in the

*Don't skimp on casing width or misuse brick. Common errors: 1: Brick between casing and window, head and jamb mismatch. 2: Casing to back of vinyl tumor, which should not exist, and crown at head is cut short. 3: J-mold vinyl casing allows sloppy end cuts, but is ugly. 4: Over-simplification of head detail. 5: Mullion casing is far too narrow, and is the result of mulling the two windows directly together rather than casing them properly.*

1

3

2

5

4

1

2

4

brick being visible between the surround and the door or window casing, making the surround look tacked on and neutralizing (or worse) any good the surround might have done for the image of the building.

The only apparent exception to these rules occurs

*Do use proper casing width and design principles. Below are several examples of well-cased windows that generally do all of the things required by this pattern in a variety of ways. 1: Ample mullion casing width. 2: Proper mullion casing width, backbanded main casing. 3: Backbanded casing. 4: Casing to pilasters with flat panels below windows. 5: Pilasters as casing with continuous sub-sill and apron below.*

3

5

when a pilaster of some sort covers one edge of the door, window, or mullion casing. In such instances, the pilaster visually becomes part of the casing width, and the casing itself can become quite narrow, sometimes less than 2". It is important, however, to avoid putting matching narrow casing on the outside of the pilaster if the pilaster abuts normal wall materials at this point. Flanking narrow casings on both sides look flimsy. Siding should be cut directly to the pilaster, or brick should run directly behind it, usually in standard running bond with no border courses whatsoever; the pilaster itself is usually all the border that is needed.

SEE 13~TRIM; 26~BRICK MOLD; 30~ENTRY SURROUNDS; 36~PALLADIAN WINDOW PROPORTIONS; 38~HEAD CASING PRINCIPLES; AND 44~SILL CASING.

## 38
## Head Casing Principles

Head casing should be equal to or wider than jamb casing, and should not be less than one-sixth of the opening width.

Some of the more refined styles allow picture-framed head and jamb casings, which means that the head and jamb must be of equal width and are mitered at the corners. They are usually detailed similarly to the architrave of the order of the building, and often they have a frieze and cornice head above, completing the entablature. In the cases of architrave casings, the width of casing is determined by the width of the opening, so the jamb casings are wider than they might otherwise be.

Most head casings that are not meant to become architraves, however, should be somewhat heavier than their jamb casings to reflect the structural nature of the opening, because a beam is almost always thicker than a column. The minimum head casing thickness is based on two issues: first, the proportion of 1:6 closely follows the structural necessities of wood construction for relatively small and relatively lightly loaded openings. Second, repeated empirical observations have shown that anything thin-

*Don't commit these common casing errors: 1: Head casing is too short, cut just to the window frame, although there's no jamb casing at all to match it to. 2: Head casing too long, with no jamb casing underneath. 3: Arch casing does not wrap brick. To avoid wrapping brick, there must be a structural masonry lintel, in which case casing is brick mold. 4: Casing far too narrow. 5: Ill-designed casing. 6: Head casing does not wrap brick (see 3).*

1

2

3

4

5

6

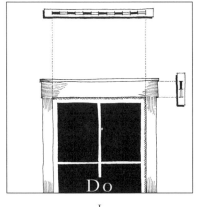

1

*Do use these or other proper head casing options: 1: Elaborate bracketed cornice over architrave casing. Architrave should match that of the primary entablature of the building, or at least be consistent with it if simpler. 2: Flat head casing with crown and bead (ends of casing may overhang slightly in similar details). 3: Simple flat head casing with simple drip above. 4: Shaped head casing. 5: Windows cased by architrave above. 6: Crowned head casing.*

2

3

4

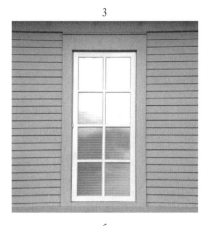

5

6

ner than 1:6 simply looks too flimsy.

The joint between the head casing and the jamb casing is also important. With the exception of architrave casings, head/jamb casing joints should typically be butted, not mitered. This reinforces the image of the lintel sitting on the doorposts. Many styles allow the end of the head casing to overhang the outside face of the jamb casing by up to 1" to further reinforce this image.

Exterior head casings require some sort of drip cap that can be flashed over to get the water away from the top of the casing. It often makes sense to make this member from 2x material that is tapered on the top to allow water to run off. A quarter round or small bed mold underneath the cap is a very simple approximation of a cornice and frieze.

SEE 13~TRIM; 26~BRICK MOLD; 30~ENTRY SURROUNDS; 36~PALLADIAN WINDOW PROPORTIONS; 37~CASING PRINCIPLES; AND 44~SILL CASING.

## 39
# MASONRY
# LINTEL PRINCIPLES

### MASONRY LINTELS SHOULD NOT BE NARROWER THAN ONE-FIFTH OF THE OPENING WIDTH.

Masonry lintels generally fall into only two categories: the square-end lintel and the jack arch, neither of which should be narrower than one-fifth of the width of the opening. As with head casings, this proportion comes both from the structural realities of relatively narrow masonry openings and from the fact that empirical observation has shown that anything less simply looks too insubstantial. The jack arch may be constructed of solid stone, stone blocks, or brick, and it is discussed in detail in 41~Jack Arches. The square-end lintel may only be constructed of solid stone. The square-end lintel supports its load by resting on the masonry on either side of the opening and acting as a simple beam. The amount of overhang (and therefore support) of the square-end lintel should be either one-half the depth of the lintel or exactly the depth of the lintel. In other words, if the lintel is 8" deep, then the overhang on either end should be either exactly 4" or exactly 8". Good local precedent is the only good reason to modify this part of the

*Don't use lintels of inappropriate width, design or materials and that could not be self-supporting. 1: Improper keystone in soldier course as lintel. 2: No attempt at a visible lintel. 3: Soldier course as lintel. 4: Brick slightly corbeled in to approximate lintel, except it is cut too short for support, even if it were real. 5: Sliver of brick between window head and frieze. 6: Improper keystone over window, but with no attempt at a visible lintel.*

DON'T

1

2

3

4

5

6

1

*Do use lintels of proper width, design and materials such as these: 1: Gothic lintels often test the lower limits of acceptable lintel thickness. 2: Masonry lintel is hidden behind elaborate wood window head. 3: Simple stone lintel. 4: Rough stone jack arch in stone wall. 5: Dressed stone lintel in natural stone wall. 6: Lintels may be articulated in innumerable ways such as this simple rectangle incised into each end. Articulation may be incised or relief.*

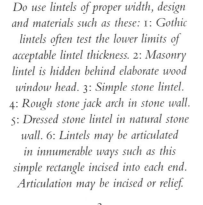

2

guideline. Keystones should never be used in square-end lintels in any condition whatsoever.

There are two occasions on which cast stone lintels or concrete lintels may be substituted for real stone lintels. First, if the proposed cast material meets either the Arm's Length Rule or the Eyes Only Rule as appropriate to the material's location in the building, then the cast material is acceptable. Second, there may be some instances in which a building is intended to appear very crude and gritty where concrete lintels may be appropriate. Due to the rough nature of the material, however, concrete should only be used in square-end lintels; it is entirely inappropriate for more refined lintels.

SEE 11~BRICK; 16~MASONRY VENEER WALLS; 17~BRICK COURSING AT WALL OPENINGS; 24~BRICK JACK ARCH; 41~JACK ARCHES; AND 43~KEYSTONES.

3

4

5

6

## 40
## ARCH
## PRINCIPLES

ARCH THICKNESS SHOULD NOT
BE LESS THAN ONE-SIXTH OF
THE OPENING WIDTH. EVERY
ARCH MUST BE SUPPORTED
IMMEDIATELY BELOW THE
ARCH.

Arches work for one reason: Their parts, whether brick or stone, are all tapered like wedges toward a radius point. Without this characteristic, they would collapse. Even veneer arches must adhere to this principle. Brick arches, if not built of gauged (tapered) brick, should usually be built of rowlocks, since their shorter height creates less of a wedge of mortar between each brick. Simple brick arches should usually be flush with the rest of the brick in the wall. More elaborate arches with header courses or other brickwork to approximate an archivolt may project slightly from the face of the wall.

Arches can be a bit thinner than masonry lintels because their shape inherently helps them to resist a greater load. As with the previous spanning member thickness guidelines (38~Head Casing Principles and 39~Masonry Lintel Principles), the one-sixth proportion was derived from both the structural logic of arches and the empirical observation of arches that are carrying a load versus veneer arches that simply appear too thin. And as with the other spanning members, arches can certainly be thicker, if this is appropriate to the style of the building.

Another common error of veneer arch construction is to support them in a structurally impossible manner. It is true

DON'T
1

*Don't build arches in the many ways that look as if they might collapse. These are a few of the legion of possible arch mistakes. 1: Irregular radius. 2: Near-miss Roman arch with keystone at wrong angle. 3: Single rowlock arch is far too thin. 4: No support at ends of arched stucco wall. This common error at McMansion entries results from the arch being used as an applique with no memory of its structural purpose. 5: Stucco arch slightly too thin.*

2

3

4

5

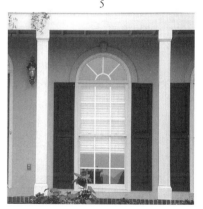

1

2

4

that veneer arches are simply a single wythe of brick, and that they are light enough to be supported with hidden steel members while performing all sorts of seemingly impossible gymnastics. But do you want to walk under something that looks as if it might fall on you? One must conclude that an

*Do build arches with proper proportions and which support themselves. The following are proper arch types:*
*1: Flat-top bowspring arch.*
*2: Elliptical arch.*
*3: Single soldier bowspring arch.*
*4: Triple rowlock bowspring arch.*
*5: Multi-rowlock full Roman arch.*

3

5

unsupported brick arch either is made of brick wallpaper or is unsafe. Most people subconsciously write it off as brick wallpaper, but their perception of the rest of the building suffers as a result.

Another common error is made in building arches of indeterminate shape. Roman arches should be a perfect half-circle, with the ends of the intrados and extrados vertical. Bowspring arches should never have an end angle of greater than 30° from vertical. Elliptical arches should be a clear ellipse, with both ends of the intrados and extrados vertical. There are exotic arch types such as the Gothic arch and the Moorish arch, but in every case, whether exotic or common, arches should strictly adhere to the rules of their type. Just building something that generally curves on top is not acceptable.

SEE 11~BRICK; 16~MASONRY VENEER WALLS; 17~BRICK COURSING AT WALL OPENINGS; 42~ARCH/EAVE ALIGNMENT; AND 43~KEYSTONES.

# 41
# JACK ARCHES

THE SIDE FACES OF JACK ARCH
KEYSTONES SHOULD CONVERGE
AT THE SAME RADIUS POINT AS
THE ENDS OF THE JACK ARCH.
THE END OF JACK ARCHES
SHOULD BE EITHER 22.5° OR
30° FROM VERTICAL.

Solid stone jack arches work in a manner similar to ordinary lintels: The jack arch acts primarily as a beam to hold up the load. The sloped ends of jack arches support the jack arch through wedging action. Segmented stone jack arches or brick jack arches, on the other hand, work more as arches, supporting the load when each member acts as a wedge. The wedge system only works if the side faces of all the wedges converge on a single radius point. Jack arches with keystones and arch ends sloped at the same angle would probably collapse if not supported by a steel angle, and they are an enormous symptom of paste-on "traditional styles" that have little to do with the actual traditions that created the styles.

The angles of the jack arch ends are important. The most common angles used by most styles are either 22.5° or 30° from vertical. Steeper angles look cartoonish and have little structural logic. Shallower angles create more horizontal

*Don't: This is an obvious 3-piece jack arch, which is not self-supporting, even if the side face angles were right.*

*Don't use jack arches which require steel angles for support.*

*Don't: Bricks are vertical, resulting in totally non-structural condition.*

*Don't: Paste-on EIFS jack arch is too thin and side face angles are wrong, resulting in a jack arch that would never be self-supporting, even if built of something stronger than foam.*

*Don't: Brick and stone side faces do not converge at a single point, so these could not be self-supporting.*

*Don't: Keystone angle is far too shallow, making convergence impossible.*

*Do use jack arches where all joints converge on a single point. If a keystone is used, make certain that the side angles of the keystone converge on the radius point of the arch.*

*Do: Textbook brick jack arch.*

thrust and are therefore less structurally stable.

Keystones may technically be used with either solid or segmented jack arches. They look most appropriate, however, in segmented jack arches, because the keystones are simply one of the segments.

SEE 11~BRICK; 16~MASONRY VENEER WALLS; 17~BRICK COURSING AT WALL OPENINGS; 24~BRICK JACK ARCH; 39~MASONRY LINTEL PRINCIPLES; AND 43~KEYSTONES.

*And another.*

*And another.*

*And another. Notice a pattern here? The old jack arches were required to be self supporting out of necessity, resulting in a great continuity of method.*

*Do: Stone jack arch.*

## 42
## ARCH/EAVE
## ALIGNMENT

**EAVE TRIM SHOULD NEVER INTERSECT AN ARCH EXCEPT TO TOUCH THE TOP OF A KEYSTONE.**

It is unfortunate that this pattern must be included in the book, because violation of it runs against every applicable principle of good detailing, but the violations continue to occur on a regular basis. Everyone has seen them repeatedly— frieze boards, cornices, or other trim boards that lop off the top of an arch as if it were not there. The Near-Miss Rule is worthy of mention here. It states: "There are few things in architecture worse than a near miss. Either engage the object precisely, or steer clear of it by a noticeable margin."

Arches, as one of the more noble elements in architecture, certainly deserve the dignity of treatment according to the Near-Miss Rule. The problem with arches is that they are obviously round on top. There are very few good ways for a straight line to engage a round object from the top without looking strange. The only really good method is to use a keystone at the top of the arch and allow the architrave or frieze trim above to precisely touch the top of the keystone. Missing the top of

*Don't break the Near-Miss Rule when placing eave trim close to the top of an arch. These are a few of the innumerable bad ways for an arch (or lintel) to collide with an eave. Look at the great amount of architectural energy that went into solving a problem that never should have happened in the last photo. This is a pattern that will cause future generations to ask: "What were they thinking?"*

*Do design the top of the keystone to precisely intersect with the eave or other element at the very top of the keystone as shown in the Do drawing if the arch and eave are less than 3 brick courses apart. 1: If there is no keystone, the top of the arch must miss the element above by at least 3 brick courses, ideally more. 2: The same principle applies to all types of lintels. 3: The lintels may also engage using the keystone rule.*

1

2

3

the keystone by an inch or by a brick or two clearly violates the Near-Miss Rule; it really must just touch the top of it.

If the arches have no keystones, then there is no choice but to leave a significant amount of brick (or other masonry) above the arch before any trim occurs. And even if the arches have keystones, a significant amount of brick above the arch is perfectly appropriate. A good rule of thumb for the appropriate amount is one-third of the width of the arch opening. In other words, if the arch opening is 8' wide, there should be at least 2'-8" of brick between the top of the arch or keystone and the bottom of the nearest trim board above.

SEE 40~ARCH PRINCIPLES AND 43~KEYSTONES.

## 43
### KEYSTONES

KEYSTONES SHOULD NEVER BE USED AS A PART OF PICTURE-FRAMED CASING. LINTELS WITH SQUARE ENDS SHOULD NEVER INCLUDE A KEYSTONE.

The structural purpose of a keystone is to act as a wedge within a structural member that works by wedging action. The aesthetic purpose is usually either to make the structural member (arch or jack arch) more prominent or to elaborate it in some other manner. Unfortunately, if the structural purpose does not exist, keystones simply look silly. For example, square-end stone lintels with keystones would probably collapse without their hidden steel support. Keystones in picture-framed casings most often read like a sad, unintentional joke on the designer.

The properly executed keystone, however, for millennia has been one of the more evocative architectural elements. It has come to symbolize many things ("This is the keystone of our strategy...," etc.) There is even the Keystone State, of course. If the idea of the keystone is this important to society, then the actuality of the keystone deserves proper detailing.

There are many proper ways to build keystones. The simplest keystone is simply a

Don't use fake, paste-on keystones. It is possible that keystones have been built in more improper ways than any other architectural element. This is but a small selection. 1: Where's the lintel? 2: Paste-on foam keystone is off-center in an arch that is far too small. 3: Keystone sits above arch that is far too small. 4: Foam keystone pasted onto soldier course. 5: Keystone in arch that is far too small and not supported at ends. 6: Keystone in soldier course.

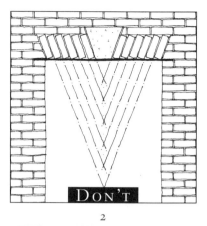

1

2

3

4

5

6

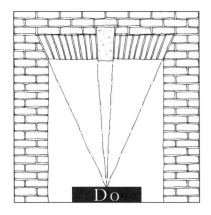

*Do use keystones in a structural manner where the side faces of all elements converge at a single point. 1: Articulated keystones have been common since antiquity. Here, the articulation is a simple incised pattern, although it can be quite elaborate. 2: Keystones used in wood headers have some freedom from structural accuracy since they are obviously decorative in nature.*

1

2

shaped stone block that is level on top and flush with the face of the arch. Keystones may also project slightly from the face of the arch. Double (or triple) keystones must project from the face of the arch and include a central keystone with narrow voussoirs to either side, all cut as a single stone. The more elaborate keystones may have either incised ornamentation or even applied acanthus scrollwork projecting from the front. The common thread is the size of the keystone: Seldom is the width of the bottom of a keystone less than one-ninth or greater than one-seventh of the overall width of the opening. Keystones are often laid out to be equal to the width of the voussoirs in stone arches. The maximum height of the keystone is twice the width of the bottom of the keystone. Keystones project slightly from the intrados of the arch and an equal amount or more from the extrados.

SEE 40~ARCH PRINCIPLES AND 42~ARCH/EAVE ALIGNMENT.

## 44
# SILL CASING

THE SILL SHOULD ACT AS A VISUAL BASE TO A WINDOW. CASING SHOULD NEVER BE PICTURE FRAMED AT THE SILL.

Windows, like nearly every other element in traditional architecture, usually have a cap, a shaft (or body), and a base. And, like most of the rest of them, this is not only the product of the reflection of the human form, but also the product of necessity. The things that a window must do to keep water out of a building are much different at the top, at the sides, and at the bottom; so one would expect each part to be very different. Traditional window heads, jambs, and sills are usually quite different, but the rush to over abstraction and over simplification found in machine-based architecture has spilled over into today's allegedly traditional architecture in the form of window casings that are the same on all sides, to the point that they are often built as a picture frame, with mitered joints in all four corners.

There is a wide variety of proper sill design. Much of it is dependent upon the style of the building, of course. However, most proper sills adhere to the following principles regardless of style: First, the jamb casing almost always

*Don't abstract or simplify window sills to the point that the sill can't do its job both visually and functionally. 1: The infamous picture-framed sill treats the sill as if it were a jamb, or a head. 2: Here, a very elaborate arch and jamb assembly rests on nothing at all. Even if the brick rowlock sill were extended to the edges of the trim above, it would still be overmatched by the visual power of the jamb detail.*

1

2

*Do design window sills to act as a visual base for the window and get the water from the window out of the wall. 1: This is a simple block subsill. Look very closely at the very subtle way that it runs barely past the edges of the jamb casing above. 2: This is a much more elegant sill detail, complete with contoured sill blocks that are the same width as the jamb casing above.*

Do

ends at the top of the sill, sitting on the "ears" of the sill rather than running past it, as described above. Masonry openings typically include a subsill of brick or stone that sits just under the bottom of the window and is sloped to shed water to the outside of the wall. Sills in masonry walls are made of either stone or brick instead of wood casing, but in any case, they should extend to the edge of the jamb casing above. Subsill designs, as do other window parts, vary with the style of the building. If the wall is wood, then the basic choice for simpler sills is whether to include an apron below the sill. An apron is a board, sometimes the width of the jamb casing or sometimes wider, that is installed horizontally below the sill. Other choices include whether to beef up the sill with a $1\frac{1}{2}$"-thick subsill in lieu of an apron, as is often done at the more vernacular end of the spectrum, or whether to include sill brackets below the sill aligned with each jamb casing, such as found on either more classical or more elaborate styles.

1

2

SEE 6~CAP, SHAFT, AND BASE; 13~TRIM; 26~BRICK MOLD; 36~PALLADIAN WINDOW PROPORTIONS; AND 37~CASING PRINCIPLES.

CHAPTER 9
~
# PORCHES AND BALCONIES

### Porch and Balcony Materials

## Porch and Balcony Configurations

## 45
## COLUMN MATERIALS AND PROPORTIONS

COLUMNS SHOULD BE BUILT OF MATERIALS THAT ENCOURAGE PROPER COLUMN DESIGNS. THIS CERTAINLY DOES NOT INCLUDE EXTRUDED ALUMINUM. CLASSICAL COLUMNS SHOULD BE BUILT TO CLASSICAL PROPORTIONS, WHICH ARE NOT FOUND IN "HOUSE COLUMNS." HOUSE COLUMNS SIMPLY SHOULD NOT EXIST.

Columns have been built of several materials over the years. Materials that are carved, turned on a lathe, or molded may be properly shaped, including the taper, or entasis, of a classical column. Extruded columns, on the other hand, cannot possibly be built correctly because the process of extrusion does not allow for any taper, nor does it allow for the finer details of non-classical column types.

The ability to taper does not guarantee proper columns, unfortunately. House columns taper, but do so entirely incorrectly. A house column is a wood column that is meant to resemble a classical column, but with highly inferior detailing, all for the purpose of being less expensive. Its capital and base details are scrawny approximations of the Tuscan order, while its entire taper occurs within the top foot or so of the shaft. For-

tunately, the advent of good molded fiberglass composite columns promises to make the house column obsolete at some point.

Proper classical columns exhibit the following proportions: The taper of the column shaft occurs over the top two-thirds of the shaft except in the Greek Doric order, where the entire shaft is tapered. In every case, the taper is circular, so that it bows slightly outward, rather than straight. The top of the shaft in all orders except the Greek Doric is five-sixths the diameter of the bottom of the shaft. The Greek Doric has no base, while the base of the other orders, measured to

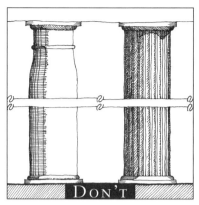
*Don't: "House columns."*

*Don't: Aluminum columns.*

*Don't: Aluminum columns.*

*Don't: Wood columns far too thin.*

*Don't: Impossibly thin pipe columns.*

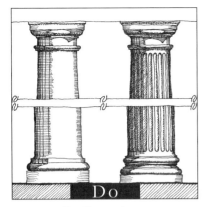

*Do: Stone columns.*

the bottom of the apophyge, should typically be one-half (or slightly more) as tall as the diameter of the column at the base. Tuscan and Roman Doric capitals should also be one-half as tall as the diameter of the column at the base, measured to the top of the astragal. Ionic capitals may

*Do: Masonry columns/stucco details.*

vary according to the version of the Ionic order, but are generally the same height or deeper. The Corinthian capital is significantly deeper.

Columns built of molded composite materials are the first good advance in column technology in centuries. Columns built of these materials are stronger than wood and do not rot. Limestone, on the other hand, has been used to build columns for thousands of years, and is still often the least expensive material to use over the life of the building, because stone is the only true no-maintenance building material.

SEE 6~ CAP, SHAFT, AND BASE; 50~COLUMN TO ENTABLATURE; 52~INTERCOLUMNIATION; 56~SQUARE COLUMN CAP AND BASE TRIM; 57~COLUMN BASE TO PORCH EDGE; AND 58~LARGE SQUARE COLUMNS.

*Do: Wood and molded columns.*

*Do: Stone lasts for centuries.*

## 46
### BEAM MATERIALS

PORCH BEAM CASINGS SHOULD
BE BUILT OF MATERIALS THAT
REFLECT THE STRUCTURAL
NATURE OF THE BEAMS,
WHICH MEANS THAT THE
GRAIN OR TEXTURE OF THE
CASING MATERIAL SHOULD BE
HORIZONTAL. THIS EXCLUDES
VERTICALLY RIBBED MATERIALS
SUCH AS VINYL.

The grain of a wood beam always runs the length of the beam because wood is much weaker in cross-grain. Metal beams usually have flanges or other ribs that run the length of the beam, because objects running perpendicular to the beam do not strengthen the beam. Even the stone beams of classical antiquity had elements that ran the length of the beams. The architrave is the structural support of the entablature. Architraves are often plain stone members with a horizontal taenia at the top running the length of the architrave. If they are elaborated, as some Ionic architraves are, for example, all the elaboration is entirely horizontal. So no matter whether the beam material has been used for ages (wood), or has been used only in more recent times (metals, especially steel), any visible texture or patterns in the beam should run the length of the beam, not across it. This even applies in the case of stone beams, which

*Don't negate the structural nature of the beam with materials that run vertically such as the vinyl beam casing shown in the Don't drawing. 1: Vinyl continuous from beam to pediment. 2: Brick as beam on front face, or is there any beam at all? 3: Conventional vinyl-wrapped beam and soffit. 4: This may be one of the strangest beam details ever built. See how quickly you can pick out the first dozen things that are wrong with this picture.*

DON'T

1

2

3

4

*Do reflect the structural nature of the beam by using material that has a horizontal grain, if any. 1: Open timber beam. 2: Classical EIFS entablature. 3: Stone entablature. 4: Concrete entablature designed to mimic stone. 5: Wood cornice and architrave, stucco frieze. A similar option on brick buildings is the stone cornice and architrave with brick frieze. 6: Wood beam built of boards to resemble timber.*

have no grain or necessary protrusions.

The worst offenders of this pattern are vinyl beam facings. The material typically used for these facings is a vinyl sheet with incised ribs spaced 4" to 6" apart. Because vinyl end joints are exceptionally ugly due to the flimsiness of the material and are impossible to conceal, vinyl installers almost always install the ribs running the short direction of the beam rather than the long direction. Coating a beam with a material such as vinyl that makes it appear nonstructural is a serious enough offense; but turning the material the wrong direction is totally intolerable and makes the beam look as if it were made of corrugated cardboard.

SEE 13~TRIM; 51~ENTABLATURE PRINCIPLES; 53~PORCH BEAM; AND 60~SEAM LOCATION AT BEAM BOTTOM.

1

2

3

4

5

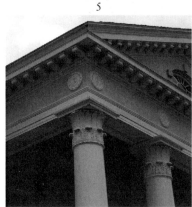

6

## 47
## PORCH CEILING
## MATERIAL

**PORCH CEILINGS (IF THEY ARE USED) SHOULD BE BUILT OF WOOD OR STUCCO.**

Porch ceilings may be unnecessary or even undesirable on some vernacular buildings if the level of detail of the building is primitive enough. If no ceiling is used and a roof covers the porch, then care must be taken to ensure that roofing nails do not protrude through the bottom of the roof deck. This can be accomplished by reducing the length of the nails if local building codes allow, or by increasing the thickness of the roof deck at the porch only. If the porch is covered by a second floor porch, the second floor porch may be constructed of boards spaced slightly apart to allow water to drain through the upper floor. If, however, a ceiling is used, then the upper level floor must be waterproof.

It is common practice in some parts of the country to use gypsum board for porch ceilings, but this material typically weathers poorly, showing joints and defects in just a few years. If a smooth porch ceiling is desired, stucco is currently the best alternative.

Tongue-and-groove beaded board or V-groove boards

*Don't ignore either the appearance or function of a porch ceiling. The porch ceiling is one of the first surfaces to greet people when they approach a building. The porch ceiling makes an impression on them before you do in most cases. Nearly all vinyl systems that have been developed to date do an unsightly job of covering things, including porch ceilings.*

DON'T

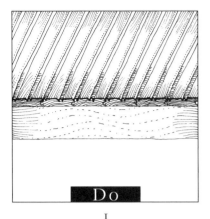

Do

*Do choose porch ceiling materials according to the location of the building within the Transect and from the list of acceptable materials. 1: Timber beams and purlins (small cross-beams) with solid floor deck above. 2: V-groove wide board ceiling. 3: Exposed framing and metal roofing. 4: Narrow beaded board ceiling. 5: Open slat ceiling. 6: Plywood grooved to resemble beaded board.*

1

2

3

4

5

6

make good porch ceilings as long as the species of wood used is appropriate for the local climate, and allows a single surface to extend to all edges of the ceiling. Exterior plywood or other flat wood surfaces selected for the local climate may also be used for porch ceilings, but require batten strips to cover joints between the boards. If full sheets of plywood are used, batten strips should be installed in such a pattern that the sheet size is not obvious. For example, for 4' x 8' sheets of plywood, batten strips could be installed either 16" or 24" on center each way. Batten strips should also be installed at all edges of the ceiling. Carpenters occasionally use thin "tongue depressor" lattice strips as ceiling batten strips, but the minimum batten strip that looks substantial is usually a 1x4, depending on the style of the building.

This pattern can vary slightly along the Transect, with the less formal ceilings such as open framing or spread boards being found more frequently at the rural end of the Transect. More refined ceilings such as beaded boards and paneled ceilings are found more often at the urban end.

SEE THE TRANSECT (PAGE 75); 13~TRIM; 37~CASING PRINCIPLES; AND 53~PORCH BEAM.

## 48
# BALCONY
# MATERIALS

### BALCONIES SHOULD BE CONSTRUCTED OF WOOD OR METAL.

Actually, there are three acceptable balcony materials, but the third is very rarely affordable: stone. True stone balconies are enormously heavy and difficult to support, making them appropriate for only the most monumental-scale buildings. Wood, because of its relative weakness, may result in heavier structural members, whereas metal balconies may be lighter and more delicate because of the relative strength of metal.

Wood balconies must be constructed of one of the "eternal woods," or of pressure-treated pine in cases where the finish of the balcony is not as important, or on more vernacular buildings. Less weather-resistant woods such as untreated pine should never be trusted on an item such as a balcony that is meant to support human weight or that ties back into the rest of the structure. Balconies that are constructed of untreated woods not resistant to weathering and then covered with sheeting, such as vinyl panels or aluminum sheeting, are even more dangerous, because the sheeting material hides

*Don't compromise the long-term safety or the immediate appearance of a balcony by using improper materials, including those that do not weather well or that cannot be easily repaired.*
*1: Featureless concrete balconies were never popular except with architects for reasons that are obvious.*
*2: This technically is a wood balcony, but look carefully - it's really just a wood railing. The balcony is entirely hidden.*

1

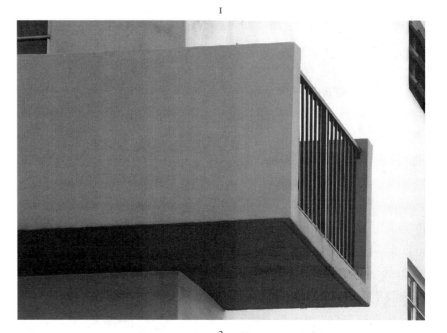

2

*Do use one of the "eternal woods," pressure-treated pine or non-rusting metal for balconies.*
*1: Simple wood balcony with angle bracket supports also carries roof above.*
*2: Metal balconies may be fabricated either simply or in all sorts of fanciful shapes as shown here. Greater care must be taken with fanciful ones to make certain that they do not become grotesque.*

1

2

deterioration. Such conditions should never even be considered. A wood balcony structure should support a wood balcony floor.

Metal balconies should ideally be constructed out of a non-rusting metal such as stainless steel or bronze, although these materials can be extremely expensive. If constructed of steel, the entire structure, including connectors such as bolts and screws, must be built of hot-dip galvanized components, with all connections treated against rust after fabrication. The zinc coating of electro-galvanized components is too thin to protect parts that are subject to any degree of use or abuse, and paint simply cannot be trusted to protect structural elements indefinitely. Metal balconies often support a concrete balcony floor, although the floor may be constructed of wood.

Balconies, especially wooden ones, often have open floor structures that allow the flooring material to be visible from the underside. If not, then the underside of the balcony should be treated similarly to a porch ceiling.

SEE 46~BEAM MATERIALS;
47~PORCH CEILING MATERIAL;
49~RAILING MATERIALS;
54~RAILING DESIGN; AND
55~BALCONY DESIGN.

## 49
# RAILING MATERIALS

RAILINGS MAY BE BUILT OF
WOOD, METAL, OR STONE, BUT
THE RAILING MATERIAL SHOULD
IN NO CASE BE HEAVIER
IN APPEARANCE THAN THE
PRIMARY ELEMENTS OF THE
PORCH OR BALCONY.

Railings may also be constructed of synthetic materials, but only if the synthetic materials meet the requirements of the Arm's Length Rule. It is especially important that the Arm's Length Rule be extended not only to the standard components of the railing system, but also to the joints where the railing system meets the wall, column, or newel post. Some railing systems currently available have acceptable rail and baluster components, but have connectors so incredibly heavy and crude that they can be seen from nearly a block away. Other railing systems have profiles that are very close to correct, but are extruded in very thin sections. These systems might be acceptable for a rooftop balustrade that human hands will never touch once the installer leaves, but they would never comply with the Arm's Length Rule because they feel so flimsy and hollow. In most cases, such systems also rattle around when touched, supporting the impression that they are insubstantial and cheap. Synthetic railing materials are most often used to approximate wood railings, since they are usually too weak to substitute for much thinner metal components.

Wood railings should be held to the same standard as wood

*Don't use railing materials that do not weather well, or that are visually incompatible with other porch or balcony components. The two examples below illustrate the current state of the art in plastic railing. Obviously, the industry has a long way to go in order to even pass the test of the Eyes Only Rule. Unfortunately, railing is something that is handled, so it must pass the more stringent test of the Arm's Length Rule.*

*Do use railing materials that are equal to or lighter in appearance than the primary porch or balcony framing. Proper railings can run the gamut from extreme simplicity to high expressiveness. 1: Wood can be used to create some of the simplest possible railings. 2: Wood can also be used to create railings in the middle ornamental ranges. 3: Metal railing can be highly expressive if designed as an assembly of thin pieces such as those shown here.*

balconies because human safety may be at stake. This means that railing components must be either constructed of one of the "eternal woods" or wood that is pressure-treated to resist decay. Railing components, because of the relative weakness of wood, seldom are thinner than $1\frac{1}{4}$".

Metal railings are often constructed of thin square or round tubular components. Metal railings, because of their thinness, are often capped with a thicker cap member of another material, often bronze or brass, which wears better with repeated hand contact than a painted rail.

Stone railings, because of the relative weakness of stone in tension, are usually visually heavy. Stone railing systems are almost always thicker than metal systems, and are usually thicker than wood, although there is significant overlap between appropriate wood member sizes and appropriate stone member sizes. Stone railings, because of the extreme rarity of stone balconies, should generally be confined to ground-level railings that are supported on masonry walls or on solid paving.

This pattern varies along the Transect, with wood railing found more often at the rural end of the Transect and metal railing occurring more frequently at the urban end.

SEE THE TRANSECT (PAGE 75); 13~TRIM; 48~BALCONY MATERIALS; 54~RAILING DESIGN; AND 55~BALCONY DESIGN.

1

2

3

## 50
## COLUMN TO ENTABLATURE

THE FACE OF THE ENTABLATURE SHOULD ALWAYS ALIGN WITH THE FACE OF THE TOP OF THE COLUMN.

Renaissance architects put forth the idea that there were certain canonical ways of constructing the classical orders, and that there should be little variation in their design. Later archaeology uncovered tremendous variety in the ancient classical orders, effectively dispelling this notion. The relationship of the column to the entablature, however, was an exception. It is nearly impossible to find examples of classical or even good traditional architecture that violate this rule. Simply stated, the top of the column shaft should align flush with the face of the beam or architrave above.

What was it about this relationship that empowered it to defy all variation in numerous cultures for thousands of years? It is a primarily visual issue, of course, but with clear structural implications. Most porch columns are in reality far stronger than they need to be in order to hold up what are typically light porch loads. If the beam is wider than the column, then it looks too heavy as if it is carrying an enormous load, and the column appears unable to sup-

*Don't make the entablature too thick or too thin as in these variations on the two basic ways of doing it wrong.*
*1: This detail gets it wrong both ways. It clearly slides the column too far out to the side. But look carefully at the shadow on the column, which shows the column slid too far in from the front.*
*2: This detail swells the entablature to where the column capitals that cannot reach either the inside or outside faces of the architrave. 3: Not only does the architrave trim board project too far out, but it hangs down too far, too, covering the abacus of the column capital. By doing so, it highlights the fact that the entablature is built of thin lumber.*
*4: This one almost gets it right, aligning the outside face of the architrave with the outside face of the abacus of the column capital. 5: This photo illustrates the great number of variations of this error. This one is very similar to 3, but not quite: Here, the architrave board covers only half of the abacus.*

DON'T

1

2

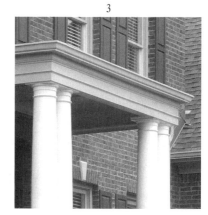

3

4

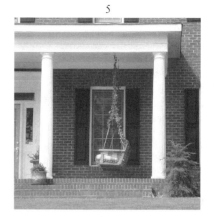

5

*Do make sure that both the inside and outside faces of the architrave match the width of the top of the column shaft. These photos represent three traditional styles, yet they all consistently align the top of the column shaft with the face of beam or face of architrave. Traditional architecture not only looks enduring, but it is enduring because of details such as these. 3: Even this photo, which depicts a very abstracted Greek Doric order, is true to this age-old rule.*

1

2

3

port it. A beam that is too thin makes the columns look clunky. Taken to the extreme, a beam that is very narrow looks like a knife blade ready to slice the column in half.

Compare this to the human body, with the column as an arm and the capital as a hand holding up a load (the beam). The vertical forearm easily holds up the beam with an upward-facing palm. The fingers are outside the beam, just as the column capital is outside the beam. A beam that sat on the fingertips would surely bend the fingers back in a most painful fashion.

Finally, there are similarities between the appearance and the structure in these situations. A beam bearing on the edge of the column capital would be just as precarious as a heavy load resting on your fingertips; it would tend to shear off the column capital. It would also introduce structural eccentricity to the column, bending it and compressing it at the same time. Eccentric column loading is an exceptionally bad idea. Which is easier to do, crush a soda straw by pushing straight down on the end of it or by pushing down on a straw you have already bent?

See 6~Cap, Shaft, and Base; 45~Column Materials and Proportions; and 53~Porch Beam.

## 51
### ENTABLATURE PRINCIPLES

EACH OF THE COMPONENTS
OF THE ENTABLATURE SHOULD
CONFORM TO CERTAIN
PRINCIPLES. THE CORNICE
SHOULD PROJECT A DIMENSION
EQUAL TO ITS HEIGHT.
THE FRIEZE MAY BE PLAIN,
ELABORATELY ORNAMENTAL,
OR ALMOST ANYTHING IN
BETWEEN. THE ARCHITRAVE
SHOULD NEVER BE TALLER
THAN THE FRIEZE AND IS
OFTEN PLAIN.

The entablature, which is the uppermost element of the classical order (entablature, column, and pedestal), is itself made up of three elements: the cornice, the frieze, and the architrave.

The frieze is elemental, meaning that it cannot be divided vertically into smaller elements. The architrave may be divided, depending on the order. The cornice, on the other hand, is always composed of three elements: the cymatium (crown), corona (fascia), and bed moldings.

The bed moldings, in turn, may be composed of either a simple bed or any one of several three-part assemblies such as corbels or modillions over a corbel or a modillion base over a bed mold. The simple bed is made up of three parts: an ovolo, a fillet, and a cavetto.

The primary function of the classical cornice is to throw water away from the wall; the bottom of the corona typically includes a drip so that any water running down the face of the cymatium and corona drips free of the frieze. The proportions of the various parts of the cornice vary from order to order and from variety to variety within each order; but the total height of all elements of the cornice exactly equals the total depth (overhang) of the cornice.

The frieze originally was the band where ceiling beams framed into the entablature. Ceiling beams, the ends of which were triglyphs, sometimes penetrated the outside surface of the frieze. In other cases, the ceiling beams did not penetrate the surface of the frieze, resulting in an uninterrupted band that could be treated in a number of decorative manners. The Tuscan frieze is a flat, unelaborated band. The Greek Doric frieze is elaborated with

*Don't: Architrave missing, overhang, etc.*

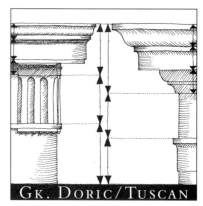

GK. DORIC/TUSCAN

*Don't: Architrave missing, etc.*

*Don't: Deep cornice, oversize dentils, etc.*

*Don't: Tiny picture-framed frieze, etc.*

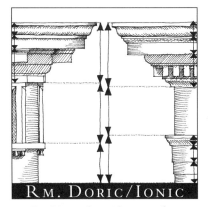

RM. DORIC/IONIC

*Do: Vernacular with open rafters.*

*Do: Vernacular with square columns.*

*Do: Simple Ionic.*

*Do: Greek Tower of the Winds order.*

triglyphs, while the Roman Doric frieze either may be flat or may contain triglyphs. The metopes, or spaces between the triglyphs, are usually flat in the Greek Doric order, but may often be enriched with various raised ornamental motifs in the Roman Doric. The Ionic frieze does not contain triglyphs, but usually is enriched with raised ornamental motifs that are typically more ornate than those of the Roman Doric. The Ionic frieze may also be pulvinated, or pillowed, either with or without raised ornament. The Corinthian and Composite friezes follow the general ornamental principles of the Ionic, but with yet greater vigor.

The architrave is the structural beam that supports the entire entablature and all the beams and rafters that frame into it. It is therefore usually a plain, massive element intended to look the part of strength as well as to perform it. The architrave is less than or equal to the height of the frieze, depending on the order and the variety of the order. Generally, Greek Doric architraves tend to be taller because the Greek Doric order is the most massive of all orders, thereby requiring a heavier beam to support it. The more delicate orders generally have narrower architraves, but never narrower than structural necessity requires. Architraves of the Tuscan and Doric orders (both Greek and Roman) are always plain, or elemental, whereas architraves of the Ionic and Corinthian orders may either be plain or be composed of three horizontal bands. In any case, however, the architrave always contains as its uppermost member the taenia, which is a narrow band that distinguishes the architrave from the frieze.

SEE 6~CAP, SHAFT, AND BASE; 50~COLUMN TO ENTABLATURE; 53~PORCH BEAM; AND 59~TRIGLYPH/ COLUMN ALIGNMENT. SEE ALSO DESCRIPTIONS OF THE CLASSICAL ORDERS OF ARCHITECTURE ON PAGES 14 TO 21 FOR A MORE THOROUGH ILLUSTRATION OF THE ENTABLATURE PRINCIPLES OF EACH ORDER.

## 52
## INTERCOLUMNIATION

INTERCOLUMNIATION SHOULD
BE VERTICALLY PROPORTIONED
EXCEPT AS CLEARLY
APPROPRIATE TO THE STYLE.

Intercolumniation techni-
cally is the measure of the
spacing of columns, measured
in modules which are equal
to the radius of the bottom of
the column shaft. But because
each classical order has a direct
relationship between column
height and column diame-
ter, intercolumniation also
is a measure of the proportion of the opening between
columns. Classical standards
of intercolumniation always
result in openings between
columns that are markedly vertical in proportion. Common
intercolumniations include
the pycnostyle (3 modules
between columns), the systyle
(4 modules), the eustyle (4½
modules), the diastyle (6 modules), and the araeostyle (8
modules). So in the case of
the Roman Doric, where the
column height is 8 times column diameter, or 16 modules,
the widest intercolumniation
(araeostyle) results in a space
between columns propor-
tioned at 16:8 or 2:1.

Classical orders were obviously built around the requirements of stone construction.
Stone is enormously strong as
a column, but much weaker
as a beam, so the vertical-

ity was as much a structural
necessity as it was a design
choice. Wood, however, is
about equally strong as a beam
and as a column. Wood structures that are not strictly classical, therefore, often have
intercolumniation wider than
2:1.

*Don't: Every bay is different, and none of them are a precise proportion. What is the purpose of the double column in the center? Double columns ordinarily are used either more than once or not at all on a porch.*

*Don't: Bays are wider than square, vary unpre-dictably, and are of uncer-tain proportions. Variable bays can sometimes be used to center on doors or windows. While this appears to be the intent of the designer at first glance, neither the door nor window actually centers in their column bays.*

*Don't: Two of the three bays are enormously too wide. Coupled with a hidden porch beam, this makes one wonder how stable the porch roof is.*

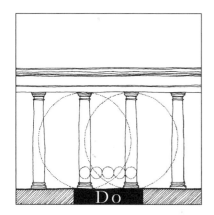

Metal structures, especially steel structures, are enormously strong compared to any previous structural system. Column heights in conventional structures are usually determined by interior building requirements, not by maximum column heights, which could typically be much taller.

Because nearly every building is wider than one floor is tall, the proportion of the space between columns can be quite horizontal with steel structures. Many Modernists consider this decidedly horizontal proportion to be a natural expression of the strength of modern materials. Traditional steel structures, however, still respect the vertical proportion of the human body by using an exceptionally thin and delicate system of columns and beams, which creates a structure that is equally expressive of the strength of steel as the Modernist version. So in no case does intercolumniation exceed a proportion of 1:1 except in a few very late traditional styles such as the California Arts & Crafts.

*Do: This exact full-scale replica of the Parthenon in Nashville, Tennessee, illustrates the subtle variations of intercolumniation found in the Greek Doric order. Compare, for example, the end bay to the one next to it.*

*Do: Variations become more pronounced as buildings become more vernacular. This double-gallery porch uses 1:1 proportion (measured upstairs) at ends to match gallery width. Intercolumniation tightens increasingly to the center of the building, then breaks out to 1:1 downstairs as a punctuation at the entry.*

*Do: If in doubt, equal intercolumniation produces a porch that, while not as subtle, certainly appears competent.*

SEE 3~SIMPLICITY OF
PROPORTION; 5~REGULAR
ARRANGEMENT OF COLUMNS
AND OPENINGS; 45~COLUMN
MATERIALS AND PROPORTIONS;
50~COLUMN TO ENTABLATURE;
57~COLUMN BASE TO PORCH
EDGE; AND 59~TRIGLYPH/
COLUMN ALIGNMENT.

[171]

## 53
## PORCH BEAM

THE BEAM AT THE TOP OF
PORCH COLUMNS WHICH
SUPPORTS THE PORCH ROOF
SHOULD BE VISIBLE FROM BOTH
THE INSIDE AND THE OUTSIDE
OF THE PORCH.

The primary reason for this pattern is quite simple: If the porch ceiling is flush with the bottom of the porch beam, then the porch beam does not look like a beam at all. A viewer subconsciously has two choices: Either there is no beam, so there must not be much weight to hold up. Or maybe there should be a beam, but there is not. The first subconscious choice dematerializes the entire structure, making it all look like so much cardboard and duct tape. The second choice makes it seem unsafe. Very few people realize that the lack of a porch beam makes them feel uncomfortable with a building. Fewer yet can explain why this is so. But they are uncomfortable nonetheless, mentally reducing the value of the building.

The solution is quite simple: Raise the porch ceiling so that a significant amount of the finish porch beam is visible from both the exterior and the interior. If the beam is part of a classical entablature, the amount exposed below the ceiling should be equal to the entablature and

*Don't leave out a visible porch beam. In every example below, lack of a proper porch beam makes it appear that the columns will punch through the roof. 1: Conventional columns, but no beam at all. 2: Massive columns, but nothing to support. 3: The dentil mold should be part of the cornice, not the beam. 4: Massive columns again with missing beam. 5: Tiny implied beam, confused columns. 6: Tiny frieze, oversized dentils, etc.*

DON'T

1

2

3

4

5

6

*Do create an element which looks as if it is supporting the porch roof:*
*1: Architrave of the full classical entablature acts as the porch beam. Some read the architrave and frieze together as the beam, but the architrave itself satisfies the structural requirement, leaving the frieze to decorative uses.*
*2: Board beam over timber column.*
*3: Simple timber beams over square columns. 4: Timber beams with brackets.*

detailed exactly like the exterior entablature. The taenia makes an excellent trim piece against the porch ceiling. The entire frieze and architrave may also be exposed if desired, although this results in extremely high porch ceilings and more costly porch beams. In cases where the entablature occurs between a first-floor porch and a second-floor porch, the depth of the porch floor structure may not allow the full architrave plus frieze to be exposed inside the porch.

More vernacular porches that include only a beam that is not a part of a full entablature should probably show the entire beam. Porch beams that are built of heavy (usually square) timbers should almost certainly be fully exposed on both outside and inside.

SEE 46~BEAM MATERIALS;
47~PORCH CEILING MATERIAL;
51~ENTABLATURE PRINCIPLES;
AND 60~SEAM LOCATION AT
BEAM BOTTOM.

1

2

3

4

## 54
## RAILING DESIGN

RAILINGS SHOULD HAVE BOTH TOP AND BOTTOM RAILS, WITH BOTTOM RAILS CLEARING THE FLOOR. BALUSTERS SHOULD BE CENTERED ON THE RAILS AND SPACED AT NO MORE THAN 4" CLEAR OPENING.

Modernist architects, in their rush to break every traditional rule of architecture that they could find, have developed some fairly nonsensical details over the past century. Many of their railing designs clearly fit into this category. The top rail, or handrail, is clearly respected because of necessity. Everything else, however, was fair game. The bottom rail was the first to go; it must have appeared too much like a base, and as any observer can see, most Modernist buildings desired neither base nor cap, only the shaft. Where balusters of some sort were retained, they usually slammed into the floor with no warning, or sometimes they wrapped around the outside of the porch or balcony floor. The most extreme example is the solid glass rail, where the handrail is supported by a sheet of glass that sits in a trough in the floor.

The problems with the new designs include the fact that they all create water problems by creating either a series of holes punched in the floor or, worse yet, a trough in the floor. Even the rail types that attach to the side of the floor must frame directly into the floor structure to get their strength, so they bring water directly to the framing. Another problem is that, because of the Modernist affinity with horizontal intercolumniation, many railings are too long to be supported at their ends, requiring support from the floor. This is much more expensive because the rail acts structurally as a cantilever, like a telephone pole, rather than as a beam, like a floor joist. This can increase the cost of the railing several times more than what it should be. Sensible tradi-

Don't: Rail too thin for balusters.

Don't: Confused rail types.

Don't: Thin aluminum rail, connections.

Don't: Pickets bypass rails.

Don't: Tubular metal handrail.

Do

Do: Creative, but simple square wood.

Do: Scrolled wood balusters.

Do: Contoured simple metal rail.

tional railings, on the other hand, attach at their ends, where water is easily shed, and are short enough between columns or newels to easily span the distance without structural gymnastics.

Wood balusters may run the gamut from simple square balusters to thick, ornately turned balusters. Wood top rails may vary from a simple, thin rail contoured to the comfort of the human hand to elaborate, multipart decorative rails. Unmodified 2x4 top rails are typically too crude for comfort and do not shed water, so they should not be used. Bottom rails typically are the simplest of the three basic

Do: Wood center panel.

Do: Balusters and rail match.

components and are often rectangular. Bottom rails for thin balusters are often vertically oriented and the same widths as the baluster, while bottom rails for thick turned balusters are often horizontally oriented. In any case, the top of the bottom rail should slope to one side or both sides, so that water does not stand on the rail.

Metal railings are often constructed of thin, square, or round tubular components. Metal railings, because of their thinness, are often capped with a thicker cap member of another material, often bronze or brass, which wears better with repeated hand contact than a painted rail.

SEE 5~REGULAR ARRANGEMENT OF COLUMNS AND OPENINGS; 6~CAP, SHAFT, AND BASE; 13~TRIM; 49~RAILING MATERIALS; 52~INTERCOLUMNIATION; AND 55~BALCONY DESIGN.

## 55
# BALCONY DESIGN

BALCONIES SHOULD PROJECT
NO MORE THAN 3' FROM
THE FACE OF THE BUILDING
AND SHOULD BE VISUALLY
SUPPORTED BY BRACKETS.

Balconies that project substantially farther than 3' from the face of the building require larger brackets to appear structurally sound than can be designed as a coherent element of most buildings. Buildings of a monumental scale, of course, can visually support larger balconies. Balconies with no visible support either appear to be so light that they would be unsafe to stand on or, if assumed to be of normal weight, look as if they might fall. In either case, they appear unsafe and unsettling.

Brackets, while required to perform visual and probably structural tasks, can nonetheless be quite creative. They should usually be built of the same material as the balcony, which should be either wood or metal as noted earlier in 48~Balcony Materials. Wood brackets, of course, will be stockier because wood is weaker than metal. The visual weight of wood brackets may vary from the solid wood scrolls of Georgian architecture to the lacy gingerbread brackets of Victorian examples. They should never be so

*Don't build balconies that have no visible means of support. All of these balconies violate at least one of the balcony rules. 1: No visible means of support. 2: Too deep, no visible means of support. 3: No visible means of support. 4: If it isn't really a balcony, then set the rails within the wall opening, not outside it. This allows objects to more easily be dropped out. 5: No visible support and a host of other problems. 6: No visible support, too deep.*

DON'T

1

2

3

4

5

6

*Do support balconies with visible structural members and limit their projection from the building wall so that they appear safe to stand on and under. All of the balconies below meet the balcony requirements in creative and substantial manners. None appears likely to fall off the building if you step on it. All engage the architecture of the overall building in meaningful ways.*

lacy, however, that they appear incapable of carrying the load. The basic building blocks of the simpler wood brackets, of course, are straight sticks of wood that may be shaped on their ends. Any curves that occur in the simpler designs are generally cut into otherwise straight sticks.

Metal brackets, on the other hand, can be quite light and delicate, and they are usually built around the capacity of metal to curve. Metal brackets, because of the strength of the material, can be extremely thin and delicate, which allows the metal to be shaped into countless fanciful, curving shapes. As noted earlier, Modernists assume that the strength of metal construction is best used to create super long horizontal shapes, but traditional architecture has shown that the strength of metal construction allows delicate, elegant shapes that simply are not possible with weaker materials. There is probably no larger collection of such shapes in the United States than that found in the French Quarter of New Orleans.

SEE APPARENT STRUCTURE (PAGE 11); 48~BALCONY MATERIALS; 49~RAILING MATERIALS; AND 54~RAILING DESIGN.

1

2

3

4

5

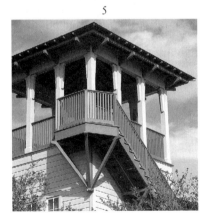

6

## 56
## SQUARE COLUMN
## CAP AND BASE TRIM

*SQUARE COLUMNS SHOULD BE
USED FOR MOST VERNACULARLY
ORIENTED STYLES. WHILE
NOT CLASSICALLY CORRECT,
THEIR CAPITAL AND BASE
TRIM SHOULD NONETHELESS
APPEAR TO BE SUPPORTING THE
LOAD JUST AS MUCH AS THEIR
CLASSICAL COUNTERPARTS DO.*

The pattern of the cap,
shaft, and base should be the
primary guide for this pattern.
Even the simplest square posts
on barns have caps of sorts:
the brackets that brace their
tops to the beams to resist the
wind. Care should be taken
in detailing to ensure that
the cap looks as if it belongs
on the top of the column or
post, and that the base looks
as if it belongs on the bottom. The braces at the top of
the barn posts, for example,
would look extremely silly if
installed at the bottom of the
posts.

There are several techniques
for creating an implied or simplified cap and base. One of
the simplest and most useful
is the chamfer. Square wood
posts are susceptible to damage at their corners, especially
if the corners are sharp-edged,
such as found on rough wood
posts. A chamfer is a bevel
cut into each corner of the
post that produces two 45°
corners about 1" to 1½" apart

rather than the original 90°
corner. The 45° corners are
much more immune to dam-
age. The starting and ending
points of the chamfered corners are important. Starting
a few inches from the top
of the post implies a column
capital above, whereas ending the chamfer slightly above

*Don't: Fluted necking.*

*Don't: Crown as echinus.*

*Don't: Overdone capital.*

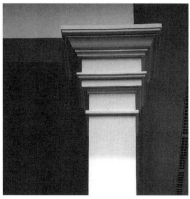
*Don't: Fluted columns, abstract capital.*

*Don't: Oversize astragal, no capital.*

*Don't: Nothing but rectangular blocks.*

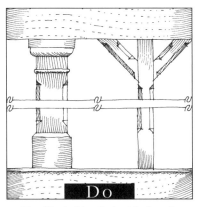

*Do: Capital implied with chamfer.*

*Do: Block over quarter round, board.*

*Do: New Urban corbels.*

*Do: Block over bed with board necking.*

*Do: Single cap, Italianate scroll.*

*Do: Double cap, Italianate detail.*

the handrail implies a pedestal below without installing a single piece of trim.

If trim is used on square posts or columns, classical columns should inform it. The cap should clearly be built of supporting pieces such as the quarter round, the cyma reversa, or the bed mold. Crowns are often used here, but they are absolutely inappropriate: Crowns are crowning shapes, not supporting shapes. Neither are base shapes appropriate here.

The square column base, obviously, should include base shapes and not supporting shapes. Base shapes include primarily the half-round and the cove. The cove may also be approximated by a horizontal chamfer at the top of a baseboard. The classical base is generally one-half as tall as the column is wide, but square column bases are often taller, approximating a short pedestal.

SEE BUILDINGS FOR PEOPLE (PAGE 10); 6~CAP, SHAFT, AND BASE; 13~TRIM; 45~COLUMN MATERIALS AND PROPORTIONS; 50~COLUMN TO ENTABLATURE; 52~INTERCOLUMNIATION; 57~COLUMN BASE TO PORCH EDGE; AND 58~LARGE SQUARE COLUMNS.

## 57
## COLUMN BASE TO PORCH EDGE

COLUMN BASES SHOULD NEVER PROTRUDE BEYOND THE EDGE OF THE PORCH FLOORING. IDEALLY, THE OUTER EDGE OF THE BASE SHOULD ALIGN WITH THE FACE OF THE PIER OR FOUNDATION BELOW.

This is one of several patterns that should be so obvious as to not require space in this book. Unfortunately, incorrect versions of this pattern continue to be built at a distressing rate. The simplest explanation is that the visual structural impossibilities of the past century have so desensitized our culture that we cannot see obvious items such as this without assistance.

The worst offenders of this pattern are the columns placed so that the column face itself overhangs the pier below. In these cases, unless the porch edge is built very strangely, the column base is almost guaranteed to project far beyond the edge of the flooring. This condition makes it appear that the column is supporting no load because a big part of it is sitting on thin air. As with other examples noted earlier, this leaves the viewer with two subconscious options: Is the part of the building that the column supports made out of something incredibly light and flimsy such as cardboard,

*Don't lay out columns so that their bases project beyond the masonry or other foundation below. Columns that project beyond their support below simply look unstable and incorrect. This error should be beyond dispute.*

DON'T

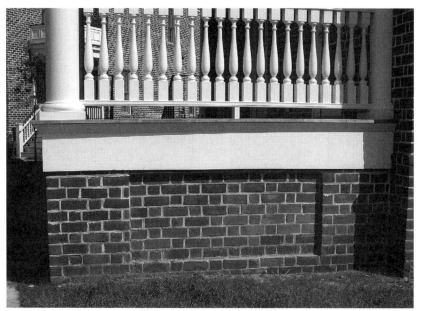

*Do detail the porch so that the face of column base projects no further than the masonry or other foundation below. As a general rule, too much base is clearly better than not enough base and the face of a column base may sit inside of the masonry base.*

*Column centers over pier: This is the ideal condition where feasible.*

*Interior columns center over brick piers, but corner columns slide near the outside corner of brick piers so that column base and outside face of pier align: In cases where piers must be notably larger than column bases because of brick coursing, this allows porch floor not to be overly large.*

*Column base sits inside of pier face: This is perfectly acceptable. Few people are disturbed when a base seems too large, but many are uncomfortable when a base seems too small.*

or is the column structurally unstable? As noted earlier, most people will not consciously state their concern in these words, but will rather have a vague sense of unease that they cannot explain.

The solution, then, involves two things. First, the pier supporting the column absolutely cannot be any smaller than the diameter of the column itself, but should actually be the same size as or larger than the outside of the column base trim. Piers that are much larger than this appear oversized. Second, if the pier is the same width as the outside of the column, then the skirt board must project at least $3/4$" beyond the pier and the porch flooring must project a short distance beyond that— probably $1/2$" to $3/4$" if no trim is installed below the flooring. This guarantees that the edge of the flooring will project beyond the base of the column by a small but acceptable distance if the columns are not enormous.

SEE APPARENT STRUCTURE (PAGE 11); 6~CAP, SHAFT, AND BASE; 45~COLUMN MATERIALS AND PROPORTIONS; 56~SQUARE COLUMN CAP AND BASE TRIM; AND 58~LARGE SQUARE COLUMNS.

## 58
## LARGE SQUARE
## COLUMNS

SQUARE COLUMNS WIDER
THAN 12" SHOULD BE BUILT
OF FRAMES AND PANELS
UNLESS THEY ARE CLASSICALLY
CORRECT MANUFACTURED
COLUMNS.

Columns that are obviously built up of wood members should be built of frames and panels because solid wood boards wider than 11¼" simply are unavailable. This leaves only panelized products such as plywood available to construct wide columns. Plywood is entirely unacceptable for all except the shortest columns, simply because it is not available in lengths greater than 8', which would require a horizontal seam on columns greater than that height.

Each of the four faces of frame-and-panel columns is constructed by building a frame of ¾" material and filling it with a wood panel. The side frame members should be at least 1x4's, but each one should be noticeably less than one-third of the width of the column. Top and bottom frame members should be wide enough to support any capital or base trim that may be installed. This usually requires the use of 1x10's or 1x12's, or in the case of very wide columns with very thick cap and base trim wider

than 11¼", the top and bottom frames may actually be spliced with the joints hidden behind the cap and base trim members.

Panels may be raised, but are often simple flat boards. The maximum column size that can be built using single boards includes a 1x12 panel

DON'T

*Don't: Panels pieced, panel stop butted to cap frame instead of picture framed.*

*Don't: Panels pieced, poor pedestal attempt, columns too thin, etc.*

*Do: Simple cap, square frame.*

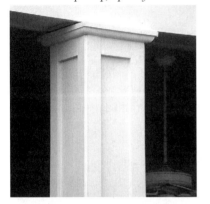

*Do: Cove echinus, simple frame.*

*Do: Simple capital is thin enough.*

*Do: Cove echinus, neck depth OK.*

*Do: Implied Greek Doric echinus.*

*Do: Almost full classical capital, base.*

and the two 1x10 side frame members (less than one-third the total column width, as noted above). The resulting column is just over 30" wide if the corners are mitered, which will satisfy needs for all but the largest columns.

Square columns of the Greek Doric order (or a vernacular approximation thereof) must almost always be built of frames and panels because a properly proportioned 12" wide Greek Doric column would be only about 5'-6" tall, which is not very useful. Greek Doric columns, of course, have no base. The only approximation of a base is the 1x10 or 1x12 base frame, which is used because narrower members simply appear too flimsy at the location on the column subject to the most abuse. Square columns of other orders usually have base trim, depending on how high style the building is. Even with more vernacular examples, cap trim and base trim (if they are used) should approximate the classical orders as with any other square column.

SEE APPARENT STRUCTURE (PAGE 11); 6~CAP, SHAFT, AND BASE; 45~COLUMN MATERIALS AND PROPORTIONS; 56~SQUARE COLUMN CAP AND BASE TRIM; AND 57~COLUMN BASE TO PORCH EDGE.

## 59
## TRIGLYPH / COLUMN ALIGNMENT

TRIGLYPHS SHOULD ALMOST ALWAYS BE CENTERED OVER COLUMNS. ADDITIONAL TRIGLYPHS SHOULD BE EQUALLY SPACED BETWEEN THE ONES THAT ARE CENTERED OVER COLUMNS.

*Don't mis-align triglyphs over columns. Lack of alignment of triglyphs over columns simply looks like a mistake. This is a detail that should be resolved by the designer during the layout of the columns.*

DON'T

The Greeks achieved a level of optical sophistication never seen again in human construction. Elements of their buildings curved and distorted by tiny amounts to correct for visual distortion when one is viewing the building from ground level. One of their refinements was a slight outward cheating of the triglyphs at the last two column bays of a building, so that the outside edge of the last triglyph was located exactly at the outside corner of the frieze. This left the last four triglyphs progressively more off-center of the columns while all other triglyphs were centered either over or between the columns below. The Romans that followed discarded this degree of sophistication, preferring instead to center all triglyphs directly over columns (if not between), which has been the standard ever since except when one is constructing a building of the Greek Doric order, of course.

There may be one or more triglyphs between columns,

*Do align triglyphs over columns. Alignment of triglyphs over columns simply looks natural. The only acceptable exception is at the end of a Greek Doric frieze as noted in the text. Note that the spaces between the triglyphs (the metopes) are wider than perfect squares in all except the bottom right photo.*

all spaced evenly. If the intercolumniation varies along the length of a colonnade, all triglyphs on the entire colonnade should be held at the exact same spacing. The pair of columns with wider intercolumniation simply have more triglyphs between them than the more narrowly spaced columns. This should result in every space between columns being of a rational proportion. To be entirely correct, the space between the triglyphs (the metope) should be a perfect square.

SEE 3~SIMPLICITY OF
PROPORTION; 4~SYMMETRY
OF THE FACE; 5~REGULAR
ARRANGEMENT OF
COLUMNS AND OPENINGS;
51~ENTABLATURE PRINCIPLES;
52~INTERCOLUMNIATION; AND
71~TRIGLYPHS.

## 60
## SEAM LOCATION AT
## BEAM BOTTOM

BUILT-UP BEAMS NATURALLY
INCLUDE SEAMS BETWEEN BEAM
COMPONENTS. SEAMS BETWEEN
THE BEAM FACES AND BEAM
BOTTOM SHOULD BE LOCATED
ON THE UNDERSIDE OF THE
BEAM.

*Don't make the beam bottom wider than the beam. Improperly placed beam bottom leaks easier and looks flimsy.*
*1: This may be one of the worst violations of this pattern. 2: This one is a bit better, but is still incorrect. It is also confusing, because the beam bottom looks like an extra (and unnecessary) taenia.*

DON'T

There are both utilitarian and visual reasons for this pattern. The utilitarian reasons are quite simple: Water runs more easily into a horizontal joint where water is entering from the side than into a vertical joint where water is entering from the bottom, simply because of gravity. Gravity pulls water out of the vertical joint, but does not prevent it from running into the horizontal one. The best wood beam bottom detail includes a beam bottom board that is rabbeted about 3/8" wide and 3/8" deep on both outside edges. When installed, the rabbets appear to be (and function as) a pair of drips, which keep rainwater from running back along the underside of the beam bottom.

One additional utilitarian reason has to do with the difficulty of installing the beam bottom exactly flush with the bottoms of both the outside and the inside beam face. The rabbets separate the beam bottom from the beam faces by

1

2

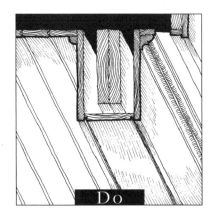

*Do install the beam bottom between the beam face boards. Who would not want to build something so that it sheds water better and looks more solid?*
*1: This is the ideal version of this pattern, where the routed edges of the beam bottom appears to be a pair of drips in a solid architrave. 2: This is more common but not quite ideal, because while solving all of the water problems, it still makes it obvious that the beam is constructed of thin lumber, not solid timbers.*

1

2

3/8", making small inaccuracies difficult to see.

The other function of this detail is visual: The beam looks more substantial if it hides the fact that it is constructed of thin boards. The double-drip beam bottom detail leaves open the possibility that the beam could be a solid wood timber with two grooves routed into its underside. A beam bottom installed below the two beam faces with a horizontal joint leaves no doubt that the beam is built of thin boards, and implies that everything else about the house is less substantial as well. The structural beam, of course, is inside the finish beam and should be fully capable of carrying the load, but the design is responsible not only for carrying the load, but also for looking as though it can.

SEE APPARENT STRUCTURE (PAGE 11); 13~TRIM; 46~BEAM MATERIALS; 51~ENTABLATURE PRINCIPLES, AND 53~PORCH BEAM.

[187]

# CHAPTER 10
~
# EAVES

## Eave Materials

[188]

# Eave Configurations

## 61
# EAVE RETURN CAP MATERIAL

**THE EAVE RETURN CAP SHOULD BE BUILT OF CONTINUOUS, UN-SEAMED METAL FLASHING.**

The eave return cap occurs at the bottom of the tympanum on gable walls. Some eaves return only a short distance on gable walls, while others return across the entire width of the wall. In either case, the cap material should be detailed so as to be unseen. Part of the issue has to do with the slope of the return cap, which is discussed later. The rest of the issue, however, has to do with the materials that are used.

It is common practice today to try to call as much attention as possible to the eave return cap. The reasons for this are unclear, but the over articulation of the eave return cap seems to have occurred hand in hand with the development of the "McMansion," the now-familiar house form that tries to put as much visual "interest" on the front wall of the house as possible, including multiple intersecting gables, two-story arched entry members, and as many circle-head windows as can possibly fit within the walls. Unfortunately, there is rarely room within the budget after the fireworks eruption on the

*Don't call attention to the eave return cap. All of the examples below turn the eave return cap on as steep an angle as is practical and accentuate it with ribbed roofing panels. In three of the four examples, the copper roofing used is far more expensive than the roofing used elsewhere on the house, all for the purpose of calling attention to a surface that should not be seen.*

*Do detail the eave return cap so that it is unseen. All of the examples below turn the eave return cap to a very shallow angle, hiding it from view. This allows it to be covered with a simple continuous piece of flashing rather than short sections of expensive ribbed roofing.*

front wall to purchase anything more than simple windows on the side and rear walls.

It should come as no surprise then, that the overheated, ill informed attempt at "traditional design" on the front wall of a McMansion would take an element that should be invisible and morph it into a "design element." The eave return cap today either is executed as shiny copper flashing with as many ribs as possible, to call more attention to it, or is executed as rough-textured "architectural" asphalt shingles. In reality, it should be nothing more than a piece of continuous flashing from one end of the return to the other, ideally with no seams at all. These practices take the notion of the Celebration of the Act of Building and turn it on its head by celebrating the wrong thing.

SEE CELEBRATION OF THE ACT OF BUILDING (PAGE 12); 1~SIMPLICITY OF MASSING; 67~EAVE RETURN; 73~METAL ROOFING MATERIAL; 74~SHINGLE ROOFING MATERIAL; AND 79~OVERLAPPING GABLES.

## 62
## TRIM UNDER
## CORNICE

THE TRIM IMMEDIATELY
BELOW THE CORNICE SHOULD
NEVER BE A CROWN MOLD. IN
MOST CASES, IT SHOULD BE A
BED MOLD OR SIMILAR SHAPE.

The crown is composed primarily of a cyma recta, or ogee, usually separated from a small cove by a fillet. The crown is reserved for a very few special places in architecture, which are always at the top, or the crown, of a collection of elements. It is appropriate, of course, at the top of a cornice. It also can be appropriate at the top of the casing of an important window. Inside, of course, a crown may be used at the very top of a wall. Beyond these locations, crown mold simply should not be used.

Unfortunately, it is common practice to install crown mold as the lowest element of the cornice, just above the frieze. This practice is purely the result of poor understanding of traditional architecture; it is virtually impossible to find crown mold at the bottom of the cornice of any buildings built before 1925.

There are a number of distinct shapes that may be used in this location, but they all have one commonality: They are shapes designed as supporting elements, not crowning

*Don't overdo the trim under the cornice, or use inappropriate shapes. Crown mold at the bottom of the cornice, rather than at the top where it belongs, is an almost totally modern phenomenon, and also an incorrect one. 1: The most common version of this error is crown under the fascia. This is akin to wearing a hat under one's chin. 2: A less common version is a collection of overdone indeterminate shapes as bed molding.*

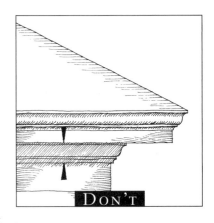

DON'T

1

2

1

3

2

*Do use bed molds specific to the order of the building, if it is a specific classical order. If not, the Tuscan convention of a simple bed (quarter round over fillet over cove) is the best option. 1: Simple bed under modillions in an Ionic entablature. 2: Large simple bed in vernacular Greek Doric cornice. 3: Small bed and block in vernacular open cornice. 4: Modillions over egg-and-dart ovolo over bead over band over cyma reversa in Corinthian.*

4

elements. The cyma reversa, or reverse ogee, is the ultimate supporting shape. It is composed of an ovolo over and transitioning smoothly into a cavetto. Separating the ovolo and cavetto by a small fillet creates the bed mold. Other appropriate shapes are the ovolo, whether circular or elliptical, with fillets above and/or below. There are more elaborate versions, of course, such as the three-part composition of cyma recta on band, ovolo with fillet, and band below. But in every case, these shapes all appear to support the load above. Finally, larger-scale cornices may be enriched with corbels, modillions, brackets, and dentils. All such enrichments should be designed consistent with the order of the architecture.

Use of a standard bed mold as the lowest member of a cornice would be a mistake in only a tiny fraction of buildings. Appropriately sized bed molds are smaller than the crowns currently being used; but as more builders learn how incorrect crowns are in this location and begin using beds instead, the cost will drop.

SEE 13~TRIM; 64~EAVE MATERIALS; 66~EAVE OVERHANG AND ENCLOSURE; 69~BRACKETS, CORBELS, AND MODILLIONS; AND 70~DENTIL SIZE AND PROPORTION.

## 63
## GUTTER AND
## DOWNSPOUT
## MATERIALS

EXPOSED GUTTERS AND
DOWNSPOUTS SHOULD BE
COPPER, GALVANIZED STEEL, OR
ALUMINUM.

Copper is the ultimate gutter material, both because it is beautiful and because the only limitation to its life is physical damage. The only downside to copper, other than cost, is the fact that once it loses its initial shine, it may take years or even decades to turn to the beautiful green patina of the copper on old buildings. It is this patina, incidentally, which forms a protective coating over the surface of the copper to prevent further corrosion. As with any metal, care should be taken to verify that there will be no galvanic action between copper and other metals with which the copper has direct physical contact.

Galvanized steel was the standard U.S. gutter material a half century ago. For many years it has been substantially cheaper than copper, and it is stronger than either copper or aluminum. Coating steel objects with zinc creates galvanized steel. Galvanized steel may be either hot-dipped or electroplated. Electroplated galvanic coatings are shiny, but they are also thin and highly susceptible to wear. Hot-

dipped galvanic coatings are much thicker and are dull and splotchy in appearance. Currently, almost all galvanized steel gutters are hot-dipped, as they should be. Unfortunately, over time, even hot-

dipped galvanic coatings will wear off, so galvanized steel gutters will someday rust.

Aluminum gutters have become the new favorite gutters in the United States, and are now the least expensive

*Don't: Plastic is weaker than metal, requiring thicker members and connectors. The thickness of the members is fairly easy to hide, but the thickness of the connections is not.*

*Don't: Transitions from one plastic component to another can get exceptionally clumsy. Many of these connectors break very easily, too, when used at ground level subject to normal abuse from people, pets, and lawn mowers.*

*Don't: One could argue that most people may someday become accustomed to the look of plastic fittings, but if the best we can hope for is to acclimate ourselves to continually less substantial construction, then what will we leave to our children?*

purely as a result of supply and demand. Aluminum is softer, so rolls of aluminum are more easily formed into gutters and can be roll-formed as opposed to galvanized steel, which must be break-formed. Break-formed metal usually can be no longer than 10', or never longer than 20', because those are the most common lengths of metal breaks. This creates frequent joints in galvanized gutters that are missing in aluminum gutters. Indeed, most aluminum gutter installations include joints only at corners. The downside to roll-forming machines is that they are quite expensive. This motivates gutter installers to buy machines only for the most common gutter shapes. This means that if a particular shape is not popular in an area, it probably will not be available in aluminum and will therefore be more expensive.

SEE 65~EAVE CONTINUITY; 66~EAVE OVERHANG AND ENCLOSURE; 67~EAVE RETURN; AND 68~GUTTER AND DOWNSPOUT SHAPES.

Do: Galvanized steel may be formed into many shapes, including the classic half-round gutter and round downspout. It is shown here painted.

Do: Galvanized steel may also be used unpainted if desired. This looks best with the most vernacular styles, which tend to be simpler, less adorned, and more utilitarian.

Do: Copper gutters and downspouts are usually left unpainted to weather to a soft green patina over the years, which protects them from corrosion indefinitely.

## 64
## EAVE MATERIALS

ALL PARTS OF THE EAVES,
INCLUDING THE FASCIA AND
THE SOFFIT, SHOULD BE BUILT
TO REFLECT EITHER STONE
CONSTRUCTION OR WOOD
CONSTRUCTION. MATERIALS
MAY INCLUDE WOOD OR
STUCCO, BUT SHOULD
CERTAINLY NOT INCLUDE
RIBBED VINYL OR ALUMINUM
SHEETS.

Stone eaves, of course, are the ultimate, but most architects and contractors go through an entire career without seeing a single stone eave. For centuries architects have been designing eaves that are built to resemble stone from materials other than stone. A quick walk around historic Charleston neighborhoods reveals numerous stucco eave details, ranging from simple eaves to full entablatures. Stucco still makes great sense here, since it can be shaped precisely without having to conform to stock molding profiles and has a surface appearance similar to stone. If scored and finished properly, a stucco entablature is indiscernible from stone.

Wood has always been the predominant eave material in the United States. All parts of wooden eaves should be constructed of one of the "eternal woods," since nothing else will endure the weather abuse that eaves must endure. This is not so difficult for the flat

*Don't fall for the claim that aluminum and vinyl are maintenance-free. They are advertised as being maintenance-free materials, but why would you want to install something distasteful that will stay that way for a long time and then eventually get much worse? Some of the aluminum and vinyl detailing problems are as follows: 1: Aluminum ripples and waves when wrapped around pressure-treated eave or rake members. And this is the best it will ever look. 2: Vinyl dentil mold has never been properly designed, although it technically could be. As is, it loudly proclaims the fact that the building is cheaply built. Vinyl salesmen may complain at this statement, but for what other reason does anyone ever use vinyl other than to supposedly save money over the life of the material? 3: Vinyl soffits have no chance of passing the test of the Eyes Only Rule. 4: It is standard practice to install vinyl siding all the way up to the soffit with no frieze whatsoever.*

1

2

3

4

*Do use proper eave materials.* 1: *Wood eaves have a long and noble history in the U.S. Their two biggest problems today are the inferiority of wood today that is genetically engineered for fast growth at the expense of durability and the lack of appropriately sized shapes for very large eaves. Synthetic replacements promise to solve the first problem. The laws of supply and demand can solve the second.* 2: *Stucco eaves have an equally long but less pervasive history here. Stucco is the only material capable of being inexpensively formed into very large shapes. It is enormously important to heed the cautions in 12~Stucco if EIFS (synthetic stucco) is used for eave details. Stone eaves are much more expensive and therefore much rarer than stucco, but have a similar appearance since the stucco eaves are intended to look like stone.* 3: *Stamped metal eaves are rare today, but show signs of making a comeback. Stock shapes are used, but they can be designed to any size.* 4: *Main Streets in the U.S. were once built with brick eaves.*

1

2

3

4

pieces, which are commonly available in weather-resistant woods. The problem occurs with special shapes, such as crowns or bed molds, which are rarely available in any material except pine, which will not endure weather, even if painted. This is one instance in which building with proper materials will cost more money at the beginning, but will save money over the life of the building.

It is becoming standard practice on lower-priced homes to construct eaves of pressure-treated pine, wrap the trim boards with aluminum, and finish the soffit with ribbed vinyl in the interest of "maintenance-free" construction. Unfortunately, this is a costly myth. It is true that these materials do not rot or require paint. It is not true, however, that they require no maintenance. The maintenance cycle may be somewhat longer, but when it does occur due to physical damage, then there is no way to repair a small area, because the replacement material will never match the weathered condition of the surrounding original materials, requiring the replacement of all eave materials on the entire house.

SEE 66~EAVE OVERHANG AND ENCLOSURE; 67~EAVE RETURN; AND 72~FRIEZE.

## 65
## EAVE CONTINUITY

EAVES SHOULD BE AS
CONTINUOUS AS POSSIBLE,
BOTH HORIZONTALLY AND
VERTICALLY.

This pattern should more than make up for the extra money spent complying with the last one. "McMansions," as described earlier, waste enormous amounts of money trying to win the subdivision's prize for throwing the greatest number of gables and roof breaks on the front of a house, all in the name of "street appeal." Many of these houses are built of brick veneer, which means that every small gable that sits on the big hip roof must have some means of supporting the brick veneer on the sides of the gable. This was not difficult in old buildings where brick walls were a foot thick or more and continued down to the foundation. Today, however, there is likely to be nothing below, requiring structural steel gymnastics to support the brick veneer. Even if the house is not coated in brick, however, something must be installed on all those walls between broken roof lines. A roof only has to break by a foot or so to cost hundreds, if not thousands of dollars. The important issue isn't how deep the break is, but how wide it is. A 1'-deep break in

Don't use hyperactive eave lines. They are built this way in the name of street appeal, but simply cost more money than calmer eave lines.

Don't: Several breaks in horizontal eaves create many roof planes. If the house is brick or stone, there can be serious problems supporting the masonry walls over roof areas below.

Don't: Multiple breaks in raking cornices also create many roof planes. The only significant difference is the shape of the additional wall areas that are created. This also creates structural problems if the walls are brick.

Don't: Eaves can also hyperactively jump up and down along the edges of a single major tent of roof mass such as this one. The structural issues may be reduced, but this is still visually tiring and costs more money than a simple roof.

*Do build simple eave lines to accompany a simple roof. This is possible on a street that is itself appealing so that the house won't be burdened with having so much "street appeal." Roof lines on beautiful streets can be calmer. Look at nearly any historic neighborhood to verify this fact.*

*A single large hip roof with two levels of entry gable and a wrap-around porch creates a gracious welcome, yet costs thousands less than multiple roof breaks.*

*Single hip roof with entry porch is simply elegant in its calmness.*

*The ultimate in simplicity is the single gable. Here, it extends to cover a double-gallery porch.*

a roof 40' wide requires 40' of roofing cuts, eave flashing, cornice, frieze, sheathing, wall studs, step flashing, counter flashing, and probably some siding thrown in for good measure— and that's if the house is coated in siding, not brick.

Traditional buildings are not beautiful because they throw more elements on the front wall than their neighbors; they are beautiful because they are well proportioned and well composed. "McMansions" may well be the first big gasp of traditional architecture upon surfacing again after almost drowning for a half-century, but it is now time to move on. And in this case, moving on to simpler roof lines and calmer details will save the owner money.

SEE 1~SIMPLICITY OF MASSING; 2~HIERARCHY OF MASSING; 3~SIMPLICITY OF PROPORTION; 64~EAVE MATERIALS; 66~EAVE OVERHANG AND ENCLOSURE; 78~BAY ROOFS; AND 79~OVERLAPPING GABLES.

## 66
### EAVE OVERHANG AND ENCLOSURE

EAVE OVERHANGS SHOULD
BE APPROPRIATE TO THE
STYLE OF THE BUILDING. THIS
WILL USUALLY BE LESS THAN
THE 18" TO 24" OVERHANGS
COMMONLY USED IN TRACT
HOUSES. CLASSICAL BUILDINGS
SHOULD USUALLY HAVE CLOSED
EAVES, WHEREAS VERNACULAR
BUILDINGS USUALLY HAVE OPEN
EAVES. EXPOSED RAFTER TAILS
SHOULD NOT EXCEED 6" IN
HEIGHT.

Buildings that speak an existing architectural language should take great care to follow the prescribed eave proportions of that language. In other words, be fluent in whatever language you choose. Classically detailed cornices should overhang no farther than their height. In other words, if the eave (not counting the frieze board) is 6" tall, it should only overhang 6". Clearly, this is a commonly violated principle. Less classically detailed eaves may overhang more, but generally not as far as tract house eaves did for decades. Open eaves are those where the rafter tails are exposed to view, whereas closed eaves have a soffit or other trim board that covers the rafter tails.

Oversized tract house eaves normally possess one Modernist architectural gene: Frank Lloyd Wright's Prairie Style eaves. Unfortunately, most

*Don't allow the eave overhang to conflict with the style of the building.*
*1: This house is vaguely Georgian, but its pork chop eaves obey none of the rules of classical eave proportion. Also, the gutters are placed too high so that a sheet of ice sliding off the roof in winter would rip the gutter off, among many other problems. 2: Pork chop eave is larger yet, with a tiny porch beam.*
*3: The Ionic columns support an entablature that's missing the architrave and that bears no resemblance to the Ionic order. 4: The eave is more reserved here, but the porch beam and arch are a mess.*
*5: Based on the width of this eave, the cornice on this attempt at classicism should be as deep as the entire entablature.*

DON'T

1

2

3

4

5

1

2

3

4

5

*Do make closed eaves on the more clas-sical buildings. They should have a cor-nice that is as deep as it is tall as shown in this drawing. As the building becomes more vernacular, the overhang generally may increase. 1: Classical Doric entab-lature rigorously follows the proportions of the order. 2: Very vernacular porch with wide, open eaves appropriate to the language. 3: This photo shows the eaves of two adjacent buildings. The one in the foreground is midrange between clas-sical and vernacular, with partially open eaves, while the one in the background is purely vernacular and totally open. 4: Large open eaves of a "peasant classical" building, are vernacular at heart, but with small ennobling details such as the scrolled rafter tails. 5: High midrange eaves are a bit wider than classical.*

tract houses are not built on the prairie, and any other stylistic genes they have are usually classical in nature, so the proportions of their eaves contradict the rest of the house and confuse the viewer. The wide overhang is inappropri-ate for almost every style other than the Prairie Style.

Eaves on classical buildings should probably be closed due to the refinement of the building. Closed eaves add at least a rafter or truss header, a fascia board, a soffit board, and a continuous vent to the open eave. Properly detailed classical eaves add a crown and a bed mold as a minimum, and probably more. Properly detailed closed eaves, there-fore, have at least six more pieces than the open eave, all of which cost money. Almost all buildings on the vernacular end of the traditional spec-trum should be built with open eaves, using the savings on other items. Even mid-range buildings can be built with open eaves: look at all the multimillion-dollar houses with open eaves in Seaside, Florida, for example. Only the most classical buildings should invariably have closed eaves.

SEE 51~ENTABLATURE PRINCIPLES; 62~TRIM UNDER CORNICE; 64~EAVE MATERIALS; 65~EAVE CONTINUITY; 72~FRIEZE; 78~BAY ROOFS; AND 79~OVERLAPPING GABLES.

## 67
## EAVE RETURN

EAVES SHOULD ALWAYS BE TRIMMED IN SUCH A MANNER THAT THE CORONA, OR FASCIA, RETURNS AROUND THE CORNER AND DIES INTO THE WALL WITHOUT THE EXCESS TRIANGLE ATTACHED TO THE RAKING CORNICE. THE SLOPE OF THE EAVE RETURN CAP SHOULD IDEALLY BE 1:12; IN NO CASE SHOULD IT BE GREATER THAN 2:12. THE CORONA, OR FASCIA, OF THE RAKING AND BOTTOM CORNICES SHOULD OCCUR IN THE SAME PLANE. THE CYMATIUM, OR CROWN, SHOULD OCCUR ONLY ON THE RAKING CORNICE.

The infamous pork chop eave has a questionable heritage and is the flagship of cheap tract house construction. Its origins may be uncertain, but its history is not. It began appearing around 1925, near the beginning of the Great Decline. By the end of World War II, it had become the only way that eave returns were trimmed in the United States. A half-century later, we're still trying to undo the damage. There are many good ways to resolve the eave with the raking cornice, all of which are specific to the style of the building. Specific styles are outside the scope of this book, so look for good examples of the style built before 1910 for the best precedent.

The cap material of the eave return was discussed earlier.

*Don't build the Pork Chop Eave. 1: Pork chop eave with picture-framed frieze. 2: Almost right, except for double crown and other minor issues. Only the cove of the crown should return; ogee should only follow the roof. 3: Pork chop, numerous other issues. 4: Eave returns, but with steep cap. 5: Raking cornice does not align with horizontal cornice. 6: Pork chop is surrounded by numerous problems and contradictions. How quickly can you count seven?*

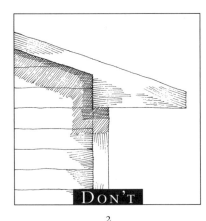

DON'T

1

2

3

4

5

6

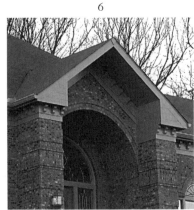

Do

1

2

*Do build proper eave returns. 1: Gable rafter approximates cymatium in this structurally expressive low classical.*
*2: Flat board as cymatium, classical bones with vernacular proportions in this midrange example. 3: Fully classical proportions and design with simple flat shapes. 4: Higher classical incorporates fully shaped classical parts.*
*5: Italianate eave return. 6: High classical components, although the dragon and eagle are admittedly not required.*

It should be a simple piece of flashing designed not to be seen. That will be possible only if the slope of the eave return cap is very low. Current practice is to install the cap at a slope of 12:12 or more. That slope should ideally be 1:12, or certainly no more than 2:12. The only exception to this pattern occurs where a gable sits on a larger roof with the outside edge of both roofs in the same plane. In this case, it is appropriate to let the eave return slope more steeply because it is, in fact, the same plane as the larger roof.

Another common eave return error is to install the raking cornice behind the horizontal cornice. The outside edge of the raking cornice should always be plumb with the outside edge of the horizontal cornice of a gable.

SEE 51~ENTABLATURE PRINCIPLES; 61~EAVE RETURN CAP MATERIAL; AND 64~EAVE MATERIALS.

3

4

5

6

## 68
## GUTTER AND
## DOWNSPOUT SHAPES

EXPOSED GUTTERS SHOULD
BE HALF-ROUND, ALTHOUGH
OGEE GUTTERS MAY BE USED IN
RARE INSTANCES WHERE THEY
ARE DETAILED CORRECTLY.
DOWNSPOUTS SHOULD BE
ROUND IN ALL CASES.

Few items except maybe the pork chop eave are as indicative of cheap tract house construction as rectangular corrugated downspouts. The corrugations are designed to give strength to a member that would otherwise be so weak that it would be easily dented and damaged. Round downspouts are stronger due simply to the inherent strength of tubular objects, and they should be the only type of downspout used.

Ogee gutters were originally designed to be part of a classical cornice, forming the cymatium. Unfortunately, they have been improperly used for so long that only a very few people understand their proper use. Properly used ogee gutters sit on a narrow ledge created by the top edge of the corona, or fascia of the cornice. A large cove should be installed immediately below the gutter, which should be oversized enough to allow it to run horizontally. If installed in this manner, the gutter and the cove work together to

*Don't misuse ogee gutter. 1: Use of the ogee gutter in this example is one of many improper elements here. See how quickly you can find ten errors in this photo. 2: Ogee gutters and crimped rectangular downspouts have become totally discredited as proper architectural elements due to their long association with cheap tract house construction. The ogee gutter could be used as a cymatium of a single size of entablature, but it is unlikely the downspout will ever recover.*

1

2

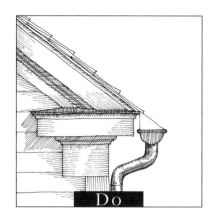

create a complete crown at the top of the corona. Dead-level gutters, however, either must be 6" wide or must have very frequent downspouts to allow for the fact that they do not slope to the downspouts. This drives the sizes of every other cornice member if the cornice is properly propor-

*Do: See how the half-round gutter tends to blend into a classical cornice and disappear? It does its job far better than the ogee gutter simply because the shape is very simple with a single gradation of shade and no sharp breaks within the shape like the ogee gutter has.*

*Do: The half-round gutter and round downspout look perfectly natural on a very vernacular building. An ogee gutter, due to its shape, can be nothing but classical, but unless used as a cymatium with appropriately sized cove below, it is an improper use of a classical shape.*

*Do: Half-round gutter tends to become part of the eave shape of a very simple midrange roof edge.*

tioned, creating a cornice that is almost too large for some single-story walls and that is only appropriate on very classical buildings.

Half-round gutters solve all these problems. Half-round gutters are not constrained to extremely classical buildings, but may be installed on vernacular buildings, including those with open eaves. Half-round gutters, because they are attached close to but not integral with the cornice, can slope to drain if necessary. They are more resistant to damage owing to their cylindrical shape. In the event of a clogged downspout, they allow overflow water to pass between them and the cornice, unlike ogee gutters that flood (and rot) the cornice. Because they are slightly detached from the cornice, they also allow the cornice to be as classically detailed as desired without detracting from the detail. The only downside is that half-round gutters are not currently used frequently enough to make it worth most installers' money to buy a roll-forming machine, which drives up the cost— for now.

SEE 63~GUTTER AND DOWNSPOUT MATERIALS.

## 69
## BRACKETS, CORBELS, AND MODILLIONS

VERNACULAR BRACKETS SHOULD EXTEND AT LEAST TO THE FASCIA, IF NOT SLIGHTLY BEYOND. THEIR HEIGHT IS OFTEN AS GREAT AS THEIR DEPTH. ITALIANATE BRACKETS FOLLOW SIMILAR GUIDELINES. CLASSICAL CORBELS OR MODILLIONS SHOULD EXTEND TO THE DRIP OF THE SOFFIT. THEIR HEIGHT IS USUALLY ONE-THIRD TO ONE-HALF OF THEIR DEPTH.

Vernacular brackets are usually constructed of square wood framing such as 4x4's. They are not just decorative, but actually support the gable rafters or eave beams, so they should project at least to the outside of the members they support. As with most things vernacular, they should be designed to make the most efficient use of the material, which generally involves framing at a 45° angle. Shallower angles are weaker, whereas steeper angles waste material. The only member that may be thinner than square is the backplate of the bracket that occurs at the wall. This member may be as little as 1½" thick.

Italianate brackets follow the same general outline as vernacular brackets, but are much more elaborate. They are nearly always carved, usu-ally in large compound curved

*Don't make the most common error of brackets, modillions, and corbels, which is not extending them to the edge of the eave. Often, this is the result of the overhang being too wide, a result of Prairie Style eave infection in styles where it does not belong. Some styles, such as Italianate, should have very wide eaves. In these cases, the brackets are simply undersized and make the building look as if the builder ran out of money while finishing the cornice.*

DON'T

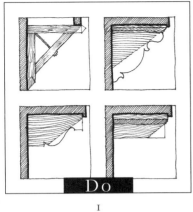

*Do properly size brackets, modillions, and corbels of all styles to extend to the back side of the fascia. Note from the drawings that properly sized elements catch sunshine at their outer faces and contours, rendering them pleasantly, while undersized elements remain forever in shadow. 1: Brick Italianate. 2: New Urban Italianate. 3: Greek Revival Classical. 4: Wooden Italianate. 5: New Urban Vernacular. 6: Federal Classical.*

shapes. Unfortunately, there are almost no good stock Italianate brackets as of the date of this writing. That will change if enough people demand them, which is likely to happen due to the current revival of the style.

"Corbel," "modillion," and "bracket" are terms that are used almost interchangeably with classical entablature details. All three words describe large supporting elements mounted under the corona and against the top member of the bed moldings. Classical corbels or modillions are often close to square when viewed from the end, but their projection is usually 2 to 3 times their height or width depending, of course, on the cornice detail. Corbels or modillions usually have plain vertical sides, but their undersides are almost always scrolled or otherwise shaped in a simple elemental pattern. Corbels or modillions may be included in the same bed moldings with dentils if properly detailed.

SEE 13~TRIM; 62~TRIM UNDER CORNICE; 64~EAVE MATERIALS; 66~EAVE OVERHANG AND ENCLOSURE; AND 70~DENTIL SIZE AND PROPORTION.

1

2

3

4

5

6

## 70
## DENTIL SIZE AND PROPORTION

DENTILS SHOULD USUALLY BE SMALL SQUARE OR VERTICALLY RECTANGULAR BLOCKS AND SHOULD BE LOCATED JUST BELOW THE CORONA AS A PART OF THE BED MOLDINGS. DENTILS SHOULD GENERALLY BE 6 TO 7.5 PERCENT OF THE HEIGHT OF THE ENTABLATURE, AND THEY SHOULD BE SQUARE IN PLAN.

Dentils are small, closely spaced blocks that are part of Ionic, Corinthian, or Composite bed moldings. Their name comes from their resemblance to human teeth, which is another reflection in architecture of elements of the human body. Dentils may be the only enrichments to the moldings, or they may be used with corbels, modillions, or brackets, and if so, they almost always occur below the corbels, modillions, or brackets. Dentils are usually square in plan and either may be perfect cubes or may be taller than they are wide and deep. Dentils should be detailed based on good examples of the order of the entablature, which will usually result in dentils between 6 and 7.5 percent of the total entablature height.

The most common dentil mistake is, unfortunately, almost the only way they are built today— the so-called

*Don't use flat 1x4 dentil blocks. Every example below is oversized in height and width but undersized in thickness. It is as if the homebuilding community has said, "By golly, if we're going to have dentils, we're going to get the biggest bang for the buck that we can get," and has made cartoons of dentils the thickness of a single trim board turned flat. 1: Vinyl dentil band. 2 - 5: Architectural buck teeth in gables. 6: Are chamfered edges sold as a "feature"?*

DON'T

1

2

3

4

5

6

**Do**

*Do proportion and size dentils so that they are very clearly based on classical proportions when the building is classical. Vernacular buildings can also have dentils, but they are based more closely on construction elements.*
*1 – 4: These are all examples from strictly classical buildings of various styles and orders. 5: Vernacular brick dentils composed of alternating rowlock brick. 6: Midrange building with exposed rafter tails acting as dentils.*

"dentil mold." Dentil mold consists of a band of wood into which the contour of the dentils is cut. This could work successfully, if not for the thickness of dentil mold: scarcely over ¼". As a result, dentil mold becomes nothing more than a cartoon of real dentils. An entablature would be better served to have no dentils of any sort than to have dentil mold.

SEE 13~TRIM;
51~ENTABLATURE PRINCIPLES;
62~TRIM UNDER CORNICE;
64~EAVE MATERIALS; AND
69~BRACKETS, CORBELS, AND
MODILLIONS.

1

2

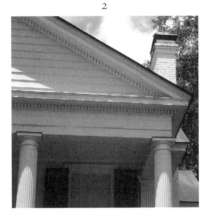

3

4

5

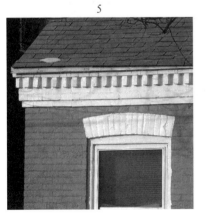

6

# TRIGLYPHS

**TRIGLYPHS SHOULD BE COMPOSED OF THREE VERTICAL PARTS.**

Triglyphs originated as the ends of triple ceiling beams that projected through the frieze and were chamfered at the edges. Triglyphs, as is obvious from their name, are composed of three parts, as they have been for over 2000 years. Triglyphs composed of any other number of parts are not really triglyphs, but are the sign of an uninformed designer or manufacturer.

Triglyphs occur only on the Doric order (both Greek and Roman). The space on the frieze between each triglyph is called the metope. Metopes may be left plain or enriched with raised ornamental motifs. Triglyphs extend the full height of the frieze, and usually they engage both the bed moldings above and the taenia and architrave below.

Engagement of the bed moldings usually consists of a thin block attached to the face of the lowest element of the bed moldings, which is usually flat. The block is required because the triglyph is usually thicker than the lowest bed element. The triglyph head block extends to the surface of the second bed element.

*Don't use the wrong number of glyphs. They are called triglyphs because they should be composed of three elements. The drawing shows more than three glyphs, separated by routed channels that are too narrow and stop short at the bottom. Also, the guttae are missing. 1: "Quadglyphs," too broad at top, thickness too shallow. 2: "Quadglyphs," and they don't match columns, thin guttae stuck on thin backboard. 3: "Quintglyphs," too few guttae, etc.*

DON'T

1

2

3

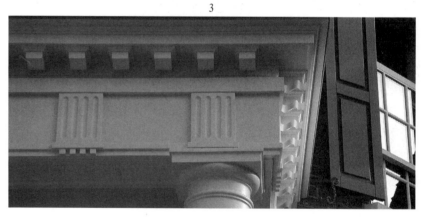

[210]

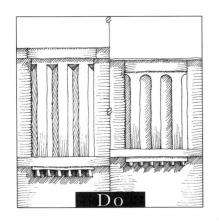

*Do build proper triglyphs. Drawing shows Roman triglyph on the left and Greek triglyph on the right, although elements have interchanged dating back to antiquity. 1: Decent modern example, except for Roman Doric placement that is too wide on an otherwise Greek Doric building. 2: Example from within the past two centuries. 3: This example was built in about 450 B.C. in the Greek colony of Paestum, Italy contemporary with the Parthenon.*

1

2

3

Engagement of the taenia and architrave consists of a narrow block the same width and thickness as the triglyph that attaches just below the triglyph. There are six equally spaced cylinders (Greek) or cones (Roman) called guttae that project from the bottom of this block, two below each glyph. Some stories place the origin of the guttae as being symbolic of blood dripping off the burnt offering. The more likely explanation is that they descended from pegs that connected the beams of timber construction that was the pattern that classical stone buildings emulated. Guttae occasionally are pyramid-shaped with flat sides rather than cones or cylinders.

Chamfers at the edge of each glyph are elliptically curved in most Greek Doric buildings, usually arched at the top. Roman Doric chamfers, however, were composed entirely of straight lines and mitered corners. Triglyphs are always evenly spaced along an entire colonnade, with columns centered under triglyphs.

SEE 5~REGULAR ARRANGEMENT OF COLUMNS AND OPENINGS; 13~TRIM; 51~ENTABLATURE PRINCIPLES; 52~INTERCOLUMNIATION; 59~TRIGLYPH/COLUMN ALIGNMENT; 64~EAVE MATERIALS; AND 72~FRIEZE.

## 72
### FRIEZE

A FRIEZE BOARD OF SOME
SORT SHOULD OCCUR BELOW
ALMOST EVERY EAVE, FROM THE
HIGHEST CLASSICAL TO THE
SIMPLEST VERNACULAR. IT IS
HARDLY EVER PROPER TO OMIT
THE FRIEZE ENTIRELY AND TO
RUN SIDING OR BRICK RIGHT
UP TO THE SOFFIT OR RAFTER
TAIL. THE FRIEZE SHOULD
NEVER BE PICTURE-FRAMED.

The frieze in a classical entablature is the flat, sometimes embellished panel between the cornice and the architrave. Often, in less classical examples, the architrave is eliminated, but the frieze typically is not. Even in the most vernacular examples, there almost always is a simple frieze board under the eave to avoid the awkward problem of siding or brick ramming directly into the soffit or rafter tails. This is an issue of both appearance and utility. Once, when brick buildings were constructed of real brick walls that were well over a foot thick, the brick wall was built first, then the roof was built upon it and the roof trim was installed last. Now, however, the walls are built, the roof is built and trimmed, and then brick veneer is laid to the underside of the trim. The top course is difficult enough to lay behind an existing frieze board, but would be more difficult if the frieze did not exist

*Don't omit or picture-frame the frieze. As with most errors, there are a number of ways of getting a frieze wrong. This page includes several. 1: Dentil strip rests directly on siding. Every cornice should have a frieze of some sort, but it is unthinkable that a cornice would be elaborate enough to have dentils without having a frieze. 2, 3: Frieze is picture-framed around eave return. This detail simply should not exist. A frieze either runs entirely horizontal under an eave or with the slope of a roof under a raking cornice, but should do nothing else. It is not a general-purpose trim board for the joint between brick and wood. 4: Here, the frieze gets twice as deep where it splats into the wall at each end. With even moderate workmanship, this sort of detail would be unnecessary. This proclaims exactly how far the woodwork misses the masonry and therefore how big a hole needs to be filled. Few details more clearly advertise inferior work. 5: Frieze is missing entirely.*

1

2

3

4

5

*Do construct a frieze at every eave and raking cornice. Friezes on more classical buildings should follow the proportion of the frieze in the appropriate classical order more closely. Generally, the classical frieze is at least as wide as the cornice. More vernacular friezes vary more widely. 1: Simple classical frieze. 2: Midrange building with partially exposed rafter tails over frieze. 3: Refined vernacular building with fully exposed rafter tails over frieze.*

and the brick had to be laid to the underside of the soffit.

Similar problems exist if the wall is finished with siding. First, if there is no frieze and the soffit is $1/4$" plywood, the soffit can sag noticeably with nothing solid to support it, depending on how the siding hits the top of the wall. If the cut is near the top of the board where the board is thin, it simply might not catch the soffit. Also, because of this same issue, the top joint becomes difficult to seal from the weather if adjoining pieces do not meet solidly. A frieze board joins properly to both soffit and siding or brick.

SEE 13~TRIM;
51~ENTABLATURE PRINCIPLES;
62~TRIM UNDER CORNICE;
64~EAVE MATERIALS; AND
71~TRIGLYPHS.

1

2

3

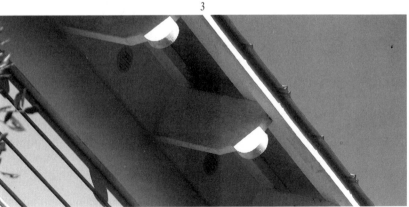

# CHAPTER 11
~
# ROOFS

## ROOF MATERIALS

# Roof Configurations

## 73
## METAL ROOFING
## MATERIAL

METAL ROOFING PANELS
SHOULD BE FLAT BETWEEN
THE PRIMARY RIBS, WITH NO
STRIATIONS OR PENCIL RIBS.

Metal roofing lay dormant in the U.S. residential market for decades, until the founding of Seaside, Florida, in the early 1980's. Seaside looked to local vernacular buildings for precedent, hoping that they might have more local wisdom to offer than the same tired old styles that had been imported to the Florida Panhandle area from elsewhere. One of the planners' discoveries was metal roofing, which reflects a high percentage of the heat of the southern sun in summer, lasts decades longer than asphalt shingles, and makes a very comforting sound when it rains. That sound is so comforting, as a matter of fact, that country musicians had been writing songs about it for decades.

Suddenly, metal roofing was all the rage. Unfortunately, most people had never dealt with it before. People would visit Seaside, then go back home and ask their roofers for metal roofing. The roofers would install it, and then the owner would notice the waviness, or "oil-canning," and would demand that the roofing be removed, insisting

that it was defective. It did not take most roofers long to learn their lesson. They realized that there was high demand for the material, but didn't want to install it twice, so they modified their rolling machines to insert small "pencil ribs" or "striations." These small ribs or breaks in

DON'T

*Don't: Striations are obvious in this standing seam roof. This looks exactly like the standing seam roofing that is used on warehouses.*

*Don't: This roofing panel is often misnamed as 5V or corrugated, but it clearly is not corrugated, nor does it contain any V's at all, much less the 5 V's per panel that gave the roofing its name. In reality, it's an indeterminate double-ribbed roofing with lots of striations.*

*Don't: This is another 5V imposter. In this case, the panel is single-ribbed with intermediate pencil-ribs instead of striations. In either case, it is an unattractive substitute for the real thing.*

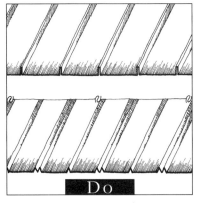

Do: True 5V roofing.

Do: True corrugated roofing.

Do: True standing seam roofing.

Do: Metal tile roofing.

the panels were techniques borrowed from metal building manufacturers to stiffen panels and prevent oil-canning on warehouse buildings.

Unfortunately, panels created with these techniques will forever look as if they belong in the warehouse district. What the owners didn't realize was that oil-canning is a natural, healthy condition of metal roofing that indicates that the roofing is moving to accommodate temperature changes. Metal roofing without oil-canning would look as unnatural as wood without grain, a tree without bark, or a beach without sand. Oil-canning is simply the natural surface texture of metal roofs.

The two acceptable metal roofing types are 5V crimp, which is the surface-attached roofing type found at Seaside, and flat-panel standing seam roofing, which is a more expensive hidden-fastener roofing type that should be installed in panels 16" to 18" wide. Standing seams should be as thin as possible ($\frac{1}{4}$" wide maximum) and as short as possible ($1\frac{1}{2}$" tall maximum). The 5V roofing and its rarer cousin, corrugated metal roofing, may be installed at slopes as low as 3:12. Standing seam metal roofing may be installed on nearly flat roofs; $\frac{1}{4}$" of slope per foot of run is usually sufficient if the seams are properly made.

SEE 74~SHINGLE ROOFING
MATERIAL AND 77~ROOF
SLOPES.

## 74
# SHINGLE ROOFING
# MATERIAL

SHINGLE ROOFING MATERIALS
SHOULD BE SLATE, WOOD
SHINGLES, OR WOOD SHAKES.
ASPHALT SHINGLES SHOULD BE
VERY STRONGLY DISCOURAGED.

Asphalt shingle roofing is
one of the really unfortunate materials that U.S. construction today has inherited
from the World War II era.
We have gotten over much
of the architectural fallout of
that period, but not asphalt
roofing. Think for a moment
about asphalt roofing: What is
the purpose of the three-tab
shingle? Why are there tabs at
all? Asphalt roofing would be
much more weather tight and
easier to install if roofers were
able to simply roll out one
roll after another that was the
same width as asphalt shingles,
but without the tabs, nailing
as they went. The answer
is that asphalt shingles are a
cheap, flimsy substitute for
slate shingles.

Recently, asphalt roofing
has also attempted to reinvent
itself as fake cedar shingles.
Nearly all the so-called "archi-
tectural-grade" shingles try to
use multiple layers of thicker
asphalt to look a little bit like
wood. The only true architectural grade shingles, however,
are made either of slate or of
wood.

*Don't: Anyone can clearly see that
the so-called "architectural grade
shingles" are a very poor fake for
the wood or slate shingles they are
meant to represent. If asphalt roofing
is unavoidable on a building, use the
lowest-profile shingle possible with the
plainest color possible so as not to draw
attention to it. Better yet, consider 5V
metal roofing, which is close to the cost
of asphalt in places where roofers have
proper experience with 5V roofing.*

DON'T

*Don't: "Architectural grade" asphalt are a cheap fake of slate shingles.*

*Don't: "Architectural grade" asphalt are a cheap fake of wood shingles.*

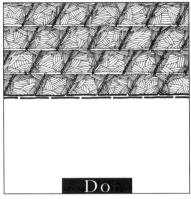

Do: Slate shingles.

*Do: The single acceptable asphalt shingle is the diamond shingle because it does not try (and fail miserably) to fake another material. Diamond shingles were widely used in the early part of the twentieth century. They are hard to find today. Wood shingles and shakes are beautiful if they tolerate the local climate. Slate shingles pay for themselves many times over because they last for centuries.*

Do: Asphalt diamond shingles.

Wood shingles or shakes, usually made of cedar, are mixed in their effectiveness. They are much more expensive than asphalt, yet scarcely last longer than asphalt in many climates in the United States. Care should be taken to research the local weathering of wood shingles before they are used.

Slate shingles, on the other hand, last many decades longer than asphalt and will not burn. There are reports of slate shingles lasting centuries, not decades, because their only natural enemy is physical abuse such as a falling tree limb, since they are made of stone. There are some promising slate-substitute materials available today which cannot be distinguished from real slate according to the Arm's Length Rule, even though the test for roofing materials should be the more generous Eyes Only Rule. The substitutes are usually made of fiber reinforced cementitious materials that should also last for decades, if not longer. Both slate and wood shingles may be used at slopes as shallow as 3:12.

SEE 73~METAL ROOFING MATERIAL; AND 77~ROOF SLOPES.

Do: Wood shingles.

Do: Wood shakes.

## 75
## TILE ROOFING
## MATERIAL

TILE ROOFING MATERIALS MAY
INCLUDE CLAY TILES, CONCRETE
TILES, OR METAL TILES.

Clay tiles are one of the most ancient of roofing types, and they have been used for centuries in some places. Properly made clay tiles may last for centuries and are fireproof. Clay tile roofing is very heavy, however, requiring heavier roof structure than most other roofing types. Its main enemy, like that of slate, is physical abuse. Maintenance traffic, for example, can crack clay tile, so rooftop equipment should be either located in areas with other roofing or removed from the roof entirely, if possible.

Clay tile roofing has one of the most distinctive appearances of any roofing type, due in part to the coarseness of the grain of the roofing. No other roofing has a height profile of several inches. Because of this, clay tile roofing cannot be used as interchangeably between styles as most roofing types, but is strongly tied to certain styles. Tile works best with stucco or masonry buildings that appear capable of supporting its considerable weight, and tile is most often identified with Mediterranean and Latin American styles

*Don't substitute plastic tiles or mis-shapen clay tiles for quality clay, concrete or metal tiles. Distinctions in tile roofing are less harsh than with other materials. Note that the tile in the top Don't illustration could be somewhat acceptable if built of clay rather than plastic. The combination of plastic, top-seamed design and shallow profile is what makes it unacceptable.*

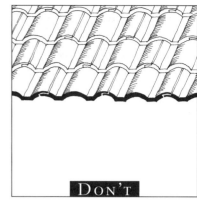

DON'T

*Don't: Dark blue plastic tile roof (with grouted ridge).*

*Don't: Mis-shaped tiles all lean slightly to the left.*

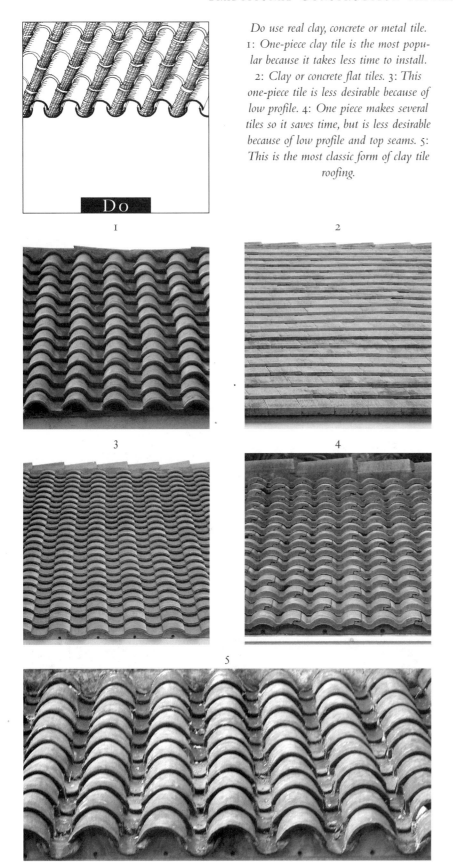

Do

1

2

3

4

5

*Do use real clay, concrete or metal tile. 1: One-piece clay tile is the most popular because it takes less time to install. 2: Clay or concrete flat tiles. 3: This one-piece tile is less desirable because of low profile. 4: One piece makes several tiles so it saves time, but is less desirable because of low profile and top seams. 5: This is the most classic form of clay tile roofing.*

that developed in areas where tile roofing is most common. Tile roofing would obviously never look proper on a clapboard Tennessee farmhouse.

Newer materials have been developed to substitute for tile roofing. These materials, however, were conceived as worthy replacements, the performance of which is equal to that of tile roofing as opposed to asphalt shingles, which were simply conceived as a cheap fake. The two most common replacement materials are concrete tiles, which are sometimes indiscernible from clay tiles, and metal tiles, which make no mistake about the fact that they are not built of clay. Clay tile or tiles of replacement materials may be composed of a single piece that looks like two or more pieces, or may be composed of individual ridge tile and valley tile, which is the purest form of tile roofing. Individual ridge and valley tile also have the highest profile, but take longer to install because there are more pieces.

SEE 74~SHINGLE ROOFING MATERIAL AND 77~ROOF SLOPES.

## 76
### RIDGE CAPS

BULBED RIDGE CAPS SHOULD
BE USED WITH 5V METAL
ROOFING. STANDING SEAM
RIDGE CAPS SHOULD BE OF THE
LOWEST PROFILE POSSIBLE.

Warehouse roofing is not
the only metal roofing mistake
made in recent years. Look
carefully at the old metal roofs,
then at many of the newer
ones. One very frequent difference lies in the nature of
the ridge caps. New ridge
caps are most often borrowed
from the warehouse district
along with the roofing, completing the image of a cheap
roof on an expensive building.
Warehouse ridge caps, however, don't just look cheap;
they also look oversized and
clunky.

5V roofing uses the bulbed
ridge cap, so named because
of the cylindrical bulb running
along the top of the cap. The
bulb is flanked by two legs of
metal about 4" wide that run
down each side of the roof.
The bulb allows the cap to be
bent to any number of typical roof slopes without being
creased, essentially creating a
"one size fits all" detail for
roof caps. The other advantage of the bulb cap is that it
can be shaped into an "eagle's
beak" at each end. The eagle's
beak not only keeps water out
of the end of the ridge cap,
but also is quite distinctive

Don't use oversized warehouse-type
ridge caps on other types of buildings.
Unacceptable ridge caps shed water
by being large enough that water
falls away from the joint between the
roofing panels at the ridge by gravity.
This makes the entire ridge cap close
to a foot wide. Many manufacturers
fabricate them with ridging to prevent
unacceptable rippling, but that in turn
makes the caps even more obtrusive.

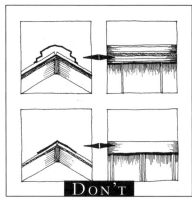

DON'T

*Don't: Wide, flat ridge cap is nearly as wide as the corner board of the bay.*

*Don't: Profiled cap ripples less but calls more attention to itself.*

[222]

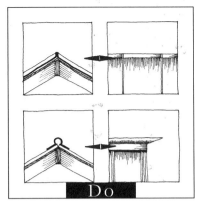

Do: Bulbed ridge cap.

Do: Eagle's beak detail.

Do: Eagle's beak detail.

*Do use low-profile or bulbed ridge caps as appropriate. The standing seam hemmed ridge is extremely low-profile, being equal in height and thickness to the standing seams themselves. Bulbed ridge cap for 5V roofing is fairly wide, but sits down tight to the V's of the roofing, so it is never more than about $^1/_2$" above the flat portion of the roof panel. The distinctive eagle's beak end detail was invented to keep water out of the bulb.*

Do: Several bulbed ridge cap conditions.

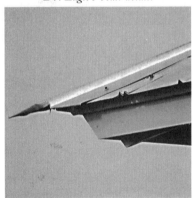

Do: Eagle's beak detail.

Do: Classic hemmed ridge.

in appearance. It is formed almost as a paper airplane is, by running the ridge cap 6" long, then folding the two corners under about the ridge of the cap, then folding under again until the "wings" are swept back and under.

Old standing seam ridges are more elegant yet, often no larger than typical standing seams. Unfortunately, this detail requires a substantial amount of fieldwork to form and crimp the ridge seams. Roofers today prefer systems that allow them to quickly throw the roof on and finish the job. If the budget allows, the old system is far preferable not only because of its clean appearance, but also because it is more waterproof. If not, the lowest-profile ridge cap available should be installed.

SEE 73~METAL ROOFING MATERIAL.

[223]

## 77
## ROOF SLOPES

ALL PRIMARY ROOF SLOPES OF
A PARTICULAR STYLE SHOULD
FALL WITHIN A RANGE OF NO
GREATER THAN 15 PERCENT.
ANCILLARY ROOF SLOPES
SHOULD BE APPROPRIATE TO
THE STYLE OF THE BUILDING,
WHICH IS IN MOST CASES
BETWEEN ONE-THIRD AND
ONE-HALF OF THE PRIMARY
ROOF SLOPE.

Most primary roof slopes are actually the same within a single building for both consistency of appearance and ease of construction. Roof slopes are strongly tied to specific styles, but each style developed in a single area, usually with consistent weather and available building materials, so the roof slopes are actually tied to climate and available materials. So what should happen to the roof slope when a particular style of building is built far from the point of origin of the style? That question is the cause of considerable debate among traditional architects.

Often, the best solution is to simply observe what has happened in the most-loved places. Over time, cultures that have migrated to other areas and have taken their styles with them have slowly modified the original styles to meet the requirements of their new homes. This approach seems the most sensible and natural, and it results in a place

*Don't vary roof slopes significantly within the same style in the same region. Arbitrary and noticeable roof slope variations within the same style in the same area simply are confusing.*

*Don't: What's the point of this variation, other than to cost more money?*

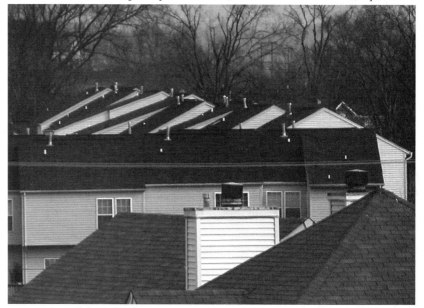

*Don't: As many slopes as above, but all in the same house!*

*Do base roof slopes on local conditions. Part of the syntax of any architectural language (style) is the roof slope rationale. This means that for a given language in a given place, all roof slopes should be about the same. Because of weather considerations, all styles in a given place will gravitate to the same general roof slope.*

*Do: Primary roof slopes at 12:12, lowest ancillary roof slopes at 4:12.*

where imported styles eventually converge on a locally ideal roof slope. Indeed, the most beautiful places on earth are often those with very similar primary roof slopes that vary by no more than 15 percent, often much less. Ancillary roof slopes may match the primary roof slope, but are more often lower when the ancillary spaces hang like saddlebags off the main volume of the building. Ancillary roof slopes are often one-half to one-third of the primary roof slope, and they are often barely steeper than the minimum allowable slope of the roofing material.

SEE 73~METAL ROOFING MATERIAL; 74~SHINGLE ROOFING MATERIAL; 75~TILE ROOFING MATERIAL; AND 78~BAY ROOFS.

*Do: Same conditions, different view.*

[225]

## 78
## BAY ROOFS

BAY ROOFS SHOULD BE
DISTINCT FROM THE PRIMARY
ROOF, AND THEY SHOULD
NORMALLY RETURN ON
THEMSELVES AT EACH END. IN
ALMOST NO CASE SHOULD THEY
BE A SHED CONTINUATION OF
THE MAIN ROOF.

The continuous shed bay roof is a remaining fragment of an extremely influential 1970's California project called Sea Ranch. This project took several steps in the right direction and opened the door for further recovery of human-based environments. Sea Ranch architecture helped to reintroduce the bay window into the lexicon of contemporary architecture, but later refinements almost always should take precedence over initial techniques. The continuous shed bay roof is clearly one such example.

Bays are most effective if they are articulated as a separate element attached to the wall, rather than confusing them with the main body of the building. This means that the peak of the bay roof should probably occur below the cornice of the main roof. This may require a lower ceiling in the bay than in the room to which it is attached, but this is usually an architectural bonus within the room, further accentuating the fact

*Don't use confusing bay roof designs. The following bay roof techniques have been used commonly in recent years, but are not desirable for reasons that should be obvious. 1: Shed continuous with main roof slope. 2: Bay pulled out to edge of main roof cornice. 3: Bay cornice with no projection whatsoever. 4: Bay roof that flares out from main roof. 5: Shed bay roof back to wall. 6: Bay roof that creates a hip in the main roof.*

DON'T

1

2

3

4

5

6

*Do make the bay roof distinct from the main roof. The following are bay roof techniques that have been developed and refined over a much longer period of time, obviously with better results. 1: Victorian bay under gable was used in several later styles. 2: Half-octagon hip in gable. 3: Nearly flat half-octagon hip against wall. 4: Flared square hip against wall. 5: Flared square hip under eave. 6: Splayed bay hip roof continuous with cornice line in gable.*

that the bay is a special, intimately scaled place for just a person or two.

Bays may be square, chamfered, or bowed. Square bays may have (from most common to least common) a hip roof, a shed roof, or a gable roof. Chamfered bays, where the side windows return to the wall at an angle (usually 45° or 60°), should almost always be roofed with a hip. A chamfered bay may occasionally be gable roofed, but it should be done only in styles such as several varieties of the Victorian that allow corner brackets to attach the chamfered side walls to the hanging corners of the gable above. Bowed bays, which are usually composed of several distinct segments but may also be curved, should be hipped. Some styles allow ancillary roofs as small as bay roofs to be almost flat, essentially causing them to disappear, even if larger ancillary roofs are steeper. All such nearly flat roofs should be finished with standing seam metal roofing.

SEE 73~METAL ROOFING MATERIAL; 74~SHINGLE ROOFING MATERIAL; AND 77~ROOF SLOPES.

1

2

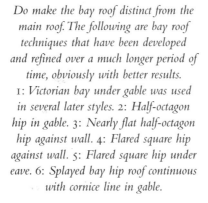

3

4

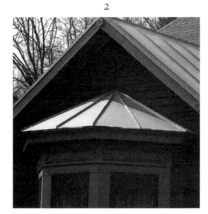

5

6

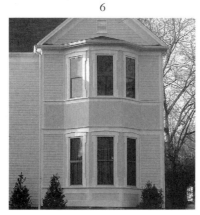

# 79
## OVERLAPPING GABLES

INAPPROPRIATE USE OF
OVERLAPPING GABLES IS ONE
OF THE GREAT SCOURGES
OF CONTEMPORARY
CONSTRUCTION. THEY SHOULD
ONLY BE USED WHEN THE
SMALLER GABLE IS PART
OF A BALCONY, PORCH, OR
ENTRANCE, OR IN THE RARE
INSTANCES WHEN THEY ARE
APPROPRIATE TO THE STYLE.

The English Arts & Crafts style of a century ago popularized the overlapping gable, which was a pattern that had appeared since medieval times in English romantic styles. The overlapping gable has recently been so influential and pervasive among non–architects that it has taken on the aura of the Victorian door: People think that they have to have one, regardless of the style of their building. As a matter of fact, the English overlapping gable, which is characterized by a smaller gable slid entirely to one side of a larger gable so that they share a roof on one side, has become a major design feature of the McMansions, a development that certainly would distress the original Arts & Crafts architects, were they alive to see it.

Very few other styles use the overlapping gable, and with good reason. It is a highly romantic feature based

*Don't use overlapping gables if they are not appropriate to the building style. Look carefully at this drawing: The core of the house is classical, but with overlapping gables growing out of it like a fungus. Also look carefully at the photos below. None of the architectural languages (styles) represented should include overlapping gables as a part of their syntax.*

Do

*Do use overlapping gables on appropriate styles only. This drawing shows an English Arts & Crafts house. The overlapping gable is a legitimate part of the English Arts & Crafts syntax. The two photos below are of houses using English medieval languages. These languages helped to spawn the Arts & Crafts language.*

strongly on the cottages of the English countryside. Because it is so specific to England, and because it excludes the entire classical end of the traditional spectrum, this pattern clearly confines itself to usefulness in only a few styles. Related styles for which this pattern is appropriate include several varieties of the Victorian. If a building is built in one of these styles, this technique can be quite powerful. Few things look as silly, however, as an overlapping gable house executed in Greek Revival details or gables growing wildly out of a Georgian house as shown in the Don't drawing.

The few exceptions for unrelated styles include gables that are part of a balcony, porch, or entrance. In each of these cases, the roof of the inner gable is usually detached from the roof of the larger gable; as a matter of fact, the smaller gable is often centered in the larger gable.

SEE 1~SIMPLICITY OF MASSING; 29~DOOR AND WINDOW STYLE VERSUS BUILDING STYLE; 65~EAVE CONTINUITY; AND 77~ROOF SLOPES.

## 80
### SKYLIGHTS

SKYLIGHTS ARE THE MOST INEFFICIENT OF GLAZING, ADMITTING THE MOST HEAT IN SUMMER AND THE LEAST IN WINTER. THEY ARE ALSO NOTORIOUSLY LEAK-PRONE AND SHOULD BE AVOIDED WHEREVER POSSIBLE. WHERE THEY MUST OCCUR, THEY SHOULD BE FLAT.

*Don't use skylights unless absolutely necessary, but in no case use the high-profile domed skylight. There is nothing beautiful about a skylight. The problem is compounded by high-profile skylights that call attention to themselves.*

DON'T

Few things are worse than a poorly performing element that calls attention to itself. Domed skylights are just such an element far too often. Flat skylights at least possess the virtue of not calling attention to themselves until they leak or make you too cold in winter or too hot in summer.

If light from above is absolutely essential, consider some form of dormer. Dormers conventionally are used to let light in horizontally to a room behind. They can also be built without floors, however, so that they admit light into a room below instead. Install a railing at the back of the dormer, and it can do both, as long as it is acceptable for the upper room to look down into the lower room. Dormers let in less light (and heat) in the summer, when the sun is high in the sky and striking vertical glass at an acute angle. The opposite is true in winter, when warmth and light are most desirable. Skylights do the exact opposite, admit-

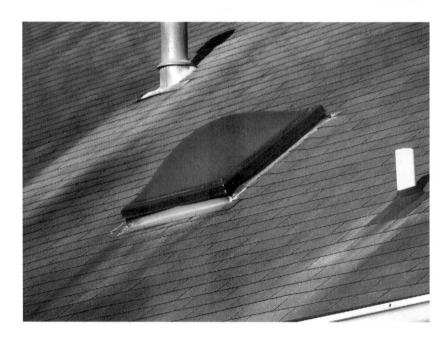

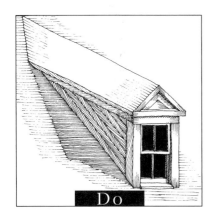

*Do use low-profile skylights if absolutely necessary. The best skylight is not a skylight at all, however, but is a dormer without a floor as discussed in detail later in this book.*

ting the most heat in summer when it is needed least from a sun high in the sky. Skylights are also dimmest in winter, when daylight is most precious. These characteristics have nothing to do with specific skylight manufacturers, but are simply the facts of life for vertical glass and nearly horizontal glass.

Another fact of nearly horizontal glass is that water does not run off it nearly so easily. Vertical glass has nowhere for water to stand, even if the glass is divided into separate panes. Horizontal glass, on the other hand, is very difficult to detail into a sash or frame without creating places for water to stand and then penetrate the system. The leaks of skylights are legendary. While leaks certainly occur in ordinary windows, they are much less frequent. Again, all this is purely a fact of the geometry of glass lying nearly flat versus glass installed vertically.

SEE 83~DORMER ROOF TRIM; 84~DORMER BODY PROPORTION; AND 85~DORMER BODY/ROOF PROPORTION.

# CHAPTER 12
~
# DORMERS

## DORMER MATERIALS

# Dormer Configurations

## 81
## DORMER JAMB
## MATERIAL

DORMER JAMB MATERIALS
SHOULD ALMOST NEVER
INCLUDE SIDING, BUT SHOULD
RATHER BE A SOLID CASING
ASSEMBLY FROM THE WINDOW
TO THE CORNER OF THE
DORMER WALL.

Dormers are similar to bays in that, because they project from the wall of a building, they should be seen primarily as framing members so that they have visual support. If they appear simply as a siding-covered box with no visible stiffening, then either the house appears to be constructed of a too-light material such as cardboard, or the dormer looks unnaturally weak. Dormers with single, strong casing boards at the corners look much more substantial than those that resemble standard windows set in a standard wall with siding.

The second reason for using a single board to case from dormer window to dormer corner is the result of the fact that dormers exist because of their windows. Usually, the windows extend almost from corner to corner. The common method is to use scrawny corner boards at the corners, 2" or narrower brick mold for window casing, and narrow slivers of siding between the two. This is significantly more

*Don't detail dormers so that siding is required between the jamb casing and the cornerboard. The dormers below represent a range of design skill, but all of them include short slivers of siding between the window casing and the dormer corner board. The dormer should be detailed so that siding in this location simply does not exist in nearly every case.*

Do

time-consuming and therefore more costly than the proper method, that is to use a single vertical jamb casing that is wide enough to extend from the edge of the sash to the corner of the dormer. One board replaces two boards plus up to a dozen little pieces of siding; there should be no question

*Do detail dormers so that they have single, strong, substantial casing boards at the corners. These examples represent a wide range of architectural languages (styles), but all have one thing in common: a single casing board or other element covers the distance between window and dormer corner without the need of siding.*

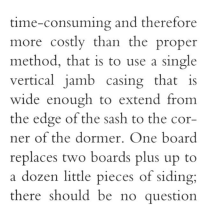

concerning which method costs most. If a single liner stud is used inside each triple-stud corner, then a 1x8 works perfectly as dormer jamb casing. If the sidewall studs are turned sideways to reduce the thickness of the walls, a 1x6 casing will work. No narrower jamb casing will work, however, without unconventional structural gymnastics to support the dormer header. Very few traditional dormer jambs are narrower than 1x6's.

The last reason is similar to some of the issues with storefront materials: The bay is a special part of a building, so it should be treated in a more refined fashion than ordinary walls are. The typical wall material of the rest of the building is usually inappropriate here.

Dormer jambs are usually plain on most buildings, but may occasionally be detailed as pilasters. In such cases, they should support an entablature or arch.

SEE 13~TRIM; 22~STOREFRONT MATERIALS; 25~BAY JAMB MATERIAL; 37~CASING PRINCIPLES; 83~DORMER ROOF TRIM; AND 84~DORMER BODY PROPORTION.

[235]

## 82
# BRICK DORMER FACE

**BRICK SHOULD BE USED FOR A DORMER FACE ONLY WHEN THE BRICK FORMS A PARAPET AT THE TOP OF THE DORMER.**

Dormers are almost always constructed entirely of wood, even when the rest of the building is built of brick. Brick clearly is too heavy a material to be safely (and legally, in most cases) supported by wood construction. As with other aspects of brick construction, its use on dormers, even if properly supported, would make it appear to be brick wallpaper, because every viewer understands that brick is a weighty material. These comments should be unnecessary, but the current rage for the mythical maintenance free material makes brick dormers a possibility.

The only exception to this rule is the brick dormer face that aligns over a brick wall below and creates a parapet wall above. This most typically occurs with the relatively rare "half-dormer," where the window is half in the wall below and half in the dormer. The eaves of the main roof intersect the dormer somewhere near the midpoint.

A single wythe of brick is inappropriate, because it creates an improper material change at an outside corner.

*Don't use brick to face a dormer unless the face terminates in a parapet wall. If the roof projects over the top of the front wall of the dormer, it is far too easy to run siding to the outside corner, creating the worst sort of vertical wall joint.*

DON'T

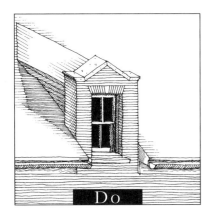

Do

*Do create a distinct parapet wall extending beyond both the sides and top of the dormer in the rare cases where a dormer is faced with brick. Dormer faces that create parapet walls above must build a masonry side return at least as wide as the parapet, creating a perfectly respectable condition. Note that the brick dormer face is most rational when it is an extension of a brick wall below as shown in the drawing and all of the photos on this page.*

A brick parapet wall, however, must be at least 8" thick. Because the scale of the dormer is smaller than the scale of an entire building, a brick parapet wall 8" thick or thicker projects at least 4", or ideally 8", beyond each side of the dormer to create a brick pilaster of sorts, when viewed from the side, and gives siding on each side of the dormer an appropriate place to die.

SEE 9~SIDING MATERIALS; 11~BRICK; 16~MASONRY VENEER WALLS; 17~BRICK COURSING AT WALL OPENINGS; 19~WALL MATERIAL JOINTS; 21~WINDOW MATERIALS; 24~BRICK JACK ARCH; 26~BRICK MOLD; 39~MASONRY LINTEL PRINCIPLES; 40~ARCH PRINCIPLES; 83~DORMER ROOF TRIM; 84~DORMER BODY PROPORTION; AND 85~DORMER BODY/ROOF PROPORTION.

[237]

## 83
## DORMER ROOF TRIM

DORMER ROOF TRIM, BEGINNING AT THE WINDOW HEAD, SHOULD BE COMPOSED OF A HEAD CASING, A SOFFIT, AND A CORONA, OR FASCIA, AT A MINIMUM. A CYMATIUM, OR CROWN, MAY BE ADDED, BUT ONLY ON THE RAKING CORNICE. SIDING SHOULD NEVER BE USED ANYWHERE ABOVE A WINDOW HEAD EXCEPT IN THE TYMPANUM OF A GABLE-FRONT DORMER.

Siding above a dormer window indicates that the dormer is very poorly proportioned and is much taller than it should be. Properly designed dormers are built of a sequence of trim pieces with no large surface areas that require siding. The first trim piece is a window head casing, which must be at least as wide as the jamb casing below, if not wider. The narrowest allowable jamb casing, as noted earlier in 81~Dormer Jamb Material, is a 1x8 with standard dormer sidewalls or a 1x6 with flat stud sidewalls.

The dormer eave above should be designed according to all principles of good eave design, and it should be a smaller version of the main roof eave in most cases. This means, among other things, that a closed-eave cornice should be as tall as it is wide. For classical buildings, the proportion of the cornice to the head casing should be

consistent with the proportion of the cornice to the frieze of the main roof, if the building has a full-height frieze. If not, the proportion of dormer cornice to window head casing should be appropriate to the order of the building.

Dormers with either bowspring or full Roman

*Don't: Circle-head windows jammed between pork chop eaves still leave blank slivers to fill with siding.*

*Don't: These dormers attempt to fill the gap, but do so with dentils, which are enrichments that should only be added to a full-featured cornice with proper cymatium, bed molds, etc. They are rare on dormers. This cornice has only a fascia and soffit, so dentils are entirely wrong here.*

*Don't: This is the raw condition of window, pork chop eave, and nothing but siding in between. The pork chops are small and therefore less offensive, but they are still wrong.*

arched window heads often incorporate jamb casings detailed as pilasters due to the formality of the dormers, the tops of which occur at the springline of the arch. This obviously leaves far too much space from the top of the pilaster to the eave of the dormer owing to the height of the arch, so a full entablature on each side wall is used which returns around the front and then into the front dormer face at the insides of the pilasters. Care should be taken in such cases to maintain the proper entablature/pilaster height proportion of 1:4. Vernacular dormer roofs usually slope at 12:12, while more classical dormer roofs typically slope less, often a slope that matches porch gable slopes, or aedicule gable slopes if they exist on the building.

SEE 13~TRIM; 38~HEAD CASING PRINCIPLES; 45~COLUMN MATERIALS AND PROPORTIONS; 50~COLUMN TO ENTABLATURE; 51~ENTABLATURE PRINCIPLES; 62~TRIM UNDER CORNICE; 64~EAVE MATERIALS; 66~EAVE OVERHANG AND ENCLOSURE; 77~ROOF SLOPES; AND 81~DORMER JAMB MATERIAL.

*Do: The dormers on this fairly vernacular midrange building have siding in the tympanum, but only after installing all of the required parts.*

*Do: The dormers on this fairly classical midrange building also have siding in the tympanum. Because this building is more refined than the first, the designer has used flush tongue and groove siding to make the joints less apparent.*

*Do: This classical dormer has a small tympanum that is filled with a single board, creating no seams at all.*

## 84
## DORMER BODY
## PROPORTION

THE BODY OF A SINGLE-
WINDOW DORMER SHOULD BE
VERTICALLY PROPORTIONED OR
SQUARE. DORMER WINDOWS
SHOULD BE PROPORTIONED
SIMILAR TO OR SLIGHTLY
SHORTER THAN TYPICAL
WINDOWS IN THE FLOOR
BELOW.

The two exceptions to this
rule are the half-round dormer and its close cousin, the
eyebrow dormer. The half-
round dormer, by definition,
has a height/width proportion
close to or exactly 1:2, while
the eyebrow dormer is wider.
Both of these types are relatively rare and are specific to
only a few styles.

Square dormers are slightly
more common and also somewhat less style-specific. The
term "square dormer" is a bit
of a misnomer, because dormers that are close to square
should usually be detailed with
a perfectly square window.
Obviously, the actual body
may vary slightly from square
depending on the widths of
the jamb casings, the head casing, and the subsill and apron.

Windows in the common
vertical dormers should be
proportioned similar to the
uppermost windows in the
wall below. If they vary from
the proportions of those windows, they should be slightly

*Don't proportion a single-window dormer to be horizontal. 1: This dormer is noticeably taller than square, yet is far too chunky for a tall dormer and is a bad match for the window size. 2: This one is even wider. It is a good match for the window height, but not for the window width. 3: This dormer is an awkward-looking over-reaction to dormers that are too wide for their height. 4: This dormer is a near miss of a square proportion with small windows.*

1

DON'T

2

3

4

*Do proportion dormer and window so that the window properly fills the dormer face. The Do drawing indicates a good dormer proportion for classical buildings. 1: This is a dormer on a fairly vernacular midrange building. It is somewhat shorter than the classical dormer, but also fills its face well with the window. 2: Dormers can be wider than square only if they entirely fill the face of the dormer with properly proportioned windows and their casings.*

shorter. This is particularly appropriate on buildings where the main-level windows are taller than the second-level windows. Dormer windows are often somewhat narrower than windows in the wall below, because larger dormer windows can create heavy-looking dormers with a chunky appearance. Narrowing the dormer windows, however, requires that their height be reduced to maintain correct window proportions.

As with the square dormers above, the dormer body proportion is driven by the window proportion. Preference should be given to getting the window proportion exactly correct and deriving the dormer body proportion from the window proportion. Multi-window dormers, which may be gabled or hipped but are more often shedded, obviously will be wider than square in most cases, and the individual window proportions should also drive this.

SEE 13~TRIM; 21~WINDOW MATERIALS; 28~DOOR AND WINDOW TYPES; 29~DOOR AND WINDOW STYLE VERSUS BUILDING STYLE; 31~WINDOW PROPORTIONS; 32~WINDOW PANE PROPORTIONS; 37~CASING PRINCIPLES; 38~HEAD CASING PRINCIPLES; AND 81~DORMER JAMB MATERIAL.

1

2

[241]

## 85
## DORMER BODY/ ROOF PROPORTION

IF DORMER EAVES ARE
PROPERLY PROPORTIONED, THE
TOTAL WIDTH OF THE DORMER
ROOF OF ALMOST ANY PROPER
STYLE SHOULD BE 25 PERCENT
TO 40 PERCENT LARGER THAN
THE WIDTH OF THE DORMER
BODY.

One of the most glaring signs of an ill-informed designer or builder is a dormer roof that is far too large for the dormer body. Unfortunately, it has been common practice for some time to build dormer roofs with the same eave detail as used for the main roof. The eave may be slightly reduced in some cases, but the conventional eave detail almost always results in a dormer roof that is enormously oversized and top-heavy, similar to the appearance of a toddler trying to wear her father's hat. This may be amusing with a young child, but it is simply awkward on a building.

Proper dormer roofs vary in proportion from about 125 percent of dormer body width to about 140 percent of dormer body width. The most effective way of measuring body/roof proportion is to the outside of the window casing and the outside of roof fascia. If the dormer jamb is properly detailed, the measurement of the dormer width at the out-

*Don't oversize the dormer roof so that it appears to be top-heavy. There are a number of unflattering ways of characterizing dormers with roofs that are too big for their bodies. Oversize tops might be cute on cartoon characters such as Dumbo the Elephant, but they certainly are not on dormers.*

DON'T

*Don't: These dormers possess a fairly good body proportion and contain no siding between window and dormer corner. But they ruin it all by oversized roofs.*

*Don't: Strangely enough, these dormers have exactly the same overhang as the dormers above, but because the dormer bodies themselves are far too wide, the proportion of roof to dormer body is actually better. Which is worse? That may be debatable, but neither is palatable.*

*Don't: Typical tract house pork chop eaves project equally too far to the gable end as they do to the eave sides. Pork chop dormer eaves do exactly the same thing, accentuating the top-heavy appearance of the dormers.*

*Do adopt modest proportions when detailing the dormer body and roof.*

*Do: Vernacular dormer roofs typically are allowed to project the farthest, and would typically be the only ones that approach the 40 percent limit.*

*Do: Classical dormer roofs typically project the least. They occasionally project less than 25 percent.*

*Do: Dormers on midrange buildings, naturally project a moderate amount. Their roof details are typified by this dormer, which contains all of the classical elements but in very simplified fashion.*

side face of window casing is exactly the same as the measurement at the outside face of the dormer since the dormer window is cased to the corner of the dormer as described in 81~Dormer Jamb Material.

These proportions may vary to the narrower side, depending on the style of the building, but almost never past the wider limit. Dormers on more vernacular buildings may fall on the wider end of this range, while dormers on more classical buildings usually fall on the narrower side.

SEE 13~TRIM; 21~WINDOW MATERIALS; 28~DOOR AND WINDOW TYPES; 29~DOOR AND WINDOW STYLE VERSUS BUILDING STYLE; 31~WINDOW PROPORTIONS; 32~WINDOW PANE PROPORTIONS; 37~CASING PRINCIPLES; 38~HEAD CASING PRINCIPLES; 51~ENTABLATURE PRINCIPLES; 62~TRIM UNDER CORNICE; 64~EAVE MATERIALS; 66~EAVE OVERHANG AND ENCLOSURE; 81~DORMER JAMB MATERIAL; AND 84~DORMER BODY PROPORTION.

## 86
## TOWER AND LANTERN PRINCIPLES

GOOD TOWERS AND LANTERNS TYPICALLY SIT ON A LOW BASE AND ARE TRIMMED TO RESEMBLE PILASTERS SURROUNDING GLAZED OR LOUVERED OPENINGS AND SUPPORTING A BEAM AND ROOF ABOVE. THEY TYPICALLY INCLUDE NO SIDING, EXCEPT POSSIBLY BELOW THE SILL HEIGHT.

Tower caps and lanterns share many of the proportioning and detailing rules of dormers. As a matter of fact, each glazed or louvered face of a tower cap, lantern, glazed cupola, or belvedere may usually be treated by using the same principles as a dormer if dormers are used on the building. Unglazed and unlouvered faces, if they exist, usually may be safely treated the same as the side walls of dormers.

The tower cap, lantern, cupola, or belvedere on more classical buildings often is built according to the principles of the aedicule, which incorporate the entire highest order of the building into a single object. Spaces between windows or louvers are articulated as pilasters as a minimum on more classical buildings, but the pilasters may also be disengaged to become free standing columns with flat casings

immediately behind in the highest-style versions.

The roof of a tower, lantern, cupola, or belvedere is usually the crowning element of a building, marking the point where the building meets the sky. This point has historically been adorned in various manners. It is often enriched

*Don't: No base, improper jamb casing, proportion far too wide.*

*Don't: Improper undersized base that follows roof, improper roof and corner trim.*

Do: Vernacular gable roof.

Do: Unusual New Urban roof.

Do: Vernacular hip roof.

with upgraded materials, such as a copper roof, and is often articulated with elements, such as finials, weathervanes, and spires. The slope of the roof depends heavily on the style of the building, but is often steeper than the main roof to make its roof surface visible from its greater height. The

Do: New Urban hip roof.

Do: Octagonal roof.

Do: New Urban hip roof and body.

roof may be further articulated by curves or breaks.

The extra attention given to towers, lanterns, cupolas, or belvederes also requires that they become "perfect" elements in other regards. Almost every such element is bilaterally symmetrical. These elements also usually strongly exhibit the cap, shaft, and base arrangement of nearly all classical objects. The roof and eave or entablature is the cap, of course. The windows or louvers and the pilasters are the shaft. The base may be articulated in a number of ways, but is always present.

SEE 6~CAP, SHAFT, AND BASE; 13~TRIM; 21~WINDOW MATERIALS; 28~DOOR AND WINDOW TYPES; 29~DOOR AND WINDOW STYLE VERSUS BUILDING STYLE; 30~ENTRY SURROUNDS; 31~WINDOW PROPORTIONS; 32~WINDOW PANE PROPORTIONS; 37~CASING PRINCIPLES; 38~HEAD CASING PRINCIPLES; 45~COLUMN MATERIALS AND PROPORTIONS; 50~COLUMN TO ENTABLATURE; 51~ENTABLATURE PRINCIPLES; 62~TRIM UNDER CORNICE; 64~EAVE MATERIALS; 66~EAVE OVERHANG AND ENCLOSURE; 77~ROOF SLOPES; 81~DORMER JAMB MATERIAL; 83~DORMER ROOF TRIM; 84~DORMER BODY PROPORTION; AND 85~DORMER BODY/ROOF PROPORTION.

# CHAPTER 13
~
# ATTACHMENTS

## ATTACHMENT MATERIALS

# ATTACHMENT CONFIGURATIONS

[247]

## 87
## FLUE MATERIALS

FLUES SHOULD BE CLAY TILE
OR GALVANIZED METAL LEFT
NATURAL OR PAINTED BLACK.

Clay tile or terra-cotta flue terminations are always preferable, of course, owing to their more substantial construction and their resultant greater life expectancies, which are usually measured in centuries, not decades. Flue terminations built of terra-cotta may be shaped in many ways and are called "chimney pots." Designs of chimney pots are enormously dependent on the style of the building. Fortunately, there are manufacturers that supply designs appropriate to most common American and European styles.

The primary drawback of clay tile or terra-cotta flue terminations is that they cannot be used with metal flues. Prefabricated metal fireplaces are by far the most common type installed today because of budget issues, and all prefabricated metal fireplaces require metal flues. Metal flues require sheet metal flue terminations. To date, no beautiful sheet metal flue termination has ever been designed. The design problems include the fact that to get cooling air into the outer shroud and out of the inner shroud of the flue, and to get smoke out of the

*Don't use metal flues that call attention to the insubstantial nature of their construction. They not only discredit themselves, but also the chimneys and the fireplaces they are attached to. This fact is recognized so widely that brick manufacturers have used metal fireplaces and flues in advertisements to discredit the construction quality of the entire house. 1: Metal flues rusting on synthetic stucco chimney. 2: Metal flues fighting for attention on wood chimney.*

1

2

1

3

5

*Do use the ideal flue top wherever possible, which is the terra-cotta chimney pot. The next step down is the plain clay tile flue. The least desirable acceptable flue cap is the simple metal cap. 1: Simple clay tile flue. 2: Simple metal cap. 3: Octagonal terra-cotta chimney pots transitioning to square at chimney. 4: Square battered chimney cap with clay tile cap. 5: Octagonal terra-cotta chimney pots. 6: Round and spiral-barreled round terra-cotta chimney pots.*

2

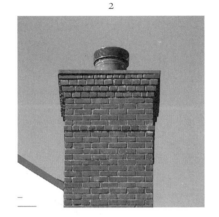

4

6

middle, the termination must necessarily be large. And it cannot have other materials immediately adjacent if it is to draw properly, so it is hard to hide. Everyone should hope for a better design to emerge. But in the meantime, the best solution may be to hide sheet metal flue terminations with brick detailing such as brick arch caps, where appropriate to the style of the building.

Sheet metal flue terminations that are painted the color of the chimney, the color of trim, or the color of some other element of the building usually look silly because everyone knows they are not built of these materials. They should therefore be left natural or painted black. Natural metal reflects the sky and therefore disappears, at least in the early years before it weathers. Black metal hides the inevitable soot from wood fires.

SEE 6~CAP, SHAFT, AND BASE; 10~STONE VENEER WALL MATERIAL; 11~BRICK; 16~MASONRY VENEER WALLS; 88~CHIMNEY MATERIALS; 92~CHIMNEY MATERIAL VERSUS DETAILING; AND 93~CHIMNEY CONFIGURATION.

# 88
## CHIMNEY MATERIALS

CHIMNEYS, WHEN VISIBLE, SHOULD BE SHEATHED IN BRICK, STONE, OR STUCCO.

Ideally, chimneys should be built of solid masonry with clay tile or refractory concrete flue liners. Solid masonry chimneys will last longer than hollow chimneys with metal flues and, when properly maintained, are much more resistant to flue fires owing to their enormously greater thermal mass. They are also obviously noncombustible, as opposed to hollow chimneys framed with wood.

Unfortunately, budget constraints now make true solid masonry chimneys unaffordable on many buildings. Hollow chimneys, while undesirable, are often simply a fact of life. The question, then, is not whether to have them, but how to detail them when budgets make them necessary. Hollow chimneys, just as masonry veneer walls, should be detailed exactly as in the solid construction they are emulating, so that it is not possible to distinguish between solid and hollow. This means that the only acceptable chimney materials are noncombustible masonry. Ideally, the chimney material should be selected from among the

*Don't use insubstantial, flammable materials such as wood or vinyl siding, which have no place in chimney construction. Such chimneys are hallmarks of cheap construction. If the chimney is an obvious cheap fake, why not simply extend a gas vent straight out through the wall behind the metal gas-burning fireplace and dispense with any pretense at a chimney? Or, if the fireplace is on the top floor, simply extend the gas vent through the roof like a plumbing vent.*

DON'T

Do

1

*Do use chimney construction that appears to be substantial, even when using a masonry veneer. 1: Stucco chimneys are appropriate in many architectural languages. They also have the advantage of requiring no masonry support since they can be frame-built. 2: Brick is the most common chimney material in the eastern U.S. 3: Natural stone chimneys are common on vernacular buildings. 4: Stucco or stone details are possible on brick chimneys.*

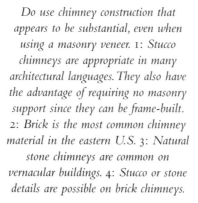

2

chimney materials used in the immediate vicinity in 1895. For most of the United States, brick is the material of choice, although natural or roughly cut stone was commonly used in some areas while stucco over masonry rubble construction was used in others. In no case were chimneys constructed of wood studs with lap siding or similar construction, which looks pitifully insubstantial next to a real brick chimney.

New solid alternatives to masonry chimneys are emerging. Most focus on refractory concrete fireboxes and flues that are prefabricated in large chunks, eliminating substantial amounts of labor and some material cost, depending on the area. In some regions, such systems are about one-half the cost of a solid brick chimney and perform just as well, if not better. As a matter of fact, most masons have lost the art of correct firebox construction because they hardly ever do it anymore. This means that prefabricated firebox and flue assemblies are likely to draw out smoke better than custom-built fireboxes.

3

4

SEE 10~STONE VENEER WALL MATERIAL; 11~BRICK; 16~MASONRY VENEER WALLS; 92~CHIMNEY MATERIAL VERSUS DETAILING; AND 93~CHIMNEY CONFIGURATION.

## 8 9
## SIGN MATERIALS

SIGNS SHOULD BE
CONSTRUCTED OF WOOD
OR METAL, OR THEY MAY
BE PAINTED ON BUILDING
WALLS OR WINDOWS WHERE
ALLOWED.

If internally lit, neon is very nimble and should usually be the light source of choice, while externally lit signs usually should be lit by incandescent or quartz incandescent lights in a visible fixture above the sign. Today, most low-quality signs consist of aluminum boxes filled with fluorescent light bulbs backlighting acrylic sheets upon which the sign graphics are placed. A close cousin is the sign composed of a series of aluminum boxes, each shaped as a letter of the business name, with colored acrylic sheet faces. Such signs have several problems. First, although fluorescent bulbs are cheaper to maintain than incandescent bulbs, fluorescent light is limited-spectrum light and is therefore less attractive than full-spectrum light such as sunlight or incandescent light. The design of aluminum box signs requires a box close to or sometimes more than a foot thick to allow the light to spread evenly over the acrylic face, rather than creating the hot spots that a thin box would cause. This necessar-

*Don't use materials meant to be seen at great distances or at great speeds on signs for human-scaled streets. Aluminum box signs are problematic because, under certain circumstances, they can be used successfully. Most of the time, however, they are not. 1: The simple rectangular aluminum box sign with a vinyl face are often of predictably poor design quality. 2: The multiple shaped box signs have been discredited for years, and are fairly uncommon today, as they should be. 3: Single letter box signs can occasionally be acceptable, depending on the design of the sign and the typefaces used. Also, translucent acrylic faces such as those shown here are the least desirable since they are most closely related to the signs in photo 1. 4: Single letter box signs with clear faces such as the sign shown here or no face at all and with exposed neon letters are the most likely types of box signs to be acceptable, depending on sign design and choice of typeface.*

1

2

3

4

*Do use materials which support pedestrian streets: 1: Painted or vinyl signs on window or door glass. 2: Painted or vinyl signs painted on sign boards mounted in various manners. 3: Signs painted on faces or fringes of awnings. 4: Exposed neon signs on painted metal or other types of sign boards or bodies. 5: Signs painted on building walls. 6: Signs inscribed on buildings (frieze sign shown here) are the oldest surviving type of sign.*

1

2

3

4

5

6

ily creates thick, clunky signs that might be appropriate for an interstate highway sign or a strip center sign meant to be viewed from great distances, but are entirely inappropriate for human-scale, pedestrian-oriented signage such as that found on a traditional American Main Street. Acrylic-faced aluminum box signs should therefore not be permitted in any place meant to be oriented to the pedestrian and human-scaled. Internally lit vinyl awning signs suffer from many of the same ugliness problems as the box sign, and they, too, should be disallowed in such places.

Traditional human-scale signs are much more nimble. Wood or metal should be the signboard material of choice. Graphics may be either painted or cut vinyl. Front-lit vinyl graphics may be subtle and elegant if designed properly, while the backlit vinyl graphics found in internally lit box or awning signs tend to be starker, almost creating a silhouette. The fact that backlighting usually brings out the worst in vinyl is one reason that back lit signs should be avoided in human-scale places.

Painted signs on building walls are now outlawed in many places, but were once some of the most memorable signs of the most-loved places. They should be allowed in certain circumstances, discussed later. Signs painted onto window glass should also be allowed.

SEE 94~ATTACHED SIGNS; 95~PROJECTING SIGNS; 96~GROUND SIGNS; AND 97~AWNING SIGNS.

## 90
## AWNING MATERIALS

### AWNINGS SHOULD BE CONSTRUCTED OF CANVAS ON A LIGHT METAL FRAME.

Plastic or other synthetic awnings look unnatural and should be avoided. They also age very poorly. This is primarily due to the fact that, when new, they are so slick and shiny that any dirt they collect or any wear they suffer causes them to look very dingy very quickly. Plastic awnings are often replaced years sooner than canvas awnings, not because they are damaged or destroyed, but because they simply look more worn.

Metal awnings also have become problematic. Many very beautiful metal awnings were designed a century ago for the entries to the Paris metro system. Design quality is clearly of highest importance here. No known mass-produced metal awning components meet the design quality standard, although this certainly is possible if someone designs such a system.

Natural canvas awnings are matte in texture. Dirt or mildew on canvas awnings tends to give the canvas a mellow patina, instead of making it look dingy. A wrinkle or sag in canvas looks much more natural than it does in plastic, which is expected to

*Don't use synthetic materials such as vinyl for awnings. Application of the Arm's Length Rule to awnings would clarify many of the awning mistakes made over the past half-century. The standard for comparison is the canvas awning. The primary strike against canvas is the fact that it only lasts about five years. The fact is that vinyl awnings also have a similar life span. 1: Metal awnings such as this have almost entirely discredited the material entirely for awning usage. In reality, it is possible to design a good fixed awning using metal, but not with currently available stock components. 2: Plastic awnings are shiny, as illustrated here. The sheen accentuates winkles, especially those found in awning fringes, so plastic awnings are usually stretched tight over a metal frame, making them appear fake or unnatural.*

I

2

*Do use canvas awnings, which look and move naturally, and have a longer lifespan of attractiveness than vinyl. Canvas awnings and their fringes ripple softly and naturally in a breeze and add life and authenticity to any street scene, and are found almost exclusively in the most desirable pedestrian streets. It is no accident that the world's most effective places at attracting visitors to their streets typically do it with canvas awnings. Canvas may be solid; it may be composed of alternately colored striped panels; it may also be composed of striped canvas. Retractable awnings are usually operated by means of a crank or electric motor which operates a folding frame.*

always be stretched as tight as a drum over the frame. Canvas awnings, for the same reason, may be outfitted with fringes that are allowed to flutter in the breeze, an action that would look positively silly in plastic. Canvas may be ordered with stripes if desired. Canvas may also be painted, either in large panels or in graphic shapes, including signs.

Awning frames come in a number of designs. Awning frames should ordinarily be light and thin, so they are best constructed of some sort of metal such as aluminum or galvanized steel. Frames should be designed so as to avoid frame members much larger than 1" in diameter, since framing tends to look clunky above this size. The ascendancy of plastic awnings in recent years required full frames. Canvas awnings have recently also been built with full frames except at the fringes. There is another type, however, that should also be considered: That is the retractable awning, which was once the most common awning type. The retractable awning can be pulled back against the building at the close of business or during a severe windstorm, significantly increasing the life of the awning.

SEE 99~AWNING CONFIGURATIONS.

## 91
## CHIMNEY HEIGHT

CHIMNEY HEIGHT SHOULD BE
APPROPRIATE TO THE STYLE
OF THE BUILDING, BUT SHALL
IN ANY CASE MEET CODE-
REQUIRED MINIMUM HEIGHTS.

Code-required chimney heights are, in most cases, shorter than those of chimneys appropriate to most traditional styles. If the building has no tower, lantern, cupola, belvedere, dormers, or other roof-top elements, then the chimneys are often the crowning element where the building meets the sky. As with other such elements, chimneys are often used to celebrate this meeting of building and sky. Short, stubby chimneys do not accomplish this task very well within most styles.

Modernists, in their rush to remove all traces of the human form from their work, embraced all things horizontal in an effort to forget the basic upright form of the standing human. Chimneys, however, were unmistakably vertical elements, carrying smoke from a lower level to the sky. Nonetheless, most Modernists did all that they could to eliminate the verticality of the chimney in several ways. First, they often built chimneys enormously wide from front to back, wasting a tremendous quantity of brick or stone. Next, they dropped

*Don't build short chimneys which look stubby and don't function as well as taller ones. Chimneys which meet minimum code requirements for chimney height typically look far too short. Increasing the width of the chimney only increases the problem and violates all principles of human-based proportions.*

DON'T

*Do base chimney height more on proportion than measure, although all code requirements clearly must be met as a minimum. Proper proportion varies according to the architectural language of the building.*

the chimney heights to the minimum allowed by code. Unfortunately, shorter chimneys do not often draw as well as taller chimneys, and chimney tops closer to the level of the roof are more likely to leave soot deposits on the roof, nearby dormers, or other rooftop items.

What, then, is an appropriate chimney height if the building codes are not a good guide? The best chimney heights are extremely tied to building style, a detailed discussion of which is beyond the scope of this book. In general, as with all other patterns, buildings based on existing architectural languages should pay special attention to the details of good precedent of that style in the area. In no case should the proportion of the chimney (in its narrow width) above the point where it penetrates the roof be less than the proportion of the first level windows of the building. In most cases, it should be 50 percent or more larger.

SEE 6~CAP, SHAFT AND BASE; 10~STONE VENEER WALL MATERIAL; 11~BRICK; 16~MASONRY VENEER WALLS; 86~TOWER AND LANTERN PRINCIPLES; 87~FLUE MATERIALS; 88~CHIMNEY MATERIALS; 92~CHIMNEY MATERIAL VERSUS DETAILING; AND 93~CHIMNEY CONFIGURATION.

## 92
## CHIMNEY MATERIAL
## VERSUS DETAILING

CHIMNEY DETAILING SHOULD
BE APPROPRIATE TO THE
MATERIALS USED, WHICH
MEANS THAT STUCCO AND
NATURAL STONE CHIMNEYS
SHOULD GENERALLY BE SIMPLER
THAN BRICK CHIMNEYS.

This is one of several patterns in this book that should be so obvious that they do not need to be included; but chimneys today continue to be built of stucco and detailed as if they were brick, and vice versa. Natural stone chimneys, because they are built of a rough material with little capability for subtlety, should be the simplest of all. Seldom is anything more than a simple one-step cap appropriate on a natural stone chimney. Natural stone chimneys, like chimneys built of other materials, often step back above the top firebox to a more slender shaft to save materials. Step-backs built of other materials usually incorporate some sort of cap for the step-back, or shoulder. Caps are often built of brick soldiers or dressed stone slabs. Stone shoulders, however, are constructed simply by corbelling the stone back a little farther with each course until the upper chimney dimension is achieved. This often creates steeper shoulders than might occur with other materials.

Stucco, because it is troweled onto a substrate masonry material, is best suited to large, plain surfaces with few or no breaks. This means that stucco chimneys, like natural stone chimneys, are usually of relatively simple design. Stucco can, however, be the most ornate of the common acceptable chimney materials because it can be shaped into any desired configuration. Stucco chimneys often incorporate special shapes at the top of the chimney, where it meets the sky. Any such shapes should be consistent with the style of the building as should be the case with any material.

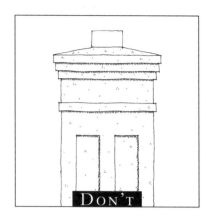

1

2

*Don't use chimney detailing incompatible with the material used. Chimney shown in drawing is stucco, but is detailed exactly as if it were brick. 1: This chimney has fallen prey to the Modernist penchant for over-simplification. There is no reason for a brick chimney to be a decapitated slab. 2: This one is much worse. Look closely. This is actually a metal chimney painted to resemble brick. Why not simply use a metal flue cap?*

1

2

*Do use chimney detailing consistent with the capabilities of the material. 1, 3, and 5 show varying degrees of complexity of brick chimney, depending on the style of the building. 2: Stone detailing (shown in this photo and in the Do drawing) tends to be simple due to the rustic nature of stone. 4: Stucco and clay tile cap using a range of clay tile capabilities. 6: Stucco chimneys have the greatest capability of refined detail due to the plastic nature of the material.*

Brick chimneys may be the most elaborate of the three, again based on the style of the building. Brick can be easily corbelled in or out, and vertical breaks and turns are relatively easy to accomplish. Chimneys often involve a higher level of brick detailing simply because they contain substantially fewer bricks than the rest of the building, making each brick feature on a chimney much less expensive than the same detail carried all around the building.

Dressed stone chimneys are so rare and expensive that they are largely beyond the scope of this book. Suffice it to say that if a budget has room for a dressed stone chimney, it probably has room for the dressed stone to be fairly ornate.

3

4

SEE 6~CAP, SHAFT, AND BASE; 10~STONE VENEER WALL MATERIAL; 11~BRICK; 16~MASONRY VENEER WALLS; 87~FLUE MATERIALS; 88~CHIMNEY MATERIALS; 91~CHIMNEY HEIGHT; AND 93~CHIMNEY CONFIGURATION.

5

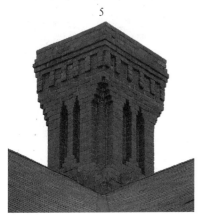

6

## 93
# CHIMNEY CONFIGURATION

CHIMNEYS SHOULD HAVE A
PROJECTING CAP AND SHOULD
EXTEND TO THE GROUND
IF LOCATED ON AN OUTSIDE
WALL.

Chimneys built of solid masonry necessarily extend to the ground, because there is usually no other good way to support the weight of the chimney. Wood box chimneys, however, are sometimes cantilevered from the wall because they are so light. Fewer things make a building look more insubstantial than chimneys that are obviously built of light, flammable materials. Chimneys should extend to the ground for this reason alone.

The pattern of classical elements being built with a cap, shaft, and base seems to require some sort of ground-level base on chimneys. Buildings built of brick or other masonry often include water table courses of various designs near the main-floor level. If so, the water table should be continued around the chimney and become its base. Buildings built of wood walls and masonry foundations, however, should have no water table or other step back whatsoever in the brick, as discussed in 18~Frame Wall/Masonry Base Alignment. Chimneys

^1 ⌄2

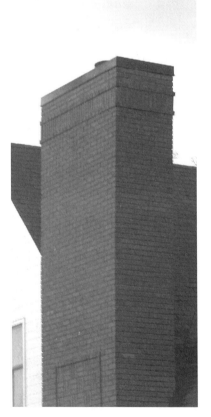

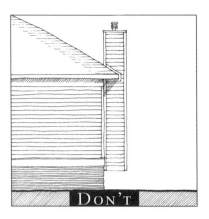

*Don't drawing illustrates the worst condition: a flat slab vinyl-sided chimney with a metal flue cap but no chimney cap that does not extend to the ground. 1: The only redeeming virtue here is the fact that by amputating the chimney, this one has been mangled almost past the point of recognition as a fireplace. 2: Modernist version of traditional chimney: flat slab shape and deeply abstracted detailing. 3: Decapitated chimney.*

3

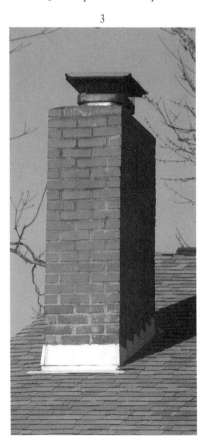

Do follow basic chimney principles according to building style. 1: Highly expressive brick chimney consistent with style of house. 2: Stucco chimney with clear base. 3: Shoulders typically occur in the vicinity of the primary eave height. 4: Some shoulders step both directions like a pyramid. 5: Simple vernacular chimney. 6: Highly expressive architect-designed chimney with all of the same pieces, but articulated much differently, showing range of expression.

built on such buildings should not have a water table either. This seems to leave the chimney without a base until one considers that the wide portion of the chimney below the shoulders actually acts visually as a large pedestal base, leaving the shaft function to the portion of the chimney above the shoulders. Some classical styles do not include shoulders, but this almost always happens on the grandest examples that are built of brick with a water table. So in either case, the chimney has a visual base.

Chimneys should also have caps of some sort, most of which should project in some way from the body of the chimney. Simple projections may be as little as a stone cap or header course projecting ⅝". No cap whatsoever, such as may be found on many Modernist buildings, leaves the chimney looking decapitated.

SEE APPARENT STRUCTURE (PAGE 11); 6~CAP, SHAFT, AND BASE; 10~STONE VENEER WALL MATERIAL; 11~BRICK; 16~MASONRY VENEER WALLS; 18~FRAME WALL/MASONRY BASE ALIGNMENT; 87~FLUE MATERIALS; 88~CHIMNEY MATERIALS; 91~CHIMNEY HEIGHT; AND 92~CHIMNEY MATERIAL VERSUS DETAILING.

## 94
## ATTACHED SIGNS

THERE ARE FOUR TYPES OF
ACCEPTABLE ATTACHED SIGNS
THAT MAY BE USED IN HUMAN-
SCALE, PEDESTRIAN-ORIENTED
PLACES: THE BAND SIGN, THE
ATTACHED BOARD SIGN, THE
WINDOW SIGN, AND THE
PAINTED WALL SIGN.

Each sign drawing at the top of each column notes the Transect zones in which the sign should occur. There are no Don'ts for these sign types because the Transect has a place for each of them. Some of these sign types may be illegal in some towns, but efforts should be made to have them approved once again.

The band sign should be the most common business sign type. It consists of a band of lettering across the entire width of the building. If lit, band signs must be front-lit with gooseneck lights. Band signs generally are installed just above the top of first-level glazing, often on an exposed beam face or entablature, if any are present. Band signs should be a maximum of 36" tall, and the bottom of the band sign should not be installed more than 12' or less than 10' above the sidewalk.

Attached board signs consist of painted or vinyl graphics on a signboard; they may be attached to any part of a building, but most commonly

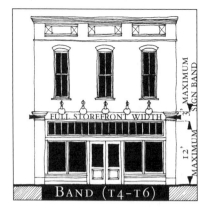

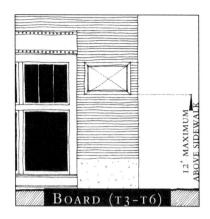

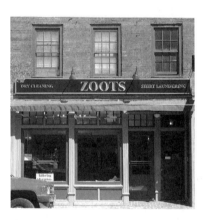

[262]

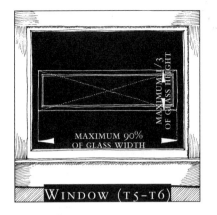

WINDOW (T5-T6)

MAXIMUM 90% OF GLASS WIDTH

MAXIMUM 1/3 OF GLASS HEIGHT

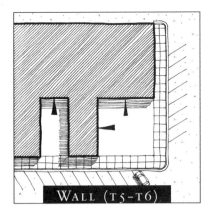

WALL (T5-T6)

GOELLNER

Drink Coca-Cola 5¢
Delicious and Refreshing

250

PLAYERS

PLAYERS

La Famiglia GIORGIO'S

WESTERN HOUSE

GOOSE NATURAL TURKEY

FRESH MEATS

BY F

CLEMENS XII PONT MAX

to a wall. An establishment may have attached signs or band signs, but not both. The cumulative square footage of all attached board signs for an establishment shall be limited to the width of the storefront multiplied by 2. No single attached board sign shall be larger than 6 square feet if the bottom of the sign is located 8' or less above the ground, 9 square feet if between 8' and 12', or 12 square feet if higher than 12' above the ground.

Window signs may be neon behind the glass or paint or vinyl applied onto the glass. Neither shall be include opaque signboards. The height of any window sign is limited to one-third the height of the glass in the sash where the sign is installed, excluding muntins. The width of any window sign is limited to 90 percent of the width of the glass in the sash where installed.

Painted wall signs may occur only on brick wall surfaces set back 40' or more from the sidewalk to allow for equal viewing by pedestrians and motorists. Because this often occurs at unbuilt gaps in the city fabric that will later be filled, these signs should be considered temporary and should not be the primary sign of the business they represent.

SEE THE TRANSECT (PAGE 75); 3~SIMPLICITY OF PROPORTION AND 89~SIGN MATERIALS.

## 95
### PROJECTING SIGNS

PROJECTING SIGNS MAY BE
ATTACHED PERPENDICULAR TO
THE FAÇADE. THE VERTICAL
CORNER SIGN IS A SPECIAL TYPE
OF PROJECTING SIGN, AS IS THE
ROOFTOP SIGN.

Each sign drawing notes the
Transect zones in which the
sign should occur. There are
no Don'ts for these sign types
because the Transect has a
place for each of them.

Standard projecting (blade)
signs may either project from
a wall or hang from an architectural element. Blade signs
hung from an architectural
element should usually be centered on that element. Blade
signs projecting from the wall
may project a maximum of
5'. The top of the blade sign
shall be between 9' and 12'
above the sidewalk. The blade
sign shall be 32" tall maximum. Blade signs shall be no
more than 4' wide. No blade
sign shall exceed 6 square feet
in urban neighborhood retail
locations or 8 square feet in
town centers or urban core
areas. In addition, brackets or
other suspension devices shall
match the sign style and shall
not be computed as part of the
allowable size of the sign.

Vertical corner signs are
the rarest sign type permitted
without an exception because
they can only occur at the
corners of blocks in town cen-

*Do provide blade signs according to
this drawing. All of the configurations
shown on both pages are desirable
depending on the location of the sign
within the Transect. See text for specific
explanations.*

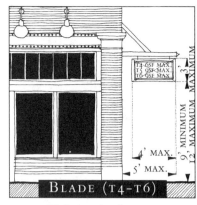
BLADE (T4-T6)

*Blade hanging from gallery.*

*Blade hanging from arm.*

*Blade hanging from roof overhang.*

*Double angle front projection blade.*

*Multiple blade signs.*

*Multiple blade signs.*

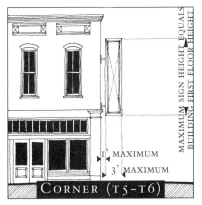

*Vertical corner sign.*

*Vertical corner sign.*

*Blade hanging from arm.*

*Do provide corner signs according to this drawing. Rooftop signs and hybrid projecting signs are allowable only in T5 and T6 Transect zones.*

*Front projection blade sign.*

*Rooftop sign.*

*Hybrid projecting sign.*

ter or urban core areas. They may project perpendicular from one side of the building or at a 45° angle to the corner. Vertical corner signs may be constructed of either signboards or metal, and they may be lit either with gooseneck lights or with surface neon. Vertical corner signs shall be mounted a minimum of 12' from the sidewalk, measured to the bottom of the sign. The height of the sign shall not exceed the first-story wall height. Vertical corner signs shall be mounted 12" maximum away from the exterior wall of the building and shall be a maximum of 3' wide.

Rooftop signs are meant to be viewed from great distances. They should be permitted only by warranted exception in locations where a major business, such as a large hotel, may be viewed at great distances such as across a major body of water.

Hybrid projecting signs are attached signs that also project out from the surface of the building more than 1 foot. Because of their increased visual impact, their size as allowed under 94~Attached Signs should be reduced by 10 percent for every foot of projection from the wall.

SEE THE TRANSECT (PAGE 75); 3~SIMPLICITY OF PROPORTION; 89~SIGN MATERIALS; AND 94~ATTACHED SIGNS.

[265]

## 96
# GROUND SIGNS

GROUND SIGNS ARE PERMITTED
ONLY IN CERTAIN UNUSUAL
SITUATIONS WITHIN HUMAN-
SCALE, PEDESTRIAN-ORIENTED
PLACES.

Each sign drawing notes the Transect zones in which the sign should occur. There are no Don'ts for these sign types because the Transect has a place for each of them.

Ground signs include pylon signs and special ground signs. Pylon signs are mounted on a pole or pylon, while special ground signs sit directly on the ground.

Pylon ground signs in human-scale, pedestrian-oriented places should be permitted only by special exceptions in cases where a place of business is not close enough to the public thoroughfare to allow an attached sign of some type that is readable from the thoroughfare. If permitted, they shall consist of an open structural framework supporting a double-sided signboard lit with gooseneck lights. Because the place is pedestrian-oriented, the bottom of the signboard should not be more than 12' above the sidewalk or finished grade. The height of the signboard should not exceed 3', and its width should not exceed 4'.

The actual signboards of the pylon ground sign may be

*Do use human-scaled pylon signs according to this drawing within the context of nearby buildings. All of the configurations shown on both pages are desirable depending on the location of the sign within the Transect. See text for specific explanations. Signs shown on this page are all pylon signs.*

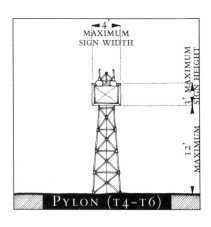

4'
MAXIMUM
SIGN WIDTH

3' MAXIMUM SIGN HEIGHT

12' MAXIMUM

PYLON (T4-T6)

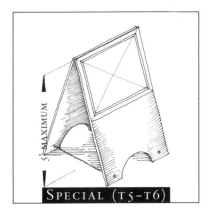

SPECIAL (T5-T6)

*Do use special signs according to this drawing. Signs shown on this page are all special ground signs. Sculptural special ground signs can be almost anything, such as the sign in the chairs below (which are actually a bit too high) and the chef sculpture with menu at the bottom of the page. Special ground signs are meant to be used adjacent to or on the sidewalk. Lettering should be small since people are intended to walk right up to the sign to read it.*

detailed as an attached board sign. In other words, the sign boards consist of painted or vinyl graphics on a wood or metal signboard. The structure may consist of a single sign pole, a double sign pole, or a trussed sign tower. Double or trussed structures should be detailed lightly so that the aggregate width of all structural members does not exceed 8" at any given location below the bottom of the signboard. Care should also be taken to design sign structures within the context of the style of the buildings they represent. Pylon ground signs should be located adjacent to the sidewalk or pathway leading to the business they represent.

Special ground signs generally take two forms: the sculptural and the A-frame sign board. In both cases, they sit directly on the ground, but are not attached to it. They may be sculptural in nature.

SEE THE TRANSECT (PAGE 75); 3~SIMPLICITY OF PROPORTION; 6~CAP, SHAFT, AND BASE; 89~SIGN MATERIALS; AND 94~ATTACHED SIGNS.

[267]

## 97
## AWNING SIGNS

SIGNAGE MAY BE PAINTED
EITHER ON THE FRINGE OF AN
AWNING OR IN THE CENTER OF
THE BODY OF THE AWNING.

Each sign drawing notes the
Transect zones in which the
sign should occur. There are
no Don'ts for these sign types
because the Transect has a
place for each of them.

Awnings shall be fabricated
of canvas on metal frames.
Awning signs shall be painted
directly on canvas. Backlit
awnings should not be permitted for reasons discussed
earlier in 89~Sign Materials.
Signs that occupy the main
body of the awning may fill
the entire body of the awning
if painted on the end of the
awning; or they may occupy
up to one-third of the awning
if painted on the side of the
awning. Signs are obviously
more effective if painted onto
solid-color awnings rather
than striped awnings, unless
the stripes are colors with little
contrast.

Signs that occupy the fringe
of the awning may fill the
entire height and width of the
fringe up to a maximum fringe
height of 9". Awning fringes
may be made of solid-color
canvas for the best signage contrast, while the awning bodies may be striped if desired.
Awning fringes often pick up
the darkest or lightest color of

Do place awning center sign on either
the side of a shed awning or the end of
a projecting arch or gable awning.
1, 2, 3, and 5: Typical applications of
this sign type. 4: While not technically
an awning, the fabric banner follows the
rules for the end of awning center signs.
They should follow the size rules of the
attached board sign. 6: These awnings
defy normal classifications because they
do not project, but the signs should be
treated as center signs.

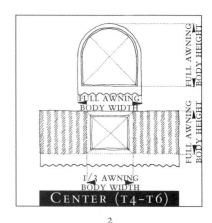

1

2

3

4

5

6

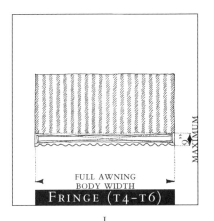

FULL AWNING
BODY WIDTH
FRINGE (T4–T6)

MAXIMUM
9"

*Do limit size of awning fringe signs because they are closer to the eye level of the pedestrian and therefore do not have to be as large. 1, 2, 5, and 6: Typical applications of the awning fringe sign. 3: Awning fringe and awning center signs may be used on the same awning at the risk of being too visually busy. 4: Hard-framed fringes such as this one are possible, but the fringe looks much better if left free to flutter in the breeze like the others here.*

the awning body stripes, and then use a contrasting sign paint color.

Awning fringe signs may actually be more effective in some cases than awning side body signs because they are closer to eye level and the letters are vertical rather than sloping back away from the viewer. This perhaps explains why awning fringe signs have historically been the most popular type of awning sign. This principle is particularly true in human-scale, pedestrian-oriented places where awnings are viewed from close distances. Automobile-oriented environments with large parking lots in front of buildings flip the equation, because motorists in the street are so far away from awnings at the storefront that they have a clearer view of the awning body, and the awning fringe is too small to be read comfortably.

SEE THE TRANSECT (PAGE 75);
3~SIMPLICITY OF PROPORTION;
89~SIGN MATERIALS;
90~AWNING MATERIALS; AND
99~AWNING CONFIGURATIONS.

1

2

3
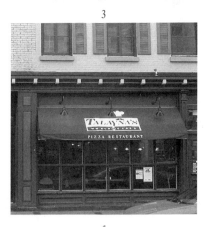

4

5

6

## 98
## ROOF PENETRATIONS

ROOF PENETRATIONS ON SLOPED ROOFS SHALL NOT BE PERMITTED WHERE VISIBLE FROM RIGHTS-OF-WAY. ALL ROOF PENETRATIONS SHOULD MATCH THE COLOR OF THE ROOF.

This is another of those common-sense principles that should be standard construction practice everywhere, but it is not. It is obviously much easier for a plumber or other tradesperson to run the exhaust or other mechanical device straight up and out the roof rather than route it to a less visible location. Modernist architecture celebrates the gadgets associated with construction, whereas traditional architecture celebrates the people who occupy the building. The gadgets are the servants, not the masters, in traditional buildings.

For properly sited buildings that create exterior living spaces in the form of court-yards, etc., one problem is the fact that a building with a public face to the street and a private face visible from outdoor living spaces, which are likely to be used frequently, has very little area to get the equipment out of the building in an unobtrusive manner. There are two general solutions to this problem. The first is either to make the

*Don't allow roof penetrations to clutter the roof. Few elements of modern construction are less attractive than the collection of things that usually penetrate the roof such as plumbing vents, gas vents, exhaust fan vents, attic vents, etc. Unfortunately, they are all necessary to the proper functioning of conveniences we consider necessary. The best we can hope for, therefore, is to properly conceal them where they are less visible. All of the photos below were taken from the street, showing roof clutter in full view of the arriving guest.*

*Do use creative methods of concealing roof clutter. Look very carefully at the left chimney cap. See the plumbing vents? If chimneys can exhaust smoke, why can they not be used to exhaust other waste gases? The fact is that chimneys may actually be the best locations for plumbing vents because they could be flashed in a much longer-lasting manner than typical roof penetrations. Also, a single chimney penetration may hold a number of exhaust vents, whereas each vent penetrates the roof and is flashed separately if installed in the conventional manner.*

private outdoor spaces narrow enough or to make the outside walls tall enough that a standing person cannot see the roof of the building from within the courtyard. This solution generally works in smaller buildings.

Larger buildings with sumptuous courtyards generally don't allow this solution. In such cases, as a second solution, roof penetrations either should be located on the backsides of wings or should be disguised. One of the best disguise methods is to build chimneys intended to exhaust something other than ashes and soot. Properly designed, such a chimney can be used to exhaust a number of gases, including bath exhaust and plumbing vents. Roof penetrations of any sort that do not go to this extreme should be painted to match the color of the roof material.

SEE BUILDINGS FOR PEOPLE (PAGE 10); 7~SITE ARRANGEMENT.

## 99
## AWNING CONFIGURATIONS

AWNINGS MAY BE EITHER
SLOPED RECTANGLES WITHOUT
END PANELS OR CURVED OR
SLOPED SHAPES WITH END
PANELS, AS IS APPROPRIATE TO
THE BUILDING STYLE. IN NO
CASE SHALL AWNINGS CONTAIN
BOTTOM PANELS.

Awnings seem to have originated as a combination of the tent and the building, designed to create a half-in, half-out space at the edge of a building. Appropriately sized awnings are extremely conducive to retail shops, since they allow shoppers to stop for a moment under shade from the sun or shelter from the rain, examining the shopkeeper's wares.

The simplest and probably earliest form of awning was the simple canvas panel, attached at the top to the side of a building and held up at the bottom by two or more poles, similar to the front flap of a tent. This type of awning, unfortunately, is a hazard to anyone walking past it because of the poles.

The next advance in awning form still used a simple canvas rectangle, but supported it with a frame cantilevered from the wall of the building so that people can walk beneath the entire awning. The most flexible version of

this awning was the rectangle of canvas mounted on a retractable frame. The awning could therefore be closed at the end of the day or retracted in the event of a serious windstorm, thereby extending its life. The great majority of shop awnings of the nineteenth century were of the

1

2

3

4

5

*Don't use oversized, overly complicated awning designs. 1: A hard-piped fringe, while not completely incorrect, it is certainly less desirable than a fringe free to flutter in the breeze. 2: This shape is not technically incorrect, but it has been used in poor taste for far too long. Avoid it in particular on houses. 3: Awning shapes such as this are far too complex, and scarcely even deserve to be called awnings. A more appropriate name might be something general like "complex vinyl external facade decoration" or the like. 4: Rounded ends, when combined with the hard-piped fringe, creates an undesirable awning. 5: Another overly complicated awning shape combination that, when covered with plastic, looks like a box sign on steroids rather than an awning. Simplicity is an enormous virtue in awning design.*

*Do keep awning design simple, of a reasonable size, and of a style appropriate to the building and the place. 1: Typical end-facing half-barrel awning with open scalloped fringe has a long record of outstanding service at the entries of restaurants and hotels. 2: The retractable awning, shown here in retracted mode, was once the mainstay of shopfront awnings. It should be reconsidered for that purpose again. 3: The flat panel awning, shown here without a fringe and laced to a rigid metal frame, is the simplest of awning types. 4: The retractable awning, shown here fully extended, also is an ideal awning for sidewalk cafes. 5: The flat panel awning may also be used with fringes such as the non-scalloped one shown here, and may be projected from the wall using two projecting rods and a hanging rod as shown, allowing fabric sag from wall to rod. 6: The window awning is now rare, but provides shade from the sun.*

^ 1 ˅ 2

3

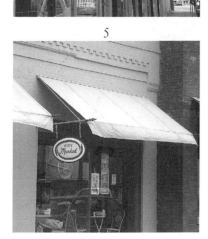

5

4

6

retractable type. This type is just beginning to be considered again, and it is likely to be a favorite in the future for the same common-sense reasons that made it a favorite a century ago.

Awnings today are usually mounted on fixed frames, which can be fabricated in several shapes. The simplest is the straight wedge sloping down and away from the building. The round quarter-barrel awning is similar, as is the elliptical quarter-barrel. Round and elliptical awnings may be turned to run away from a building and are then converted to half-barrels as shown in image 1 on this page. They reach out to the curb while providing full end signage to the street and fringe signage to the pedestrians walking under it on the sidewalk. Such awnings may have half-dome ends installed on their street ends.

All these awning types may have fringes that hang below the lowest support frame. Awning fringes probably owe their existence to tent-building traditions at least as old as medieval times. In no case should awnings have bottoms, which serve no purpose except to trap moisture and encourage mildew and rot.

SEE 90~AWNING MATERIALS
AND 97~AWNING SIGNS.

# 100
# LIGHTING

LIGHTING SHOULD BE
EXPRESSIVE OF ITS FUNCTION
AND OF ITS LOCATION BETWEEN
THE URBAN CORE AND THE
WILDERNESS. OUTBUILDINGS
SHOULD BE EQUIPPED WITH
OUTSIDE LIGHTS FACING THE
ALLEY OR LANE.

Lighting design today often draws no distinction between the urban and rural ends of the Transect. This is a huge mistake. Lighting in T6 and T5 zones should be expected to be brighter, often all through the night. Main Street lighting naturally should be bright enough, consistent enough, and late enough to allow the last customers of downtown nightspots to get home safely. T4 neighborhood areas should be darker, but not entirely dark. Lamp posts should be lower and not quite as bright, although wall- or ceiling-mounted porch lights may supplement them. Ground-mounted floodlights are appropriate only for grand civic buildings such as a state capitol building or a city hall, and they should never be used on walls of private residences that can be seen from any public thoroughfare. Small mushroom-type ground lights, however, are perfectly appropriate. As one approaches the T3 outskirts of town, however, municipal street lighting

*Don't use light fixtures in inappropriate locations on the Transect, such as floodlights in T3 suburban outskirts. Equally incorrect are dark sky ordinances applied to T5 Main Streets or T6 downtown areas, which need higher levels of light late into the night to maintain healthy levels of safe activity. Careless light fixture design that throws much of the light up into the sky is simply inefficient and wasteful, but exterior lighting should not be prohibited or unsafely limited in town and city center areas. The following fixtures are bad almost everywhere: 1: The corner floodlights of 1970's suburban fame do several things very poorly. Because of having to light everything from the eave of the house, they are inefficient and must over-light everything to get enough light on the subject. Because of not being pointed directly downward, they throw objectionable glare at the neighbors and are ugly. 2: Ground-mounted floodlights are bad dark-sky violators and should be reserved for buildings of great civic importance such as courthouses and city halls.*

1

2

*Do use light fixtures appropriate to their Transect zone and the style of their buildings. This is one of many patterns where there are many more good options than bad ones, including the following: 1: Hanging porch lights have a long and splendid history that predates electricity. 2: Surface sconces over garage doors do not have to be overpowering because they put the light right on the subject, lighting the way into the garage more safely than a glaring eave floodlight off to the side. 3: The wall sconce beside the door has perhaps the longest history. It is highly effective not only because it clearly lights the act of unlocking the door without a person having to stand in their own shadow, but it is the most effective way of lighting a visitor's face when someone is answering the door. 4: The gooseneck light is the most effective type of sign light, putting light exactly where it needs to be with very little glare. 5: The gate post lamp effectively marks the entry to a fence with low wattage. 6: Mushroom path lights are efficient, requiring low wattage.*

1: T2 – T5

2: T3 – T6

3: T2 – T6

4: T5 – T6

5: T2 – T4

6: T2 – T5

should be reduced to the point of being entirely eliminated at the town limit. No lighting except an occasional soft porch light leaves the rural night sky full of stars.

One of the greatest lost opportunities of recent lighting design was the fetish for hidden lighting. Just as Modernist architects liked to hide the apparent support of stairs, hide the water-shedding function of roofs, and hide the structural support of windows, handrails, etc., they also tried to hide light sources behind coves and in tin cans. When lights simply could not be hidden for some reason, such as in the case of a freestanding pole light, they used the minimal possible fixture— the obligatory white ball. A casual observer would conclude that most Modernists were uncomfortable with light fixtures.

Humans have, however, celebrated the act of building almost since the dawn of civilization, at least until a century ago. It is perfectly natural and appropriate to use light fixtures that are visible, expressive, and beautiful. The most important word of caution is simply to verify that the style of the fixtures is consistent with the style of the building.

SEE CELEBRATION OF THE ACT OF BUILDING (PAGE 12); AND THE TRANSECT (PAGE 75).

# CHAPTER 14
~
# SITEWORK

## SITEWORK MATERIALS

## Sitework Configurations

## 101
## FENCE MATERIALS

FENCES SHOULD BE BUILT
ENTIRELY OF WOOD, OR OF
METAL IN A CAST-IRON STYLE,
POSSIBLY WITH MASONRY
OR STUCCO PIERS AND BASE.
COLORS SHOULD MATCH LOCAL
PRECEDENT OR STANDARD.

Fences should be designed according to their location on the Transect. There are a few fence materials, shown on this page, which are not appropriate anywhere on the Transect, but most fence materials are appropriate at some point.

Hedgerows are the most natural types of fences, and are appropriate in T1 - T4. Hedgerows in the countryside are usually nothing more than hedge plants, and they may be head-high or taller. Neighborhood hedges often have wood corner posts and gateposts.

Wilderness wood fences (T1) may consist of nothing more than rails stacked against rock piles. Rural wood fences (T2) either may be barbed wire or wire mesh on rough cedar fence posts or may be cedar split rails fitted into fence posts spaced 8' or so apart. Fences are not often used on the outskirts of town, because residents of suburban areas do not have to worry about keeping cows out of the front yard and their houses are far enough apart that there is no need for psychological protection from the street. Wood fences should pick up again in the general neighborhood (T4) areas of town. Fences allow houses to pull close to each other and close to the street without residents feeling threatened while sitting on their front porch. As a matter of fact, it could be argued that the combination of front porch and fence was the glue that once held society together in countless U.S. towns. Wood fences in these areas are decidedly different from their country cousins. All fence components in T4 are dressed lumber. Fence posts are 4x4's or 6x6's with either pyramid cut or applied caps, but are still spaced 8'

*Don't build fences of materials incompatible with the Transect zone, or of a mix of incompatible materials.*
*1: Mix of incompatible materials (in this case, tubular steel newels, wrought and cast iron gate, and wood picket fence)*
*2: Tubular aluminum, with all its regrettable crimped details.*
*3: Chain-link fencing: the most regrettable material of all.*

*Do use wood, wrought or cast iron with masonry or stone piers for fences as the Transect and local precedent allow.*
*4: Stone corner posts with metal fencing.*
*5: Stucco corner posts with hedge.*
*6: Classic picket fence with dog board base.*
*7: Paneled wood posts with pickets and dog board base.*
*8: Timber posts, picket gate, and hedge.*
*9: Timber post, picket fence, and brick base.*

1

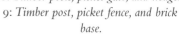

2

3

or less apart. Two or possibly three frame members run horizontally from post to post. Vertical pickets complete the fence, cut to a dozen widths and countless top shapes. Wood fences generally fade from use as the neighborhood streets approach Main Street (T5.) They are nowhere to be found in the T6 urban core.

Metal fences generally are a more urban creature, occurring most often in general neighborhood areas and along the main street, if there are any fences there. Fences of any sort are rare in the urban core, but if they exist, they certainly will be metal. Acceptable metal fencing may be built between brick or stone piers, or it may simply span between wrought iron fence posts. The fencing itself is similar to wood fencing, except with thinner members. Two or sometimes three horizontal rails span between piers or posts, and vertical pickets penetrate the rails to complete the system, often with decorative caps in the shape of arrowheads, spearheads, or other shapes.

Fences anywhere closer to downtown than the outskirts are designed entirely for humans, and they should be shorter than fences designed to keep large animals contained. Careful study has shown that fences are attractive as long as no single vertical element of the fence panel is ideally more than 40" tall or absolutely no more than 42" tall. Taller fences may be composed of picket panels over a brick, stone, or stucco base, for example.

4

5

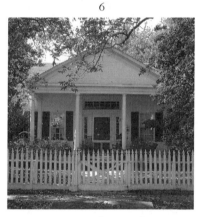

6

7

8

9

SEE THE TRANSECT (PAGE 75); 6~CAP, SHAFT, AND BASE; 104~FRONTAGE FENCE DESIGN; 105~NEIGHBORS' FENCE DESIGN; 106~PRIVATE YARD FENCE DESIGN; 107~GARDEN WALL DESIGN; AND 108~LANE OR ALLEY FENCE DESIGN.

## 102
## WALL MATERIALS

WALLS IN THE LANDSCAPE
SHALL MATCH THE BUILDING
FOUNDATION WALL UNLESS
LOCAL PRECEDENT MAKES
STONE APPROPRIATE WITH
BUILDINGS OF ANOTHER
MATERIAL.

Walls should be designed according to their location on the Transect. As with fences, there are relatively few wall materials that are inappropriate anywhere. Most are appropriate at some point on the rural to urban Transect.

Stockade walls similar to those currently used for backyard privacy fences were originally designed as temporary walls, and they were never meant to adorn a private outdoor room, but rather to contain livestock, hence their name. Walls that contain either private outdoor space or the street should be built of materials nobler and more durable than those used to contain livestock. Generally, these materials may be natural stone, concrete, stucco, brick, or dressed stone, in order of least formal to most formal. Landscape walls constructed of the same material as that of the building foundation make a lot of sense because they are able to intersect with and spring from the building foundation where appropriate in a seamless fashion. Local wall

*Don't misuse wall materials with poor techniques or use materials incompatible with local precedent or with each other.*

*1: Technically, this wall should not be unacceptable, because the materials are stone, brick, and stucco. The use of the materials, however, is abysmal. The stone is actually cast stone (concrete) for the finials. The brick is crude and poorly used, showing its cores like dirty laundry, and the stucco is thinly laid over concrete block, exposing almost every joint upon close inspection.*

*2: The stockade wall was never meant to contain humans but rather livestock in T2. Its task should not be changed.*

*3: The concrete block wall is simply ugly. Concrete blocks may be hard and efficient, but nobody has ever accused them of being beautiful. They should be used only in places where the only concerns are hardness and efficiency such as industrial districts.*

1

2

3

[280]

*Do employ good craftsmanship and respect local precedent when choosing wall materials.*
*1: Stone with brick header course overlaid with vegetation: a most civilized full-height wall (T2 – T4).*
*2: Stacked-stone wall: conceived in the wilderness of T1 and the countryside of T2, it can expand to other areas of the Transect if properly used.*
*3: Stucco overlaid on masonry wall: perhaps the most common good wall in the world (T2 – T6).*
*4: Masonry wall with metal top: classic recipe for softening a tall wall (T4 – T6).*
*5: Stone, stucco, and iron, all obeying the rule of 40" heights, create a very elegant wall (T5 – T6).*
*6: The wall of green: Miami Beach, Florida, has made a landscaping career of the living wall. Maybe other places should, too (T3 – T4).*

material precedent, however, should be highly respected as long as it is not wood.

Masonry landscape walls are subject to the same 40" height limitation as fences. This may seem difficult because walls often must be taller than 40". This limit, however, applies to only a single panel of the wall, not the entire wall. An 8' wall, for example, might be composed of an 8" cap over a 40" top wall panel over an 8" double water table over a 40" base.

Tall masonry landscape walls require either occasional buttressing or heavy reinforcing to keep them upright. The most attractive option is to build piers into the wall that act as buttresses. Piers may be somewhat taller than the fence panels and should be capped with some sort of brick or stone capital.

SEE THE TRANSECT (PAGE 75); 6~CAP, SHAFT, AND BASE; 104~FRONTAGE FENCE DESIGN; 105~NEIGHBORS' FENCE DESIGN; 106~PRIVATE YARD FENCE DESIGN; 107~GARDEN WALL DESIGN; AND 108~LANE OR ALLEY FENCE DESIGN.

1

2

3

4

5

6

# 103
# SIDEWALK
# MATERIALS

**SIDEWALK MATERIALS SHOULD
BE APPROPRIATE TO THE
BUILDING'S LOCATION IN THE
URBAN/RURAL TRANSECT.**

Sidewalks should vary tremendously from the urban core to the wilderness of the Transect. Materials illustrated on opposite page are noted with appropriate Transect zones. Sidewalks technically do not exist in the wilderness (T1) or the countryside (T2) because there is nowhere to walk to. But there are occasional pathways in these areas. Wilderness pathways are nothing more than worn tracks in the grass or underbrush. They are usually both too long and too lightly traveled to merit the cost of any sort of finishing material.

Rural paths are not much more formal. Paths in coastal country are often no more than raked sand. Rural paths further upland near a stream or other waterway might be built of loose river gravel. Rural paths near the southern piney woods may be pine straw. Clearly, they are usually made of locally available materials because, similar to the wilderness paths, they are usually both too long and too lightly traveled to merit importing expensive materials.

Suburban (T3) areas on the outskirts of towns usually spread buildings too far apart to really be walkable, so sidewalks are rare there. When they do occur, they are often built of the cheapest durable material, which is usually concrete. Paths there often follow suit.

General neighborhood areas (T4) closer to Main Street are the first to regularly incorporate sidewalks into the urban fabric; buildings are close enough here for them to make sense. Because sidewalk lengths per house are not enormous, sidewalk materials can vary with the affluence of the

*Sand walk, pine straw planting strip, concrete curb, asphalt paving: Transect zone?*

*Concrete sidewalk on the beach? What's the point: fried feet? A clear Transect violation.*

^T2–T3 *boardwalk.* ⌄T2 *sand path.*

^T3–T5 *asphalt.* ⌄T3–T6 *concrete.*

T4–T6 *brick walk.*

T2–T4 *stone walk.*

T2–T3 *gravel path.*

T1–T2 *straw path.*

neighborhood. Most are still concrete, to be sure, but some are occasionally brick pavers on sand beds or possibly slate slabs. General neighborhood sidewalks are usually flanked by a planting strip or "grazing strip" on the street side and a narrow annual flower strip between the sidewalk and the frontage fence.

Main Street (T5) sidewalks and those in the T6 urban center usually run from building face to the back of the curb. They are the most likely of all sidewalks to be built of higher-quality materials because of the upscale character of streetscape that can be created in a U.S. Main Street. Just as with the general neighborhood, the material upgrades generally consist of brick pavers or stone slabs. Concrete pavers may also be used.

Urban core sidewalks also run from building to street, but they are typically wider than the Main Street sidewalks. They are torn up more often to service the larger, denser buildings, and they take more abuse because of the increased traffic, so they are almost always built of plain concrete.

SEE CELEBRATION OF THE ACT OF BUILDING (PAGE 12) AND THE TRANSECT (PAGE 75).

## 104
## FRONTAGE FENCE
## DESIGN

FRONTAGE FENCES VARY
GREATLY BY TRANSECT ZONE,
AND THEY SHOULD BE OF A
DIFFERENT DESIGN FROM THOSE
OF NEIGHBORING FENCES.

Frontage fences are those that occur at the front of a lot and at a side street frontage. Frontage fences occur in all Transect zones, but they are by far most common in general neighborhood areas (T4.) Frontage fences are a popular palette for personal expression. Variation in design, beginning with the shape of the top of the picket, should be strongly encouraged between adjacent properties. Fences must be composed of individual panels no taller than 40", although 36" is preferable. Hedges may violate height limits in every zone because of being made of living material. Transect rules are as follows:

T1 and T2 frontage fences are built of rustic materials that often have to restrain animals, so they are 48" to 60" tall. Each board is seen as a single panel, so horizontal rail fences do not violate the 40" panel height limitation.

T3 frontage fences shall be no more than 36" tall, and may retain the character of more rural board or hedgerow fences, or they may be constructed of pickets.

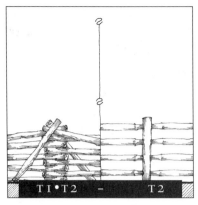

T1•T2 – T2

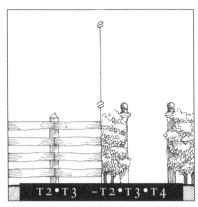

T2•T3 –T2•T3•T4

*Classic* T4 *picket fence.*

*T4 picket with 10" dog board.*

*T3–T4 picket with board gate.*

T4 *picket fence with 12" dog board.*

T3 *rail fence.*

T3 *hedge fence with picket gate.*

[284]

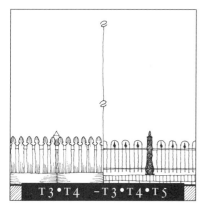
T4-T5 *metal fence with metal newels.*

T4 *picket with wood gate.*

T4 *swooped picket and gate.*

*Timber newels and* T4 *wood pickets.*

T3-T4 *wood picket on timber newels.*

T5-T6 *stucco on masonry walls.*

T4 frontage fences shall be no more than 48" tall if composed of 3 panels or more, nor more than 40" tall if built of 1- or 2-panel (picket and dog board) designs. They typically occur 12" to 18" inside the sidewalk, leaving a band of earth for annual flowers or ground cover. They may step farther back from the sidewalk at gates, either on an angle or at a right angle, leaving a paved area for potted plants or other welcoming objects. This also leaves room for someone to step out of the path of kids riding bikes down the sidewalk to open the gate.

A dog board keeps small dogs from crawling under the fence and acts as a visual base. It is installed tight down to the ground. Fence pickets should overlap the dog board and be tacked to it occasionally to strengthen the picket panel.

T5 and T6 frontage fences are built tight to the sidewalk and are masonry and/or metal. They may be as tall as 80" if the top panel is made of thin iron pickets that allow uninterrupted view or 60" tall if entirely solid. The 40" maximum panel height shall be measured at the shortest picket where picket tops arch up or down in a panel.

SEE THE TRANSECT (PAGE 75);
6~CAP, SHAFT, AND BASE;
101~FENCE MATERIALS; AND
102~WALL MATERIALS.

## 105
## NEIGHBORS' FENCE
## DESIGN

NEIGHBORS' FENCES MAY BE UP TO 18" TALLER THAN FRONTAGE FENCES, BUT MUST TAPER DOWN TO THE HEIGHT OF THE FRONTAGE FENCE WHERE THEY MEET. NEIGHBORS' FENCES MAY BE BUILT WITH A SLIGHTLY LESS ELABORATE DESIGN THAN THE FRONTAGE FENCE.

Neighbors' fences are those that occur between front yards of two adjoining lots. There are no Don'ts for neighbors' fences because the Transect has several places for them. They are by far most common in general neighborhood areas (T4,) but may also occur occasionally in suburban areas (T3.) When built in Main Street (T5) or downtown (T6) areas, they follow the same rules as the garden wall. They run from the frontage fence to the private yard fence, if any, or if not, they turn into the front corner of the house or building. Neighbors' fences are often planted against on one or both sides, which explains why they may need to be taller than frontage fences. It also helps to explain why they may be built to a lesser standard of finish: They will seldom be seen if the planting is heavy. Even if simpler, however, they should still be appropriate to the location of the house within the Transect.

*When a neighbors' fence occurs between yards with no frontage fences, extend the neighbors' fence down toward ground level. Many creative methods may be used such as the two shown in these photos.*

*Picket neighbors' fence tapering down to ground level.*

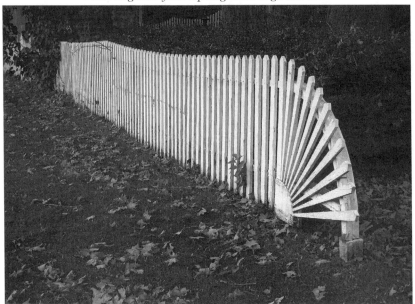

*Board-and-picket neighbors' fence tapering down to post height.*

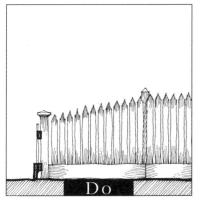

*When a neighbors' fence occurs between yards with at least one frontage fence, reduce the neighbors' fence to no greater than the height of the frontage fence as it approaches the frontage fence as shown in this drawing and these photos.*

*Picket neighbors' fence and frontage fence.*

In other words, a neighbors' fence shouldn't be a split cedar rail in T4.

The taper of the taller neighbors' fence usually occurs in a straight line from the last neighbors' fence post to the frontage fence post where they intersect. The reason for the taper should be exceptionally obvious: If the fence did not taper, the fence post where the neighbors' fence intersected the frontage fence would have to be substantially taller, ruining the appearance of the frontage fence. But back to the taper: There are cases where the taper is actually an elegant S-curve or some other shape cut out of a wider top fence rail. Such instances should clearly occur in the more elaborate fences.

SEE THE TRANSECT (PAGE 75);
6~CAP, SHAFT, AND BASE;
101~FENCE MATERIALS;
102~WALL MATERIALS; AND
107~GARDEN WALL DESIGN.

*Board neighbors' fence with picket frontage fence.*

## 106
## PRIVATE YARD
## FENCE DESIGN

PRIVATE YARD FENCES MAY BE
UP TO 72" TALL, THEY MAY
NOT BE CONSTRUCTED IN
FRONT OF THE FRONT WALL
OF THE BUILDING WHEN
SCREENING THE FRONT OF THE
PRIVATE YARD, OR IN FRONT
OF THE SIDE FACE OF THE
BUILDING WHEN SCREENING
THE SIDE OF THE PRIVATE YARD
FROM A SIDE STREET.

Private yard fences are those
that occur between a private
yard and a street frontage.
The private yard is defined as
that area lying inside of the
nearest major outside corner
of the building. T3 private
yard fences may be hedges or
wood. T4 private yard fences
may be wood. T5 and T6
private yard fences may be
masonry and follow the rules
of 107~Garden Walls, or may
also be wood.

Private yard fences are the
only wood fences allowed to
be entirely view-proof; they
are usually constructed of pickets set tight together. They are
also the only fences of any sort
allowed to be built of panels
taller than 40", but if a single
tall panel is used, shrubs at
least 32" tall should be planted
along the outside of the private yard fence, which will
yield an exposed fence panel
height of no more than 40"
above the tops of the shrubs.
A 1x6 or 1x8 middle rail may

*Do use a middle rail to divide the
vertical boards of a private yard fence
into panels no taller than 40" each.
In reality, the vertical boards may run
through behind the middle rail, but the
rail both provides the visual break and
also strengthens the fence.*

*T4 private yard picket fence in background, picket frontage fence in foreground.*

*T3 private yard wire mesh fence for training vining plants as a hedge.*

*Do use solid planting to accomplish the 40" height limit in a private yard fence. The planting material should expose no more than 40" of the fence at any location.*

Do

T4 *brick and metal picket fence for training vining plants as a hedge.*

T4 *wood lattice private yard fence.*

be applied to the outside of the private yard fence both to strengthen the panel and to break the tall panel into two segments shorter than 40" if landscaping might not immediately cover the entire fence panel. In such cases, a 1x10 or 1x12 dog board should be used at the base.

It is permissible to detail private yard fences with shaped picket tops, just as would be done with a picket frontage fence. It is preferable, however, to use flattop pickets with a top rail above on taller versions of the private yard fence, since the tallest private yard fences are approaching the height of walls. The only taller fences are stockade fences, and as mentioned earlier, these should be enclosing livestock, not humans. Private yard fences on corner lots shall return to the nearest corner of the garage or carport structure.

SEE THE TRANSECT (PAGE 75);
6~CAP, SHAFT, AND BASE;
101~FENCE MATERIALS;
102~WALL MATERIALS; AND
107~GARDEN WALL DESIGN.

## 107
# GARDEN WALL
# DESIGN

GARDEN WALLS MAY BE UP
TO 96" TALL IN T3 AND T4
AND UP TO 120" TALL IN
T5 AND T6. THEY MAY NOT
BE CONSTRUCTED IN FRONT
OF THE FRONT WALL OF THE
BUILDING. EXTERIOR SURFACES
OF GARDEN WALLS MAY NOT
BE ENTIRELY FLAT, BUT MUST
BE ARTICULATED IN A MANNER
APPROPRIATE TO THE STYLE OF
THE BUILDING. GARDEN WALLS
SHOULD BE CONSTRUCTED OF
BRICK, STONE, OR A STUCCO
FINISH ON A MASONRY
STRUCTURE.

Garden walls are those walls
that occur between the private
yards of two adjoining lots.
They occur along the same
property line as neighbors'
fences; they begin at or near
the front face of the house
or building where the neighbors' fence ends. They usually
extend back to the lane or
alley fence.

Garden walls are the tallest
walls built in the landscape, and
therefore they must be reinforced with piers as discussed
earlier. Piers should be a minimum of 16" square or quite
possibly larger, which allows a
single 8" concrete pier block
to be installed in the center
of the pier and reinforced. If
the piers are spaced closely
enough, the wall may be one
wythe thick. If not, then the
wall should be two wythes
thick. Check local conditions

*Do compose T3 and T4 garden walls
of wood pickets set above brick bases
between brick pilasters, which should be
no less than 16" square. Pilaster caps
are usually brick with a mortar wash,
but may also be stone when the building
they are attached to is very classical.*

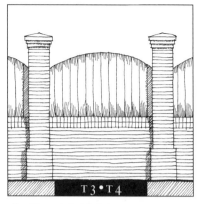

T5 *stucco on masonry garden wall with metal picket top.*

T4 *brick garden wall.*

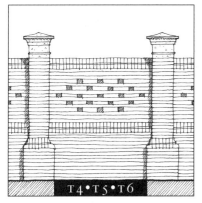

T4 *wood garden wall with brick base and pilasters.*

*Do build garden walls entirely of brick. This is an option in T4, but is a requirement in T5 and T6. Recesses shown in the top brick panel typically do not extend all the way through the wall for privacy. If used, they provide visual texture and a better foothold for vining plants.*

and structural loading requirements with a structural engineer. A double-wythe wall is thick enough to incorporate decorative patterns similar to the empty Flemish bond, where the omitted bricks usually leave holes in the wall in a decorative pattern. With a double-wythe wall, however, the coursing can be offset so that the empty holes are blind. In other words, a hole on one side of the wall matches a solid brick on the other side, which preserves privacy.

Pilasters, as noted earlier, should be capped with some sort of capital. This may be something as simple as a square concrete or stone slab, or it may be as elaborate as a carved stone pilaster capital. The midpoint is a capital created with brick corbels and protected by a sloped mortar wash on top.

106~Private Yard Fences may be built in lieu of garden walls where the budget does not allow a garden wall. Note, however, that wood fences do not absorb sound nearly so well as masonry, so private yard fences do not provide as much acoustical privacy as garden walls. Private yard fences in this location may be a maximum of 80" tall.

T3 *brick garden wall with wood panels in some locations.*

SEE THE TRANSECT, (PAGE 75); 6~CAP, SHAFT, AND BASE; AND 102~WALL MATERIALS.

## 108
## LANE OR ALLEY
## FENCE DESIGN

YARD EQUIPMENT SHOULD
NOT BE VISIBLE FROM PUBLIC
RIGHTS-OF-WAY. TRASH AND
RECYCLING CONTAINERS
SHOULD BE LOCATED WITHIN
PERMANENT ENCLOSURES
WHEN NOT WITHIN AN ALLEY
OR LANE. THE LANE OR ALLEY
FENCE MUST BE SOLID BELOW
A HEIGHT OF 54" AND MUST
INCORPORATE A 1X8 MINIMUM
DOG BOARD. IF EXTENDED
ABOVE 54", THE LANE FENCE
MUST BE BUILT OF AN OPEN,
LATTICE- OR TRELLIS-TYPE
DESIGN.

The lane or alley fence
occurs on the rear property
line between the garden wall
and the nearest corner of the
garage or carport. The lane
fence is found in general neighborhood (T4) areas, while the
alley fence is found in Main
Street (T5) and downtown
(T6) areas. These fences are
usually responsible for screening yard equipment such as
HVAC equipment, utility
meters, clotheslines, satellite
dishes, play equipment, hot
tubs, and the like.

Because the lane fence is
tight to the property line,
it would be oppressive if it
were solid to its maximum
allowable height of 80". A
6" minimum middle rail with
a 1X cap should be installed
at a top height of 54". The
dog board should be 8" mini-

*Do compose T4 lane fences of a solid
wood fence to 54" with an optional
open lattice above as shown in this
drawing.*

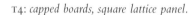

*T4: capped boards, square lattice panel.*

*T4: capped boards, no lattice panel.*

*T5: brick wall, no lattice panel.*

*T4: capped boards, square picket panel.*

*T4: capped boards with board frame, square picket panel: Textbook alley fence design.*

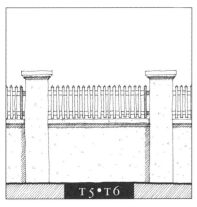

T5•T6

*Do compose T5 and T6 alley fences of brick or stucco on masonry with the same optional lattice panel above, built of either wood or metal. If the lattice panel is used, masonry pilasters should extend above the top of the lattice panel.*

*T4: hedge as lane fence.*

*T5: metal fence to 54" is lighter option.*

*T4: framed boards, no lattice panel.*

*Too high at left, OK at right.*

*T4: capped boards, horizontal lattice with open gate.*

mum, which yields a maximum panel height between the two of 40". The panel may be constructed of vertical pickets butted tight, similar to the private yard fence. The upper, more open panel, if used, may be either an open wire trellis or a wood lattice. Vines may be trained over either of these elements to provide further privacy. The top of the top rail over the lattice or trellis may extend to a maximum height of 80". Fence posts must be at least 4x4's, but probably should be larger square posts because of wind loading; check local conditions. Hedges may also be used as lane fences.

The alley fence is one major variation of the lane fence. Lanes are typically narrow paved thoroughfares with grass to either side. Lanes are typically found in T4 or sometimes T3 areas. Alleys are paved from property line to property line and are found in town center and urban core areas. Alley fences are expected to be taller and less transparent, so the garden wall design may be used for the alley fence if desired. If not, the other alley fence option is to use the private yard fence to a height of 80".

SEE THE TRANSECT (PAGE 75);
6~CAP, SHAFT, AND BASE;
101~FENCE MATERIALS; AND
102~WALL MATERIALS.

# BIBLIOGRAPHY

Adam, Robert, *Classical Architecture*, Harry N. Abrams, 1990

Alexander, Christopher, *A Pattern Language*, Oxford University Press, 1977

Alexander, Christopher, *The Timeless Way of Building*, Oxford University Press, 1979

Benjamin, Asher, *The American Builder's Companion*, Dover Publications, Inc., 1969

Benjamin, Asher, *Practice of Architecture: The Builders Guide*, Da Capo Press, 1994

Brooks, Hugh, *Illustrated Encyclopedic Dictionary of Building and Construction Terms*, Prentice Hall, 1976

Calloway, Stephen, *The Elements of Style*, Simon & Schuster, 1996

Chitham, Robert, *The Classical Orders of Architecture*, Rizzoli, 1995

Duany Plater-Zyberk & Company, *The Lexicon of the New Urbanism*, Duany Plater-Zyberk & Company, 2002

Fletcher, Sir Banister, *A History of Architecture*, Scribners, 1975

Harris, Cyril M., *Dictionary of Architecture and Construction*, McGraw-Hill, 1975

Harris, Cyril M., *Illustrated Dictionary of Historic Architecture*, Dover Publications, Inc., 1977

InfoPlease, http://www.infoplease.com

Neufeldt, Victoria, *Webster's New World Dictionary*, Simon & Schuster, Inc., 1988

Plattus, Alan J., *The American Vitruvius: An Architect's Handbook of Civic Art*, Princeton Architectural Press, 1922

Rattner, Donald M., *Moldings: The Atomic Units of Classical Architecture*, http://www.traditional-building.com/article/moldings.htm

Rifkind, Carole, *A Field Guide to American Architecture*, Bonanza Books, 1980

Summerson, John, *The Classical Language of Architecture*, MIT Press, 1995

Ware, William R., *The American Vignola*, Dover Publications, Inc., 1994

## ABOUT THE AUTHORS

Stephen A. Mouzon and Susan M. Henderson are architects and town planners, and are principals of PlaceMakers, which is headquartered in Miami, Florida. Steve is a founder of the New Urban Guild. He has authored or contributed to a number of publications in recent years, including the *Public Works Manual*, *Charles Barrett: The Architectural Drawings*, *Biltmore Estate Homes*, and *1001 Traditional Construction Details*. He continues to shoot the photographic *Catalog of the Most-Loved Places*, which currently includes over 25,000 digital images in 52 volumes. The PlaceMakers Pattern Books are currently the only Transect-based pattern books in existence and are meant to be companion pieces to this book.